The Poverty of
American Politics

THE POVERTY OF AMERICAN POLITICS

A Theoretical Interpretation

H. Mark Roelofs

Temple University Press
Philadelphia

Temple University Press, Philadelphia 19122
Copyright © 1992 by Temple University. All rights reserved
Published 1992
Printed in the United States of America

The paper used in this publication meets the minimum requirements of
American National Standard for Information Sciences—Permanence of Paper
for Printed Library Materials, ANSI Z39.49–1984 ⊗

Library of Congress Cataloging-in-Publication Data
Roelofs, H. Mark.
    The poverty of American politics : a theoretical interpretation /
H. Mark Roelofs.
      p. cm.
    Includes index.
    ISBN 0-87722-877-9 (alk. paper).—ISBN 0-87722-878-7 (pbk. :
alk. paper)
      1. United States—Politics and government. 2. Values—United
States. I. Title.
JK271.R537 1992
320.973—dc20   91-10039

For

Sarah

and

Olga, Cora, Gurion, Dan, Seth

and

Sarah, Andrew, Ann, Luke, Portia

and

Contents

Preface

Given the post-bicentennial and post–Cold War context in which this book has been written, prudence suggests that it begin with a clear statement of what it is not. This book is not a celebration of the American Constitution, not a post-bicentennial celebration of it, and certainly not a post–Cold War victory celebration of it. On the contrary, this book is exclusively an interpretation, and as such, it will take sides on many issues. But good interpretation is not simply evaluative. Good interpretation is reasoned, analytical, explanatory evaluation. To this end, this book is an effort to identify and boldly and unblinkingly to take the measure of the American political system as a whole, in all its complexity, at a time when at least some thoughtful Americans are considerably distressed over how their government and its various processes are operating.

This book is a critical interpretation of the American political system from the point of view of the political system itself and of its citizens, with their own traditionally given values and aspirations. The conclusion is that in terms of those values, the American political system shortchanges itself and, even more, shortchanges its citizenry.

The book's concern, however, is not to show factually how the system has shortchanged itself and its citizens. That is a straightforward, listing kind of business that has been done virtually constantly over the years in newspapers and journals, in official reports, and in countless exposés taking up one issue or incident or figure or program or some grouping of these after another. The book's aim is to show comprehensively why and with what significance the American political system shortchanges itself. Its aim is to show critically why the system falls short of its own aspirations, why it must fall short, by design, in theory. Its aim is to explain *in concept* why American politics is a poor sort of politics, to demonstrate intellectually, not just empirically, its poverty. It is, in short, an interpretation of the *theory* of American politics, and it is that theory that is found to be defective.

In briefest compass, the explanation advanced for the poverty of the American political system is the congenital tendency of its dominant elements to operate simultaneously at two different, disjointed, and mutually contradictory levels. One level we will call the mythic level of social democracy; the other, the ideological level of liberal democracy. Each of these levels is itself fundamentally flawed as a governing system. But it is the division between them that most cripples American politics by infecting all its controlling figures—its executives, legislators, judges, and all the lesser officials—with a kind of ongoing schizophrenia. This division forces upon them a double subjectivity, a false, perpetually self-deceiving, theatrical quality that more or less constantly distinguishes—with more or less constant contradiction—between the onstage roles political officials play before the public and their offstage roles with each other.

Because of this deep-seated and, in the end, elaborately institutionalized fissure in the American political system, the resulting political practice, so the argument runs, is marked by confusion and frustration, inflammatory bombast unrelated to positive performance, spells of military adventurism, and a host of other symptoms, including generous quantities of double talk, double-dealing, hypocrisies, and corruption. Additionally, it is a style and process of politics essentially incapable of controlling and managing the bureaucratic arms of government to even ordinary standards of long-term constancy and competence. It is a politics much too often scarred by grandiose failure and lack of meaningful accomplishment. In this perspective American politics is, in sum, a politics of contradiction and paradox, of impoverishing, self-diminishing paradox.

This is a bleak picture but not an unfamiliar one. The conclusion that American politics is in trouble is for many observers a commonplace of our times. The philosophical problem, however, is to back up that evaluation not with a long bill of particulars but with critical, explanatory analysis that establishes comprehensively the whys and wherefores of its validity.

How can we, in this era of post-bicentennial and post–Cold War celebrations, initiate a critically interpretive dialogue of this sort about American politics? It will not be easy, because the more that things have gone wrong—and the more that we have been forced to admit that they have gone wrong—the more defensive and blind we as a nation have become. Doggedly, we insist that there are overriding virtues to our political system. Implacably, defensively, we become heels-dug-in conservatives.

In consequence, the American political system has become over the years more than complex, intricate, and involuted in countless ways. It has also become a political system heavily encrusted with obscurantist rhetoric. Politicians and other public figures, obviously and for their own purposes, pour on this kind of talk at every op-

portunity. But so do the standard college-level American government textbooks. Turn to the chapters in any of them on the formation of the Constitution, and sentences like this abound: "On one
point almost all students of the founding era are agreed: The
framers offered in the Constitution perhaps the most brilliant example of collective intellectual genius—combining both theory and
practice—in the history of the Western world."[1]

By powerful, inescapable, patriotic tradition, modern-day textbooks are required to say such things. But notice the narrowing effect that a sentence of this sort must have on any study undertaken
in its wake. Collective intellectual genius combining theory and practice cannot plausibly be held responsible for disasters or even strings
of mistakes. If it is genius we are to study, then our questions must
be confined, on the one hand, to queries about intellectual sources,
and, on the other, to speculations about how the works of that genius went on to produce national greatness. That is not the road to
free, open, critical interpretation.

With this kind of rhetoric so extensive and intense in the public
discussion of the American political system, should we make the effort to cut through it? Why not be content to join the celebratory
chorus? Why not, with new flourishes, rephrase the familiar assertions about the genius of the founders and the dynamic vitality and
infinite adaptability of their handiwork?

It can be readily admitted that there is much in American political experience that can be construed in positive ways. There is much
about American politics for which Americans can be profoundly
grateful and of which they can be justly proud before the whole
world. Particularly when it comes to the size, affluence, and secular
comfort of our middle class, Americans can afford to be smug. But
in our politics there also have been persistent problems and recurrent difficulties about which all Americans, it can be reasonably argued, should be deeply worried. Consider just the last few decades,
during which there has been a succession of quagmirian experiences
in foreign policy, with associated power and character scandals at the
highest levels. There has been a sustained pattern of national and
local elections of unrivaled irrelevance and fatuousness. There has
been a national budgetary process repeated year after year that defies rational explanation, let alone defense.

These and armfuls of other similarly disturbing problems amply
justify increasing public concern over whether the American political
system will be able to meet, even in minimal ways, the challenges that
loom ahead: economic problems on an international scale, population and immigration explosions, disease epidemics, new kinds of

foreign-affairs problems, ecological crises of unprecedented dimensions, and the tangled, threatening residues of problems never adequately faced in the past, such as racism, urban decay, street and white-collar crime, chronic unemployment patterns, drug abuse, homelessness, and governmental corruption. Serious, critical analysis, interpretation, and evaluation of the capacities, strengths, and weaknesses of the American political system are overdue. That kind of analysis and interpretation by distinguished scholars has been attempted sporadically in the past.[2] It now appears to be desperately necessary and surely should be widely encouraged among all political scientists for sustained public discussion.

Yet it is not being so encouraged. Why? The problem, in a word, is patriotism.

Excessive patriotism, emotional, possessive, and self-righteous—the last refuge of scoundrels—is not a bookish business and need not detain us here. But patriotism, in the technical sense of a socially presumed commitment to a nation's political system, is an altogether different issue and presents major obstacles to all attempts at constitutional analysis. If players in a game honorably argue whether a ball should be called in or out, they are arguing about who is to win, who is to lose, within the context and rules of the game they all accept. But if one of them questions the rules themselves or where the lines are to be drawn, suddenly the game itself, whether it can be played at all, is at issue.

The same kind of constraint is at issue in constitutional criticism and interpretation. Even in societies otherwise much given to pluralism and freedom of expression, certain types of questions can be raised only at great risk. No matter what degree of dissension is permitted on questions of who is to rule and how, the closer the discussion goes to truly fundamental constitutional principles, the closer it comes to disturbing the general consensus without which no government is possible. "We hold these truths to be self-evident," intoned Thomas Jefferson in the Declaration of Independence, and well he might. In writing these words, he was doing what he could at that time to create a nation out of thirteen fractious colonies. He was aiming to constitute a community, a governing consensus. So he planted a standard to which the whole citizen body of the new nation, without thought, question, or argument, could repair.

The critic who before a broad audience questions a society's first principles attacks not only those principles but also the mood of certainty and acceptance that glues a society into its initial cohesion. Such critics may turn out to be more right than their neighbors, but, socially, they veer dangerously toward being minorities of even less than one.

How can constitutional critics be heard? Is it possible, past all the admittedly necessary rhetoric, to make before the general public the case that our society's fundamental principles may not be self-evidently true, may in fact be wrong and be the permanent source of much confusion and pain in both thought and action?

Perhaps we can begin by agreeing for the purposes of what follows that we are all patriots, whether we be politicians or students, citizens or scholars, that we all want the best for our country. That is why some of us are worried enough to take up the tasks of reading, writing, and pondering critical constitutional analysis and interpretation. So let us also assert that if the arguments of this book should be taken seriously even by a small number of citizens, we will have embarked on an enterprise that may have in the long term profound consequences at a practical level of political reform or reconstruction.

The reader may therefore want to bear in mind some suggestions for practical change in the American political system. Here is a list of possibilities. Some of them have been widely discussed; others are virtually unheard of in the American context. They are put here in an ascending order of comprehensiveness.

1. A series of "tinkering," coordinated adjustments should be made to the lengths of the terms served by members of the House of Representatives, the Senate, and the presidency; primary elections should be nationally scheduled and controlled; the electoral college should be abolished; campaigns should be mostly publicly financed; and elections held on Sundays. All this and more should be done with an eye to encouraging party solidarity, official patterns of responsibility, and meaningful election dialogue.

2. The present federal system of states should be abolished and replaced with a new system of local government based on a dozen or more metropolitan districts carved around the present cities of Boston, New York, Chicago, and others, each of which would be essentially self-governing. The remainder of the nation should then be divided into vast provinces corresponding to the nation's great river basins, within which urban areas, small cities, and rural regions would receive appropriate measures of powers and responsibilities for self-management and be otherwise supported and serviced by the national government.

3. A skillfully drawn amendment should be added to the Constitution to coalesce the two houses of Congress into one body to which members of the executive cabinet would be held collectively responsible, thereby transforming the American national government from a presidential system into a cabinet system, such as Canada's.

4. The Preamble of the Constitution should be radically rethought and fundamentally rewritten to encompass and incorporate

an updated understanding of the powers and responsibilities of a modern government in a large, highly developed, technologically, culturally, and morally advanced nation beset by seemingly intractable social and economic problems. This is a supremely difficult and radical suggestion. It would require rethinking the most profound fundamentals of American political thought and commitment. And it would entail recasting the powers and responsibilities of the several branches of government, especially of Congress, as well as of the whole government itself. Its full impact on the Bill of Rights and the Fourteenth Amendment would also be problematic. Ultimately, such a rewriting would require the recasting of our understandings of the responsibility of our various governments, national, state, and local, and of their relations to the major institutions of private life, the family, schools and universities, churches, the press, and all the corporate institutions of our so-called free-enterprise capitalist system.

5. Washington, D.C., should be preserved as a city of monuments and museums, and the operative capital of the nation should be moved to some more central location, such as St. Louis or Denver. Its powers should be radically reduced and made mostly subservient to the United Nations. Meanwhile, the whole of the United States should be allowed to "Balkanize" into a loose association of regional and ethnic, largely self-governing, almost tribal entities.

A list like this is a refreshment to the political imagination, an invitation to think what you like. However, such a list is of only incidental concern in this book. It is almost a joke. Who would take any of its items, even the first, seriously? It is included here only to assure the reader that, intellectually, alternatives to present arrangements do exist. But this is not a "how-to-fix-it" book. It is much too early by far in the national dialogue to start thinking about the "how" of reform. Why reform, why the American political system might need fixing, is still an open and unresolved question. In consequence, this book will focus exclusively on trying to understand and critically interpret the American political system as it now stands. In our late twentieth-century context, that is a daunting challenge in itself.

Acknowledgments

The ideas expressed in this book have been developing in my mind for some time. My first effort to write them out was a critical essay published by Little, Brown in 1976 under the title *Ideology and Myth in American Politics: A Critique of a National Political Mind.* In 1983, Gerald Houseman and I wrote a textbook based on these ideas that was titled *The American Political System: Myth and Ideology,* published by Macmillan. More recently, in an essay titled "The American Political System: A Systematic Ambiguity," published in the summer 1986 issue of *The Review of Politics,* I tried to spell out a complete if abstract statement of the theory developing out of these books.

Readers familiar with these earlier efforts will readily note that here I have borrowed liberally from them. But this is in every sense a new book, a culminating effort to state a whole theory without gap or break. More exactly than before, I have tried to apply this theory to the analysis of the nation's practical political institutions. And finally, I have tried to draw without limp or qualification the appropriate evaluative conclusions.

Any effort of this sort, even one so sharply focused on letting an author find and express a singular perspective developed over a long period, is still a collaborative effort. In writing this book, I have had exceptional assistance. My major collaborator was Ellen Carnaghan, colleague, advisor, and friend; but also editor, research assistant, and trusted machine operator. Andrea Az and Sharon McNamara are skilled typists who gave much and would have given more help if schedules had been different. Ralph Straetz, friend of many years, read every chapter and gave valuable—and valued—advice and comment. So, too, did my new colleague Barbara Hinckley. In the book's final stages of preparation, Marla Brettschneider, Patricia Moynagh, and Chris Stadler were of invaluable assistance, giving unstintingly of their sharp, critical intelligence, breadth of factual information, and infectious enthusiasm. I am also grateful to the staff at Temple University Press, especially Jane Cullen, who acquired the manuscript, and Debby Stuart, who saw it through the press. My wife, Sarah, not only encouraged me always to say what I meant, but also, by her sensitivity, saved me from many errors. But having said all that, it remains important to add—this being the kind of book that it is—that I alone am responsible for its mistakes and for what it says.

The Poverty of
American Politics

Introduction: The Great Paradoxes

The thesis of this book is that the American political system is best interpreted as a two-sided biformity, as a paradox. It is a double system of principles, institutions, and processes that are in near constant contradiction with each other.

The conclusion of this book, to which its thesis points as an explanation, is that American politics is impoverished. The thesis is the meat of the book. Its conclusion is its preoccupation, right from the start, but is of direct concern only in its final three chapters.

The paradoxical quality of American political life is fundamental. It amounts to a national schizophrenia. It stems from contradictions between the most fundamental principles on which the system is built and extends and expresses itself through tensions and oppositions in every level of the system's institutions and working processes.

The paradox of American politics is also systematic. It is not random or inexplicable. It amounts to what may be termed a systematic ambiguity, and this in a double sense. When the system is under certain kinds of stress, it, to a remarkable degree, systematically operates almost exclusively on one side of its great internal paradox; when it is under another kind of stress, it systematically switches over and functions on the other side of its paradox. Moreover, these two modes or styles of politics are, within themselves, comprehensive, coherent, fully integrated political systems—despite the fact that systematically they contradict each other from top to bottom.

The notion that there are paradoxical elements in American political life is a staple of the textbooks and has been discussed by scholars from many perspectives over many decades. What makes this book's discussion different is the insistence that all the often-noted paradoxical elements add up to one grand systematic paradox rooted in the nation's founding principles and systematically extending to virtually every facet of its daily functioning.

The central paradox of American politics is that it is driven to be both an egalitarian, community-loving social democracy seeking broad goals of social justice, and, at the same time, a freedom-loving, privatistic, interest-seeking liberal democracy with powerfully sustained elitist tendencies. Since that is the book's substance, and since

1

it is an assertion of such breadth, it would be wise to illustrate its meaning in practical detail immediately.

Here are five particular paradoxes of the American political system, going from the most fundamental to the apparently merely practical. The point of the argument of the chapters that follow will be to show that this is not a mere list of unrelated features of American politics but a list of elements that interact and mutually support each other within a single, all-encompassing political system, albeit one that is fundamentally schizophrenic.

1. Is America a religious, specifically, a Judaic-Christian nation? The answer is yes and no, indeed, emphatically yes and emphatically no.

Emphatically, from John Winthrop's sermon on the Arbella to the Gettysburg Address and beyond to the present day, there are, in the American tradition, not only repeated but continuous commitments to religious values and perspectives. These commitments are not simply to some vague, generalized, quasi-religious feeling. Quite specifically, all denominational multiplicity and differentiation to the contrary notwithstanding, the predominant American religious commitment is to an evangelical, biblical "Protestantism" that has infected not only all the major religious institutions but many other aspects of American life as well. The core emphasis of this Protestantism is on an individualism, a personal religiosity, but it has had persistent tendencies toward public expression as well. In consequence, from the beginning, American politics has been generously decorated and legitimated by religious symbols, rituals, references, and personages. America's "civil religion" is an essential element of its total political life. As fundamentally, much American public policy has been born of religious motives and has sought religious objectives. This has been most obviously true in our formulation and justification of national foreign policy, but it is true as well in many other areas of national concern, such as the civil rights movements and the institutions and programs of the welfare state.

Yet, emphatically, America is not, especially in a political sense, a Christian republic, much less specifically a Protestant one. One need look no further than to the nation's founding documents, the Declaration of Independence and the Constitution, for conclusive evidence on this point. It is not only that there is in these documents no announcement or affirmation of religious intent, of any determination to create in America a government in God's design or even a society that could be an exemplar of Christian living. In these two documents, God is mentioned only three times, each time indirectly and only in passing, and religion twice, both times to exclude it (Ar-

ticle VI and the First Amendment). What is conclusive is the affirmation, emphatic and unambiguous, that these documents do make
about the proper objectives of political life. Those objectives are
strictly mundane. Government is to service and protect human wants
and satisfactions. The Declaration calls them in sum "life, liberty,
and the pursuit of happiness" and then goes on to illustrate these
vague terms by listing in vivid practical detail the oppressions committed by George III against his American subjects. The list is worth
reading with care, if only to point up the fact that in and amongst all
the crimes charged against the king, such as plundering his people,
oppressing them with standing armies, neglecting their government,
and the like, not once is he charged with suppressing their religious
freedom or imposing on them a faith contrary to that lodged in their
hearts. The Constitution is even plainer. Its Preamble and, even
more obviously, Section 8 of Article I, which lists the powers (and
inferentially the duties) of Congress, make plain that this is a mer-
cantilist document designed to sustain a society of merchants,
farmers, and other property-oriented entrepreneurs. To try to label
America, in light of this kind of evidence, any kind of Christian democracy or republic or nation would be more than false; it would be
an outrageous perversion of the facts. What these facts show is that
America is, purely and simply, a secular state, the first and the oldest
example of that in the modern world. Insofar as America is a democracy—in this perspective—it is so not because of any religious
enthusiasm in it for a common life but because of its commitment to
an "enlightened," "worldly," freedom-loving, secular individualism.

The evidence that America, emphatically, is and, with equal evidence, is not a Christian nation is the root paradox of the American
political system. It is the fundamental ambiguity to which the country's founders did not attend, and it has never been resolved. We will
examine it and return to it again and again throughout this book.
The other paradoxes that we should notice in this initial list can be
stated more simply.

2. Is America a democracy? The answer is yes, of course—but
ambiguously, so ambiguously in fact that it often appears not to be a
democracy at all.

Americans, as democrats, believe in and with a high degree of
success practice a life of personal freedom under law. The inevitable
result, in the free race of life, is that many win but most do not, and
often enough the winners in time become entrenched elites, permanently more "free" than the rest, economically, socially, and politically. Americans, as democrats, also believe in equality, a powerfully
social egalitarianism that insists that without distinction we are all in

this society of ours together. So, in the name of equality, do we level the elites? Or do we blind ourselves to those demands and practice our freedom? Either way, the situation is an affront to basic moral imperatives of our political life—and a paradox. What is the fundamental meaning of one man, one vote? What is its practical meaning? Does it have any at all?

3. At the level of constitutional principle, how is America's national government organized? By the doctrine of separation of powers? Everyone knows that it is, not only from grade school civics courses, but from the plain appearance of Articles I, II, and III in the Constitution itself. But then we must wonder how Article I of the Constitution, after assigning Congress, in its first words "All legislative Powers," can give the president, in Section 7, the major legislative power of the veto. Textbook after textbook says that this is just an example of separation of powers being "modified" by the principle of "checks and balances." "Modified"? The sole repository of executive power becomes a major legislative figure? Maybe "adulterated" would be a better word, or "contradicted." There is a little-examined paradox in this matter that, when opened up, will be found to have had a very broad impact on the whole of the national government's constitutional structure and its resulting processes.

4. At the level of institutional practice, is the modern American presidency strong or weak? Too strong or too weak? Not only the textbooks but most of the major commentaries uniformly agree that the modern American presidency represents almost a pinnacle of power, that by being commander of this and chief of that in area after area the president becomes almost a kind of constitutional emperor. This impression is vastly reinforced by general popular concern over who was or might become president in this or that hour of crisis in the life of the nation. Is it a mere accident of speech that we talk of the Roosevelt "administration," the Eisenhower "era," and the Reagan "revolution"? But turn from the textbook chapters of the books detailing presidential powers to other chapters more concerned with outlining the constraints within which actual presidents operate, and a very different picture emerges. In this picture, presidents are constrained on every side. They are constrained not only by the press and wayward public opinion but also by recalcitrant congressional committees steadfastly pursuing their own agendas. They are constrained by courts ready to trump major policies with rulings of unconstitutionality. Above all, they are constrained by an inchoate bureaucracy whose endless divisions inertially pursue fragmented goals in silent and seemingly permanent alliance with private interests over whom the president has only the most tangential

authority. And where in the picture of supposed vast presidential power are we to put the vaunted "grassroots" independence of America's eighty thousand or more state and local governments?

5. At the level of political practice, are political parties essential to the vitality and meaningfulness of American democracy, to the viability of our electoral dialogues? If so, then why do American political parties, as organizations, hardly exist, as their confused condition in cities and states across the land uniformly attests? American political parties in practice are barely more than fictive entities, vague coalitions of scrambling or entrenched, independently situated, political actors each with his or her own sources of support and sets of objectives. Is the vision of America as a bipartisan political democracy then simply a myth that is believed not because it is true but because it is socially useful, even necessary, even while in fact being demonstrably false?

To explain paradoxes of the order of these five, we will need concepts that can grasp each opposing side. Myth is one such concept. It legitimizes government. Ideology is another. It defines governmental power and guides its operation. But these terms need to be carefully delineated and also contrasted to what else is in American politics.

Chapter 1 will work out these definitions in detail. As the book progresses, we will systematically use the concept of myth to grasp at the practical level the legitimizing side of American politics and the concept of ideology to grasp the working side of American government. We will see the actual, practical, paradoxical historical tensions between American myth and American ideology as the source of the nation's perpetual political schizophrenia. We will see why and how this schizophrenia, this internal tension of American politics, far from being a source of vitality and renewal, is a source of perpetual self-delusion and political impoverishment. And we will see also how the endless struggles between the mythic and ideological elements in American politics constitute so many perpetually inconclusive contests to control and manage the nation's governmental bureaucracies. In this light, it can be seen that "myth" and "ideology" are the key conceptual terms in this book's total argument.

What in practice has been given as content to American myth and ideology has been determined partly by logical requirements dictated by their respective functions in the political system as a whole, but mostly by history. In America, myth has been largely defined or at least profoundly colored by the nation's Protestant heritage. Ideology in America, on the other hand, has been largely defined by the nation's secular commitments, or, as these will be labeled in the chapters to come, America's "Bourgeois" ethos. Detailing the Protestant content of American myth and the Bourgeois content of American ideology, and the essential irreconcilability of the imperatives that they respectively impose on the American citizen, is the task of Chapter 2.

Chapter 3 carries the argument into the expressly political realm by outlining the contradictory visions of democracy that develop out of American myth and ideology. The Protestant element in American myth calls not only for a democracy of social egalitarianism but also for one in which "the people" are "sovereign"; and the secular, Bourgeois element in American ideology calls for a democracy of personal freedom under law. In these terms, so far as America responds to its mythic call, it becomes a social democracy. So far as it responds to its ideological summons, it is, with important contradiction, a liberal democracy.

Chapter 4 carries the argument still further into the political realm, to the level of institutions and processes. Protestant mythic social democracy in America has worked out over the years patterns of politics featuring heroic presidents congregating the sovereign people in crusades to the higher ground of social justice. Political parties are also featured in these mythic patterns, as are elections and their campaigns. Together, these elements constitute a vision of American democracy as a system of popular government, of a government by, for, of, and responsible to the people.

The style of this mythic view of American democracy is at every point to be contrasted with what is called up by America's Bourgeois, secular liberal democracy. That ideological democracy focuses, at the institutional and process level, on Congress and other legislative bodies, and on these not as law-making bodies but as arenas and agencies for the harmonization of the competing claims of elite-dominated interest groups. These bodies, in this light, do not so much service citizens as they represent client groups and thereby constitute a system that can be technically termed representative government, even if one with a strong elitist bias.

These first four chapters thus lay out the ambiguous principles of the American political system. Part II applies these principles in their systematic ambiguity to the major institutions of American government, from the courts through the presidency and Congress to local government and their accompanying bureaucracies. Five chapters take up these institutions one by one. The general effect of this analysis will be to make us feel that we are looking at American government through bifocal glasses.

The institution least susceptible to this bifocal effect is the court system, discussed in Chapter 5. As a general rule, the courts and judges of America are charged with and hew close to the line of conserving the law by settling disputes in terms of the law, positive, actual, and known. This is essentially an ideological function dictated by the emphasis on constitutionalism (rule within limits prescribed by law) featured in liberal democracy. By executing this function faithfully, the courts become an essential element of stability in a system otherwise wracked by ambiguity and contradictory tensions. But it must be added that the courts, and most especially the Supreme Court in Washington, with some regularity are called on to perform not only routine mythic roles but sometimes momentous ones as well.

In contrast, the presidency, discussed in Chapter 6, is called daily to grand, mythic roles. Promulgating the nation's living myth is that office's primary function. And in this role, the presidency appears vastly powerful. On the other hand, in its ideological role, which the office also has in some abundance, the office is surprisingly ineffective.

Congress (Chapter 7), in its turn, often appears incredibly clumsy in its legislative role. But that is its true role only in myth. In liberal democratic ideology, it is the nation's paradigm instrument for harmonizing the conflicting claims of the competing interests, and in this role it is a sustained and proficient success, for what that may be worth.

Local government (Chapter 8) in America is true grassroots democracy—in myth. In ideology and at the same time, it is dominated by parochial barons who are frequently as small-minded as they are self-serving.

And through it all, America's civil and military servants (Chapter 9), the nation's bureaucracy, national, state, and local, rationally and professionally competent as they may be, go about their work fundamentally either frustrated by "political" constraints or blinded by inadequate political leadership. The overall result of their efforts is often a crazy quilt of national, foreign, domestic, and local policies that, top heavy with technological proficiency, make little sense.

Interpretive conclusions along these lines might be welcomed in some quarters. Timeworn technical debates about American government can now be resolved by saying both sides are right. Not only can the president be shown to be both strong and weak, but Congress can be shown to be both inefficient and proficient. Strong cases can now be made out, too, that the United States is both a federation and a confederation, simultaneously, albeit at different levels of analysis; that the federal government employs as an organizing principle separation of powers, but also, at a different level of analysis, some other theory as well, and so forth.

Nevertheless, all this analysis points finally to painful conclusions. The general impression the first two parts of the book should leave with the reader is of a political system cleanly bifurcated between a full scale of contradictory components generating between them a perpetual tension. Some readers may find satisfaction in the relative success that the system has had not only in perpetuating but also, for the most part, in containing that tension. But other readers may already be wondering about the costs that must be paid to achieve what is at best only a limited success.

Evaluating the American political system will be the direct concern of the three chapters of Part III. The perspective adopted is that of the American citizen. But *civis Americanus* is a complicated figure. To be a citizen is to hold an office, to don an institutionalized, official dress, as much as with any other office in the system. As such, the status of citizen is caught up in and subject to the conflicts and contradictions that afflict the system generally. In consequence, the American citizen confronts the political system from a perspective that mirrors the schizophrenia of the system itself. Like it, part Bourgeois, part Protestant, the citizen will want to have it both ways. In consequence, he or she is bound to be disappointed, for either way, the other way will always be ready with a negative judgment. But the situation is more grievous than that. Both sides of the American political system, when taken separately and judged in their own terms, are defective. Moreover, both fall short of the standards citizens may bring to bear independently, the ones they derive from their own professional work experience. These rational-professional standards are shared by the government's own civil and military employees, and in their perspective American government's endlessly repeated scenes of bureaucratic and programmatic incompetence and confusion will seem simply appalling.

Throughout this discussion, it must be remembered that the aim of the argument is to establish American political failures not as empirical facts but as theoretical necessities, as design faults. The die was cast in the beginning.

I
FUNDAMENTALS

The American political system is a whole, a single system. Essentially, the system is a power construct and has two sides, a mythic side that creates and legitimizes power and an ideological side that guides power's exercise, its use in governance. American history has filled up the two sides of our political system with radically different contents, the mythic side with a largely Protestant content and the ideological side with a thoroughly secular, Bourgeois content. This means that America is a democracy ambiguously. In its mythic aspirations it is a social democracy; in its practical ideological operations it is a liberal democracy. These contrasting democratic visions have not only differing central values, social equality versus personal freedom, but also differing patterns of political institutions and operational styles. American social democracy calls for a broadly participatory popular government institutionalized in patterns of confederation and the presidential leadership characteristic of separation of powers. American liberal democracy calls for a much more narrowly elitist government based on competing interests institutionalized in the pattern of federalism and mixed government.

1
Power

If we are to understand the American political system, if we are to cut through the rhetoric that over the years has encrusted it, we had best begin by going back to fundamentals, by ensuring that we have a firm grip on the basic abstract principles of modern politics. The first of these is that the United States is a nation-state; therefore, like all modern, sovereign nation-states, it is in essence a power construct. What does this mean?

It means two things. First, America has a relatively developed and stable political culture. Second, within America's national boundaries the established governments, federal, state, and local, command obedience and can elicit the cooperation of the bulk of the population.

More specifically, by saying that the United States is a construct, we mean that the American people have been, in their historical situation, sufficiently instructed and disciplined intellectually and morally to sustain identifiable and definable patterns of political behavior and goals. By saying that this construct is centrally a power construct, we mean that, within the established general patterns of American political culture, specific patterns of deference and leadership, legitimization and governance, have been both firmly established and also are largely observed.

In other words, power is not force. Force, pure, brute push, can be exercised in a cultural vacuum. Power cannot. Power is a cultural construct.[1] Taking apart this riddle will yield for us the distinction between myth, on the one hand, and ideology, on the other, the two great concepts on which the whole analysis of American politics in this book is built. We must proceed with this definition with care.

Power and Force

Power is a loose word. America is said to be the most powerful nation in the world. Our military might is so great, we could blow up all our enemies many times over. At home, heavily armed and elaborately equipped police are everywhere. Yet it often appears that our government has very little power. We implore our allies overseas to assist us in this or that project, and very little happens. We trade

11

arms for hostages and end up with a large deficit of arms and a net loss of hostages. And at home, despite all the police, crime rates soar. It is power in this second more amorphous, weaker sense that mostly concerns us here. How do governments get people to obey? Of their own free will? To do what they are *told*, just by the asking?

Force needs no cultural context in which to be exercised because there is no need to communicate with its object; I can just hit it, push it, move it, in a word, force it. If I have arrived at the point where my small child has to be picked up kicking and screaming and simply placed into bed by force, saying "It'stimetogotobed!" will add nothing to the effectiveness or efficiency of what I am doing. Equally, if America has arrived at the point where it believes it has to blockade, invade, or shell and bomb some little country to get its way, issuing communiqués afterward explaining why will not disguise or change what it has done. For all our military pyrotechnics, we acted from a position of political weakness; we were reduced to getting compliance by force.

On the other hand, in my case, if my child smiles sweetly at my command, turns off the TV, and toddles off upstairs, all in response only to my words "Time for beddy-bys," those words are key to a total and complex situation. And the astonishment of sundry in-laws and grandparents at this performance will be a measure of both their awe at my power over the child and of their curiosity about the dialogues I must have had previously with the child to establish the possibility of what they had just seen. They would have to believe that I could have that kind of control over the child only on the basis of some carefully nurtured companionship between us in which we had come to a stabilized understanding about who we were in relationship to each other in our shared home.

Equally, if the United States urgently calls a conference of assorted nations about a particular project, and, lo, they all come and, moreover, after due discussion, all do their assigned roles, the world would be astonished at this display of American leadership "power." It would wonder too at the skilled diplomacy that must have lain behind the conference and that had created the community of interest that made possible its success.

The cultural context, within which this kind of control by one person or nation over the conduct of others can exist, constitutes "a shared field of meaning." This shared field of meaning is a sine qua non of people acting together in power relationships. No doubt observers could simply watch and record the physical processes of what goes on in these situations, and that might be interesting. But any humanistic understanding of the processes in them requires going

beyond physical appearances and grasping the concepts and meanings that lie behind the appearances and that give those appearances
their structure and relationships.[2] To start with, in my case, both
child and parent have to understand what the terms, "child" and
"parent," mean, both separately and in relationship to each other,
and to have the mental dexterity to situate themselves in relationship
to each other by using these concepts. Furthermore, before the situation can proceed, a whole range of other terms have to be understood and employed—"command," "obedience," "bed," "time,"
"sleep," and so on—some of which involve extraordinarily complex
ideas. Equally with our example of the supposed international conference, explicit understandings of basic terms of international relations, such as "sovereignty" and "national interest," would have to
exist and be assured mutual respect. Furthermore, specific understandings of the immediate situation and of its perils and pitfalls
would have to be achieved before joint action could be undertaken.

Notice, finally, in all this the role of the bystanders. It is only
apparently passive. In fact, it is both positive and substantial. They
are the audience, more or less approving, before whom the situation
is played out. We can speculate that even my tender-aged child is
sensitive to the smiles and nods of approval that greet docile behavior. Gaining that approval may well be a partial motive for good
behavior. The same may well be true of the parent, for parents also
have roles to learn and to demonstrate proficiency in before approving audiences. Equally, being seen—or not, as the case may be—as a
staunch and trusted American ally is a major element in modern
foreign relations.

What this analysis demonstrates is that even very simple "political" situations are in fact highly complex. They are also fragile. The
child could become irritable, and self-control could break down; the
parent could also become impatient; a busybody relative could seek
to take over the situation. The control or power relationship would
collapse, and once again mere force would be required to advance
affairs to a tolerable conclusion.

Within each party's perception of the shared field of meaning,
the power relationship itself appears as a transactional relationship,
in which one speaks and the other responds, both in ways appropriate to and within the limits of their established relationship. How did
the possibility of this happening come about? The only possible answer is, by some kind of nurtured consent, by agreement.

This merely abstract statement should still strike at least some
Americans as surprising. Americans have learned from the Declaration of Independence that governments derive their just powers

from the consent of the governed. What we are saying here is that all power, all government—just or otherwise—is by consent, and that the only open and interesting question is how the consent is obtained.

Let us shift to another example. Think of a team of police officers telling me to halt. This is a proverbial example among political scientists because the presumption that the police officers have guns, that is, classic instruments of brute force, is a convenient complication.

Suppose I obey the officers' command. Why? Here is a list of possible explanations:

I know them as old friends, and I generally do simple things my friends ask me to do; or

I am a philosopher and have learned from the great books that there is no freedom except within the color of the law, which the officers' uniforms and badges represent; or

I have also learned from the great books that the alternative to obedience to the law is social chaos; or

It is just habit. I am one of those people who automatically obeys authority figures of any kind, athletic coaches, teachers, parents, even librarians, let alone police officers; or

One of these particular police officers is known to me as a candidate for future public office whose decisions might decisively influence the fate of my business; or

One of these particular police officers is known to me as a person, who, off duty, is a local religious teacher of great saintliness who might well give me spiritual guidance and might lead me out of evil ways into a meaningful life; or

I know that I have done something wrong and that I deserve to be apprehended and punished. If I am not, what is life and law all about? or

Frankly, I am scared to death of all those guns; or

All, or any combination, of the above.

What this list demonstrates by its variety and comprehensiveness is that there has to be some *reason* for my obedience. Even if I do a rapid set of calculations, weighing chances of escape against probabilities of punishment, I am persuading myself to obey. If in a power relationship I am to be "coerced," it must be in some sense and for some reason by my consent. Proof of this can be seen in the possibility that I might decide not to obey. If that happens, the officers will physically subdue me, if necessary using their guns, all this in *absence* of a reason sufficient to persuade me to obey.

But are not their guns already a factor in the situation, just by my knowing they are there? Of course. But in their holsters, they were important as symbols, a communication that might just as well have been printed, saying, "Obey, or else . . ." A threat of force is a communication, part of a "dialogue of persuasion." The use of force is simply that, a brute fact, nothing more, requiring no cultural context for its interpretation and calling for no response. A threat of force is a message that there may be still worse to come, which to be effected must be within the limits of a shared culture received, understood, and, decisively, assented to.

None of this is an introduction to a discussion about the differences between good and bad reasons for obedience. Our concern is only to show that those who obey, whether for good reasons or bad ones, have to be persuaded to do so. Power, in other words, as opposed to force, cannot be had unless, through some kind of dialogue of persuasion, it is given, and given precisely by those over whom it is to be exercised.

Moreover, power cannot be exercised until after it has been given, until after the dialogue of persuasion has been favorably resolved. That process might be virtually instantaneous—in a flash I see the police officers' uniforms, see that I am outnumbered, see their guns, and decide to give in. Or the process might be protracted over many hours—if I am heavily armed and holed up with hostages behind sturdy walls. Either way, the dialogue of persuasion is logically prior to and distinct from the dialogue of governance, the cry of "Halt!" or whatever, and my specific response to it. First, I recognize the authority figure as being that, that is, to use the technical term, I legitimize the power; and only then, second, do I obey, that is, allow my behavior to be governed by the received commands. Analytically, legitimation, the dialogue of authority acceptance, and governance, the dialogue of ruling, are clear and theoretically distinct elements in power relationships.

That power constructs can thus be seen bifurcating into distinct dialogues or elements, legitimization and governance, is a matter of great analytical importance to this book. It means we can track through the American political system using these concepts as tools of classification and analysis. It means, too, at the practical level, that the conventionalized content these concepts have been given in the actual conditions of American politics may have been determined

mostly by historical accidents rather than by purely logical requirements. American concepts of conventional legitimization and governance will have to be examined for what they factually are. The argument to come will show that in historical fact American patterns
of political legitimization are radically and systematically at variance
with their corresponding patterns of political governance.

The significance of these possibilities is greatly enhanced by a
further abstract characteristic these elements in the power construct
share. This is that they are qualitative concepts. Force is a quantitative concept. No doubt there are more or less subtle differences between force applied by a hammer, by a rock, or by a fist, but the
amount of force each of them applies is measurable and comparable
in specific units. It is true that common expression often conveys the
impression that power as we have been defining it here can also be
quantified. We say that a certain person is the most powerful leader
in his or her community, or that someone's power grew significantly
in a certain period. But this kind of talk, implying as it does that
power is a substance that holders of it can carry around with them
wherever they go, is highly misleading.

Exercisable power of governance is conditional on both the legitimization agreement creating it and also the field of meaning within
which it appears. These conditions restrict the extent and content of
any particular grant of power. A police officer, commissioned as
such in a field of meaning and acknowledged as such by persons
encountered in line of duty, had best act like a police officer, that is,
in accordance with common understandings of what police officers
are, if the deference due the rank is to be received. Equally, on a
larger scene, the president of the United States is, by constitutional
mandate, commander in chief of the armed forces. That may sound
like a grant of huge—and quantifiable—power. But actual presidents many times have had to learn, sometimes to their chagrin, that
their exercise of the powers coming to them from this title is sharply
restricted by qualitative constraints, that is, by debates and conten-
tions among their Washington colleagues and subordinates about
just exactly what a "commander in chief" can and cannot do. In consequence, the power of the president as actual commander in chief
of American military might is not so much halved or quartered from
what it first appears; it is *definably* different. How different it in fact
is can only be determined by a qualitative examination of the context
within which its use was attempted.

These considerations should make it even plainer that the theoretical distinctiveness of the legitimization and governance elements
in the power construct open up practical possibilities for every kind

and degree of ambiguity, confusion, and argument. If power could be quantified, like force, and then doled out with precision and clarity, few of these problems would arise. But power is assigned and exercised through understandings of concepts derived by only more or less identically socialized individuals from their only more or less shared fields of meaning—which in turn are only more or less coherently and consistently formed. Studying American government is not a matter of locating and *measuring* power; it is a matter of determining and *defining* relationships and responsibilities of often mind-boggling complexity and contradiction.

There is no need to illustrate any of these possibilities now. In a sense this whole book is an illustration of them. What we can do now is pull together the purely abstract argument developed thus far with these summarizing definitions.

- Power is a transactional relationship within which, in a shared field of meaning, a willing inferior allows an acknowledged superior to direct in certain ways and within certain limits his or her behavior.

- Legitimization is, in the power relationship, the dialogic element by which the inferior in it comes to acknowledge, through one process of persuasion or another, the more or less articulated rights of the superior to direct the inferior's behavior.

- Governance is, in the power relationship, the dialogic element by which the directive rights of the superior are exercised over the inferior.

Boiled down, power is a relationship in which you, for some more or less persuasive reason, do as you are told.

Myth and Ideology

The essence of what we have so far been arguing is that power is always to be understood as embedded in the total social and political context in which it is exercised. This is to suggest that the power of a Soviet leader in that country may be radically different, not just in extent but also in quality, from the power of an American leader. It is even to suggest that, within a given country, the power of a given leader in a certain period may be very different from the power of earlier or subsequent leaders holding the same office. Nevertheless, if only because of the viscosity with which cultural contexts develop and change over time, power relationships throughout societies tend, within limits set for individual variations, toward stability.

Within any historically developed community, parents, children, police, citizens, presidents, and premiers all tend recognizably to obtain and use power in standardized ways.

The standardized conceptions of power may change quite rapidly in some societies, and very slowly in others. An assertion of this book, to be developed throughout its length, is that the American standards by which power is developed and exercised have, all appearances to the contrary notwithstanding, changed hardly at all since the nation's founding.

Politically, in other words, America is an extraordinarily viscous nation. The patterns by which Americans learned collectively to recognize and legitimize power and to allow for its exercise in governance were set early on and, once set, have changed hardly at all. To grasp the totality of this grand fact we are employing in this book the two terms "myth" and "ideology." As mentioned in the Introduction, by myth we mean the total process by which Americans traditionally legitimize themselves and the power constructs they erect over themselves, and by ideology we mean the total process by which Americans traditionally have come to govern themselves in actual daily practice.

Myth itself divides into two stages, one having to do with the identification of the people as a people in history, and the other having to do with the legitimization of governments and their powers. In both stages, in the United States, the dialogues are conducted almost exclusively in historical terms.

The identification of the people as a people begins with their memory of themselves, of their beginning and progress through the years, of their heroes and triumphs, their villains and disasters, in a word, their times together. This is their saga, the story of the nation, as embellished by folk tale and song. By the celebration and reiteration of it, by the endless sharing and remembrance of it, citizens young and old come almost physically to participate in their common saga and develop a powerful sense of their unity and identity as a people distinctive, even exceptional, among the peoples of the world. Out of it also has come, so deep and pervasive is the saga, a profound sense of national commitment, of national purpose, a widely shared belief that, as a people of historic particularity and style, Americans have a distinct contribution to make to history, in a word, a national mission. In the old language of the New England divines, we were sent together, as a nation, on an errand into the wilderness.

A nation's legitimate sense of itself as rooted in the memory of its saga and the anticipation of its mission can be, and often is, much reinforced by the coincidence of the people sharing a common language, racial type, religion and other cultural traits, and, most importantly, a common land with defined boundaries. But these factors are only relatively important, as the American experience shows, and one or more of them are often missing in particular nations. The essence of legitimate nationhood is the shared memory and anticipation, the shared saga and mission, the sense that we came out of that past together and together are on our way forward.

It must be stressed that this sense of national identity in history is a subjective phenomenon. Objectively, professional historians tell the facts as they find them and place them in an orderly, linear time frame. But saga and national mission are not rooted in linear time frames; they are rooted in shared, subjective memory and anticipation, in a people's sense that their current identity comes to them out of their felt and believed past and their felt and believed future. The "facts" of saga may or may not be objectively true in every case in the eyes of historians, and the anticipations of mission by the same standards may or may not be reasonable. But, to the people involved, historically and politically, truth and rationality are not immediately relevant criteria. The assertions of a saga and mission are necessary beliefs, essential to national identity and unity, primary to legitimate nationhood.

Legitimization of a nation's governing regime is the second major element of myth. This, too, is a reiterated process of both remembrance and anticipation, a process by which, repeatedly, often virtually day by day, a regime, both as a particular group of ruling persons and as an ongoing set of rulers, is placed in and measured against the people's sense of its historical context. In this light, political myth, or, more broadly, the mythic level of political activity, is given a clear function in the political system: the legitimization of both people and government, ruled and rulers. It is to give all participants a sense of place and, more important, a sense of worth, both in their own eyes and in the regard they have for each other.[3] Without that sense of self-worth and mutual regard among its operatives, the political system as a whole could not begin to govern. This, no doubt, applies especially to those citizens and leaders active in the political process, but it tends to rub off too on even the most passive and apathetic of citizens.

To be effective, myth in all its aspects must be traditionalized and routinized. It is not only that the certainty of it must be guaranteed by having citizens learn it by rote. They have to be assured that all their fellow citizens have learned and come to believe and put their trust as social beings in the same myth. That does not happen completely in practice, but it is remarkable how close even highly pluralistic societies can come to this mark. And it is worth remarking in passing how stifling especially intellectuals, oblivious to its social utility, can find this process.

Routinization of the myth that identifies and legitimizes the people is achieved mostly by conventionalizing its content. The songs and stories celebrating the saga and the hopes of the mission are set down in standardized form and symbolized in monuments and catch phrases. It is a straightforward business, mostly "educational," but nonetheless amazing in the directness with which it is undertaken. It is an experience for any social scientist to stand by the steps of the Capitol in Washington on a summer morning and watch citizens from all over the country deposited there busload by busload, like pilgrims drawn to Mecca, and hear them lectured by their youthful tour guides, phrase by identical phrase, about what they are seeing.

Routinization of the myth legitimizing rulers and their regimes has to be both a more flexible and a more precise business and is, therefore, more institutionalized than simply conventionalized. What has to be routinized here is the way in which rulers and their regimes are personally selected and legitimated. The most obvious part of this process, in democratic societies and many dictatorial ones, too, is elections, but many other techniques are used as well. Virtually every public move the president of the United States makes contains more or less significant mythic elements. Just by having their picture taken while they are seated in the Oval Office, a president and his associates transmit a message, a highly traditionalized appeal, to the American people: "I am your president—the only one you have! And this is *my* crew!" But even elections can become highly stylized, nowhere more so than in America. An argument of later chapters of this book is that American presidential elections in particular are in fact so highly mythically stylized that there is hardly room in them for anything other than style.

The role of all the major institutions of acculturation—schools, churches, family, popular literature, and, above all, the daily press and TV and radio broadcasting—in this total process is crucial. Especially the press seems duty bound to take with utmost seriousness even the most trivial and meaningless aspects of the political process, the more to enhance its mythic significance. The press alone seems able to elevate, for example, primary-election results—which may in fact have as much significance as baseball scores—to the level of "news" in which the fate of the republic is made to seem as if hanging in the balance.

A nation's political myth, in the light of the present argument, can thus be given a condensed definition as the elements of a political system that, in routinized, conventionalized, and institutionalized ways, identify the people as a nation and legitimize their rulers. As such, it deserves one final observation: myth, as the philosophers say, is value laden, so much so that it often appears to be no more than national prejudice. Its imperatives often seem preemptory about how one should dress, act, speak, even think to be regarded as a good citizen or to run a successful election campaign. But this characteristic of myth is inevitable if myth is to function effectively in a highly complex modern society full of distractions. And once again, without an effective myth to ensure its popular legitimization, the political system as a whole could not begin to operate.

The actual operation of the political system at the level of doing daily business and getting it done is, as we have said, governance, and in any historically developed nation-state this too is and must be traditionalized, routinized, and, above all, institutionalized. This side of political systems has been so assiduously studied and reported on by political scientists, and the constitutions of modern states around the world are so exclusively concerned to give it legal effect, that only one of its general characteristics need detain us here. As much as the mythic side, the governance or operational side of political systems is value laden. And the governance values of a political system are as preemptory as anything on the mythic side. Even in the most ruthless and apparently utterly lawless dictatorship, there is still the one requirement at least that only the dictator shall dictate. In democracies, the comparable imperatives are more diffuse and ambiguous but no less insistent for all that. Law and tradition combine to demand that there are right ways and wrong ways in which to get the government's business done. All this is reason enough for calling this side of an operative political system its "ideology," its traditionalized and institutionalized ways for getting done the government's daily work of legislating laws, executing programs, and adjudicating disputes.

Describing "ideology" this way is to give it a broad meaning, broader than usual. Usually, ideology refers to the specific and rigidly defined program of a party or particular groups of people (ideologues). In the present context, the word covers that traditional meaning, but also, more loosely, it is extended to cover all programs *and* institutions in a political system that are geared to getting things done, to the actual work of governance. By this definition, ideology is most simply equated with the shared mental constructs by which a people ensures, sustains, and executes governmental performance.[4]

The Reality of Myth and Ideology

There is a powerful verbal tendency, once something has been identified as "myth," to contrast it to "reality." Equally, what we have defined as ideology some readers may tend to contrast to "ideals" or "rhetoric." These contrasts may in turn be quickly confused with a series of contrasts well known to traditional study of American politics, such as "the theory and practice of American government" or "promise and performance in the American political system." But these traditional distinctions are not helpful. Some of them are logically absurd: is there a theory and practice of gravity? Others are seriously misleading: can we simply let it go that the huge gap between the aspirations and the performance of American government is nothing more than a natural human failing, a case of the spirit being willing but the flesh weak? In this book, distinctions of this type, for all their verbal facility, will be adamantly avoided.

Myth, for all its apparent "idealism," is real, as historically real and as politically functional as any other part of the political system. By the same taken, ideology, as defined in this book, for all its apparent "realism" and concern for "practicality," is in the end as value laden as myth. But that does not make ideology as we have defined it any less real a part of the political system. Whether exactly observed here or there, it remains the actual set of institutional and programmatic imperatives the system historically has for directing citizens and their rulers about how they should go about getting the business of government done. The same is true of myth. Whether observed in the breach exactly or not, real, historically given myth continues to instruct how and why and where and by whom the political system as a whole should be legitimated.

The definitions of power and its elements, myth and ideology, given in this chapter constitute a framework for analysis by which we can confront and take apart the political systems of modern nation-states, and especially that of the United States. These terms are conceptual tools by which we can do intellectual justice to the complexities and the paradoxes in political systems. America is not exceptional among modern nation-states because it has a myth and an ideology. All nation-states as power constructs have these. America is exceptional because of the content that its history has poured into these abstract concepts and because of the extraordinary tensions that have thereby developed between them. It is this strange content given to American myth and ideology that we will now begin to survey.

2
The Protestant/Bourgeois Complex

The general thesis to be advanced in this chapter is that the content poured into American power constructs was essentially an individualism divided between its Protestant and Bourgeois components. Moreover, to a remarkable degree, historically and practically, the Protestant elements of that individualism came to occupy and fill up almost exclusively the legitimation, mythic side of American power constructs, while the Bourgeois elements of that same individualism were with equal exclusiveness pouring into and filling up the governance, ideological side of those constructs.

The particular thesis to be advanced in this chapter is that the Protestant and Bourgeois elements of American individualism are, simultaneously, radically united in their celebration of the autonomy of the individual, and, as radically, divided by the absolute irreconcilability of the demands they respectively place on the individual. In consequence, American individualism, the rock on which all else in the American political system is built, is itself, at core, radically schizophrenic. All the other great paradoxes of the American political system can be traced back to this original confusion.

It might be thought that America's fundamental paradox, its central schizophrenia, is the source of a positive tension, a dynamic, vital, creative dialectic. But we will find that, practically, this has not proved to be true, nor, given the logical character of the elements involved, could it have.

Consensus/Cleavage

To understand the significance of the theses of this chapter requires a brief survey of American studies scholarship. The reason for this is that American political experience from the beginning was taken with great seriousness by all concerned, by both citizens and scholars. From the beginning, like it or not, intentionally or not, Americans of all walks of life were taught by scholars and came themselves almost unanimously to believe that their political experiment held lessons for all mankind, that their nation, in John Winthrop's words, would be "a city upon a hill." The American nation was in its founding a gauntlet thrown down to time. From 1776 forward, citizens struggled with this responsibility—and so also did scholars. Jefferson proclaimed it in the Declaration of Independence, but so too did Tocqueville and, between them, Crèvecoeur.[1] On these issues, very directly, America's first scholars spoke both to and for the people.

To these founding convictions of America's mission, the Civil War was a catastrophe almost beyond measure. How could a divided, shattered America be a beacon to the ages? Lincoln, in the closing phrases of the Gettysburg Address, by rhetorical *force majeure*, proclaimed his answer to this question ("We here highly resolve that . . . this nation, under God, shall have a new birth of freedom. . . ."). The professional scholarly answer came later but no less emphatically. Like Lincoln's, it was an attempt to speak to the ambiguities of American political experience by mostly denying that they existed. In 1893, in the still-extending wake of the war, Frederick Jackson Turner delivered a paper to the American Historical Association titled "The Significance of the Frontier in American History." In its first paragraph, Turner declared, abundant evidence to the contrary notwithstanding:

> Up to our own day American history has been in a large degree the history of the colonization of the Great West. The existence of an area of free land, its continuous regression, and the advance of the American settlement westward, explained American development.[2]

Turner went further. He claimed:

> From the conditions of frontier life came intellectual traits of profound importance. . . . That coarseness and strength combined with acuteness and inquisitiveness; that practical, inventive turn of mind, quick to find expedients; that masterful grasp of material things, lacking in the artistic but powerful to effect great ends; that restless, nervous energy; that dominant individualism, working for good and for evil, and withal that buoyancy and exuberance which comes with freedom.[3]

Turner's celebration of the American frontier, his insistence that what was exceptional and enduring in American experience came not by transport in any ship from Europe but sprang fresh and clean from the frontier, from the division between the advancing, overly civilized East and the always retreating but democratizing West, was an immediate success. It brought him academic stature and popular acclaim. It became a standard in American historical scholarship and passed over in many forms into the folklore of the nation. It defined in broadly acceptable, consensual terms the meaning of America. But there was a price.

To play up the East/West character of American experience, Turner had to play down the North/South divisions of the Civil War. He did this with surprising boldness. He admitted that in the period from 1850 to the end of the war, slavery "rose to primary," but, he insisted, "far from exclusive importance." More positively, he argued, "When American history comes to be rightly viewed it will be seen that the slavery question is an incident" and repeated once again, "The growth of nationalism and the evolution of American political institutions were dependent on the advance of the frontier."[4]

However persuasive in their own terms, these arguments do not resolve the underlying issue. The American Civil War was a fact. To say that it was more or less important than some other fact or facts does not remove the reality of its having happened. And so the question hangs, why did it happen? More particularly, in Turner's context, how could it happen in a nation supposedly shaped by a single formative experience? The more Turner labors to make the frontier the distinguishing feature of American political life, the more he uses it to explain the consensual character of the American experience, the more inexplicable he makes the Civil War—and all other instances of national division in America.

Because of these weaknesses in Turner's theory, but even more because of painfully obvious developments in American post–Civil War industrial and political life, a rival theory explaining American history was soon put forward. It was championed by a group of scholars known as the "progressive historians," although its number included political scientists, students of American literature, philosophers, and journalists. This academic group had important connections in the political arena, first in the Progressive parties in Wisconsin and New York, then through the scholar/politician figure of Woodrow Wilson, and on down through much of the rhetoric and practice of the New Deal.

The progressive theory, like Turner's, began with an insistence that there was something fresh and characteristically American about the nation's commitment to a democratic vision. And like Turner's, this theory held that the commitment to the democratic vision had been there from the nation's earliest colonial days. However, it immediately went on to assert, often in strident terms, that the fulfillment of this vision had been seriously impeded by elites entrenched in the churches, universities, and business corporations, as well as in local, state, and the federal governments, most especially in the court system, the United States Senate, and even the presidency. Therefore, against Turner, the proponents of this rival theory came to focus directly on the divisiveness of the American political experience. They held that what was meaningful and significant about American politics was that it was persistently a democratic/ oligarchical struggle in which there had been many victories and not a few defeats.

Vernon Parrington, in his massive history of American litera- ture, *Main Currents in American Thought,* written in the 1920s, began his history of this struggle by drawing a line.

> The line of liberalism in colonial America runs through Roger Williams, Benjamin Franklin, and Thomas Jefferson. . . . Over against these pro- tagonists of liberalism must be set the complementary figures of John Cotton, Jonathan Edwards, and Alexander Hamilton, men whose gran- diose dreams envisaged different ends for America and who followed different paths.[5]

In the 1940s, Arthur Schlesinger, Jr., carried the line forward. Seeking to explain the presidency of Andrew Jackson and the sup- posed revolutionary surges it represented, Schlesinger wrote:

> The Jacksonians believed that there was a deep-rooted conflict in soci- ety between the "producing" and "non-producing" classes—the farmers and laborers, on the one hand, and the business community on the other. . . .

> The specific problem was to control the power of the capitalistic groups, mainly Eastern, for the benefit of the non-capitalist groups, farmers and laboring men, East, West and South . . . Jacksonian democracy was . . . a . . . phase of that enduring struggle between the business commu- nity and the rest of society which is the guarantee of freedom in a lib- eral capitalist state.[6]

As these quotations make clear, the struggle this theory sees in American society is to be understood in part as a power struggle, a contest between opposing interests for positions of social, economic, and political control. But the struggle is also said to be philosophical. American experience is to be interpreted, this theory holds, as a con- flict between those with a democratic vision for the nation and those "whose grandiose dreams," in Parrington's words, "envisaged differ- ent ends for America."[7] It is not immediately apparent from these words what these other ends for America were. The scholars we have quoted viewed the struggle from its "progressive" side. There is another view, and it is important to notice an example of it.

Samuel Huntington, a contemporary scholar, may be thought to speak for this other view. In *American Politics: The Promise of Dishar- mony,* he speaks with an unmistakable "conservative" slant. The fulcrum of his argument is what he calls the "IvI" gap, the discrepancy he sees in American political life between its ideals and its institutions. He implicitly accepts the notion that the dominant, populist, democratic majority in America has defined the nation's ideals, or, as he calls them in sum, the nation's political "creed." But he distinguishes this creed sharply from the nation's practical system of governmental institutions. Our ideals and our institutions are, he thinks, antithetical, and their opposition has created "the central themes of American political thought."[8]

> American liberal and democratic ideas form a standing and powerful indictment of almost all political institutions, including American ones. No government can exist without some measure of hierarchy, inequality, arbitrary power, secrecy, deception, and established patterns of superordination and subordination. The American Creed, however, challenges the legitimacy of all these characteristics of government in general. They run counter to the nature of highly bureaucratized and centralized modern government. They run counter to both the original and inherited nature of American government.[9]

Huntington comes close to an analytic definition of the American creed in this paragraph:

> The basic ideas of the American Creed—equality, liberty, individualism, constitutionalism, democracy—clearly do not constitute a systematic ideology, and they do not necessarily have any logical consistency. . . . Precisely because it is not an intellectualized ideology, the American Creed can live with . . . inconsistencies.[10]

It is Huntington's claim that the items listed here as constituting the American Creed, for all their inconsistency with each other, share the common theme of opposition to governmental power. But his analysis does not go beyond this. The spareness of it must prompt the curious reader to wonder what inspired the Americans to have any government at all.

Americans do have a government, and Huntington, as the first quotation above indicates, assumes it will exhibit "some measure of hierarchy, inequality, arbitrary power, secrecy, deception," and so forth. That is a problem rooted in "the imperfections of human nature."[11] Because these characteristics are necessities of government, the United States can never live up to its creedal ideals. But again the analysis stops short. The special characteristics of American government, its Madisonian logic, its principles of federalism and separation of powers, its granting of constitutional review powers to the courts, its massive and hugely expensive system of popular elections, do not engage Huntington's sustained attention.

What we are up against here is the unwillingness, perhaps even the inability, of prominent scholars to tell us with precision and comprehensiveness what it is that divides America. The original progressives charged that the country was in danger of being taken over by sinister elitists. But who were those elitists? Did they actively reject the American democratic dream? It is not clear that even Huntington, who appears to be some kind of elitist, does that. More seriously, it is not clear what, by siding with the prerogatives of the nation's institutions, he does believe—other than that governments must govern.

There is a major, substantive reason for all these imprecisions. The fact of the matter is that there is virtually no difference at the philosophical level between the combatants in the progressives' democratic/oligarchical struggle or in Huntington's "IvI" gap. Let a former progressive, Richard Hofstadter, make the case:

> [My] studies in the ideology of American statesmanship have convinced me of the need for a reinterpretation of our political traditions which emphasizes the common climate of American opinion. The existence of such a climate of opinion has been much obscured by the tendency to place political conflict in the foreground of history. . . . However much at odds on specific issues, the major political traditions have shared a belief in the rights of property, the philosophy of economic individualism, the value of competition; they have accepted the economic virtues of capitalist culture as necessary qualities of man.[12]

The argument is persuasive. Let us agree that there is a broad moral and political consensus in America. But then and equally, there still can be no denying the fact of divisiveness in America. That fact stands, too. Can we deny that we had a civil war? Thus, side by side, in America, there is consensus and cleavage. How can their simultaneous presence as major features of American political experience be explained?

The Consensus Complex

That is the problem to which, in this book, the Protestant/Bourgeois complex will be held to be the solution. Just as we approached the problem by way of an excursion into American studies scholarship, so now we will approach the solution by the same route and for the same reasons. As before, the scholars' confusions mirror those of the people.

Turner, no doubt inadvertently, was the founder of a recognizable school interpreting American experience. His theory about the frontier was ecological, almost anti-intellectual. Certainly some of his direct descendants are on record believing that the genius of American politics is specifically its nonphilosophical character, as if what made American politics tick was a kind of mindless pragmatism.[13] But Turner himself, as quoted before, referred to the frontiersman's "intellectual traits of individualism," and Turner's celebration of Western democratic vistas could hardly have been simply in terms of deserts and empty valleys. Democracy wherever practiced is a lifestyle of definable mental characteristics. In time, a variety of scholars came to believe that it was in those definable mental characteristics of American democracy that the national consensus was to be found. Moreover, breaking ranks on this point at least with Turner, they recognized these ideas as largely European imports. This did not mean that they dismissed or even denigrated Turner's insight about the powerful influence of the frontier on the development of American character. On the contrary, what they came to insist was that the exceptional features of American politics grew quite precisely from the collision between imported European ideas and the raw American environment. In a word, they effectively labeled America a provincial society of European origins. The national consensus, the ground of American politics, was now seen to be a provincialized European theory of liberal democracy.

Much the most able proponent of this view was Louis Hartz. The title of his most important book, *The Liberal Tradition in America,* stated precisely what he wanted to study, European liberalism, or, more exactly, seventeenth-eighteenth-century Lockean liberalism, in its American environment.[14]

Hartz has three major propositions about the American consensus. The first is that the core values of American liberalism are those of Locke (individualism, security of property, etc.). This first thesis further asserts that the act of exporting Lockean liberalism out of the England in which it originated deprived it of the philosophical environment that had given it a specific social and political purpose and a context of modification and containment. Thus, American liberalism, in this view, while indeed pure Locke, was effectively also a truncated Locke, a Locke stripped of its English context and general social meanings.

This first proposition sets up Hartz's second, that American liberalism, by being planted in America's provincial environment, became isolated not only from its originating environment but also, in America's emptiness, from all other possible competitors. In consequence, it underwent a subtle but important change. English liberalism had been originally a radicalism, an appropriately bellicose testament of a middle class bent on redefining the meaning of wealth, the functions of government, and much else in a still profoundly feudal world. In America, without a fight, it became the dominant idea of the ruling class—and of almost everybody else as well. Subtly but very importantly, it became, epistemologically, the exclusive truth, the "self-evident truth," and also, socially, essentially conservative.

Nevertheless, even in its new context and stance, American liberalism remained stylistically what it had been in England, radical, still bellicose. However, having in fact in its new world no visible enemies, it was forced to invent invisible ones. It developed a paranoid style (the phrase actually is Hofstadter's) and the national attachment to it became "irrational" and "bizarre."[15]

This is Hartz's third major proposition, his conclusion. To understand it, it is important to remember that Hartz wrote his book in the 1950s, when McCarthyism and red scares rode high, and the execution of the Rosenbergs for treason turned into a national blood rite. More broadly, this was Hartz's attempt to deal with cleavage in the American consensus. His claim was that, having no real enemies, since we were all agreed on the principles of liberalism, irrationally we fought each other. Our dissensions were caused by a natural pugnacity inflamed by periodic bouts of hysteria, even hallucination.

Hartz's three propositions make up a persuasive argument. Certainly the national consensus on an adversarial, competitive, private, individualistic capitalism bent on a Lockean understanding of personal freedom cannot be denied. It runs straight through the mainstream of American politics right down to the present. Equally, the persistently hysterical element in American politics seems beyond denial. It is a constant feature of our periodic bouts of national fright that communists and other aliens are boring from within. As certainly, it is a feature of the fears of those on the other wing of American politics that the nation's birthright to democracy is about to be stolen by native-born fascists. Disproportionate response to merely perceived threats is a standing feature of American politics going back to and including the Revolution itself. But can a tendency to hysteria explain the depth and ferocity of the Civil War? Can hysteria explain the genuine feelings of embattlement that ordinary voters experience in a presidential election? America's "bizarre" commitment to its liberalism can explain some of the nation's experience with division, but not all, and certainly not its destructive intensity and frequency.

Nevertheless, it is impossible to reject any of Hartz's theses. One by one and in sum, they are not only logically persuasive but also supported by an abundance of evidence. However, it is possible to go beyond them. Hartz was a historian, and his propositions are so phrased, interpreted, and applied. If those same propositions are interpreted and applied philosophically, they can be given important extension.

Hartz can be charged with having not taken the individualism he found in Locke and then in America with full philosophical serious-ness. Individualism is not a mere brute egoism, a simple overriding concern for the needs of the self to seek and hold property. Philo-sophically, like all the great "isms," individualism is a comprehensive and complex view of how society as a whole is to be understood. Even as it puts its central emphasis on the welfare of the individual, it remains essentially a moral vision of how societies as organized wholes should be assembled, energized, and evaluated. No doubt, its primary and immediate concern is to situate individuals, but always it situates them in whole social contexts. Its principal ethical demand is directed to society and its managers that they construct their insti-tutions and organize their processes on the basis of individual needs.

This social dimension to the individualistic philosophy means that a society that adopts this philosophy as a way of life is far more attuned, far more consistently and comprehensively defining and constraining of individual behavior than the label "individualism"— or Hartz—implies. Just because individualistic societies have a weak sense of the social good does not mean that they are not "societies." As much as any other, they are held together by traditionalized pat-terns of acceptable behavior, language, shared religious outlook, and so forth. To be a free man or woman, to be a free individual in a strictly individualistic society requires as much acculturation and training as would being an aristocrat in a long-established feudal so-ciety.

Because Hartz did not philosophically sense the social dimen-sions of individualism in America, he missed most of the imperatives American society lays on individuals that define what it means to be successful, respectable human beings, truly "free" individuals. He caught some of these imperatives, of course; it could be argued that, by noticing that the free individual was expected to gain and secure property, he in fact caught the core value of America's Bourgeois civilization. But Hartz did not discuss the specificity with which this core value is fastened on the "free" American individual, nor did he notice and specify a whole list of other imperatives American Bour-geois civilization imposes. Much more seriously, he missed altogether a second range of imperatives American civilization imposes on its "free" individuals, namely, the religious values of a generalized Pro-testantism.

In other words, eighteenth-century Lockean liberalism's individualism was a far more complex affair than Hartz imagined. At its heart lay a large and complex amalgam of both Protestant and Bourgeois values. Hartz is right in saying that the whole of English liberalism came to this country as intellectual baggage in virtually every English-speaking ship arriving on these shores. He is right, too, in saying that once here it was exposed to the cruel embarrassment of an empty social context that set little restraint on its extremes. But he seems to have had no conception of what was being released here, what agony within liberalism was being allowed to uncoil in the American provincial environment.

The Protestant Ethos

Hartz is not alone in failing to pick up the Protestant component in American political individualism. Most scholars, especially of the founding period, do the same. They simply take it for granted that the Declaration of Independence and the Constitution are essentially secular documents, conclude without discussion that American politics generally must be secular as well, and go on from there. In this they are much reinforced by the omnipresent Jeffersonian doctrine that in the United States there is and always ought to be a separation of church and state. But in this book we are going to have to wrestle repeatedly with the fact that this doctrine is itself both a political and a religious statement. Moreover, its words, in highly misleading ways, can be seen to serve the purposes of both institutions. We are going to have to wrestle, too, with the fact that the Declaration of Independence and the Constitution are, indeed, secular documents—a matter of considerable import in itself—but they establish a government in a nation that has been from its very earliest days profoundly Protestant in commitment and outlook and that, in important ways, remains so even now. But before beginning any of that discussion, the notion that America is a Protestant community must be established and explained.

European observers have talked for many years knowingly and at length about the intimate relationship in liberal democratic societies between Protestantism and capitalism.[16] Max Weber, in particular, made popular the expression "the Protestant work ethic" as the core value of these societies. But this phrase conflates two moralities, one Protestant, the other Bourgeois, even if in readily recognizable patterns. It will be exceptionally important for the particular analytical purposes of this book to resist this too easy conflation and to hold the Bourgeois and Protestant ethoses distinct. We must be especially careful always to note that Protestantism's primary commandment was not to work but to *love*.

What must not be obscured are Protestantism's own themes. For all its extraordinary denominational diversities, Protestantism generally was initiated theologically by an effort to recover Christianity's biblical, as opposed to its Greek-philosophical, heritage. The commonality of this effort gave even Protestantism's political doctrines a certain substantive uniformity. Much the most important example of this is its individualism. In the biblical Protestant tradition, salvation comes by faith, and faith is an act of individual autonomy, of individual choice. Some Protestant sects more than others, on the question of detecting who had achieved salvation, put an emphasis on the arbitrary, predestined nature of election; but such arguments were mostly meant to demonstrate the absolute, unappealable power of God. They were also meant to show that salvation could not be earned by simply running through some formula or ritual of "good works." The root of the matter remained that the individual had to choose personally, gladly, and in faith to approach God, to live a godly life and be a godly person. Evangelical acceptance of Jesus as lord and savior, through his word as preached in the Gospel, is the underlying theme of all forms of Protestantism.

Immediately allied to this root individualism and effectively no more than an articulation of it is Protestantism's understanding of human egalitarianism. In this mundane world, practical necessities will inspire various distinctions between people, based on talent, age, sex, wealth, political status, and so forth. But these distinctions, even when incorporated into church structures, are of passing significance, of interest only in the interims of life. Before God, on the threshold of infinite mystery, all persons meet one measure only, a stature at once filled with the dignity of being human but also humbled before the majesty of the creator. Protestants learned this doctrine not only from the New Testament but also from the Old, and in particular from the announcement of the New Covenant in Jeremiah:

> In those days they shall no longer say: "The fathers have eaten sour grapes, and the children's teeth are set on edge."

> But every one shall die for his own sin, each man who eats sour grapes, his teeth shall be set on edge.

> Behold, the days are coming, says the LORD when I will make a new covenant with the house of Israel and the house of Judah. . . . I will put my law within them, and I will write it upon their hearts; and I will be

their God, and they shall be my people. No longer shall each man teach his neighbor and each his brother, saying, "Know the LORD" for they shall all know me, from the least of them to the greatest. (31:29–34)[17]

Protestant radical, egalitarian individualism issues into the Gospel's law of love. This is the central commandment of the Sermon on the Mount, and it is repeated many times elsewhere. It is a commandment that is specific to the Bible in both form and consequence. In form, it is a requirement not just that we love those who love us—even sinners do that—but specifically that we should love our enemies, that we should not have or sustain adversarial relationships with them, that we should instead "pray for them that persecute" us. (Matt. 5:43–45) This is as radical a call for love as can be made, and, in a political perspective, it can be seen as issuing into a call for community based on positive fellowship, on a set of willful choices by all concerned actively to love one another. There is a utopian edge to the biblical, Protestant call for loving communities that borders, in a political perspective, on foolishness. But Protestants were sustained by their conception of the loving God who, by his love, would enable people of all orders and ranks to overcome self and to love God and one another without limit or pause.

These three doctrines, radical individualism, radical egalitarianism, and radical loving communitarianism, underlie all forms of Protestantism. They underlie most particularly John Winthrop's sermon "A Model of Christian Charity," delivered on the high seas in the ship Arbella in 1630.[18] This document deserves to be recognized as much as Jefferson's as a declaration founding the new American community. Perhaps it should be called formally "America's First Declaration of Independence." For like Jefferson, Winthrop announces powerfully the principles that would define the new community. Even more than Jefferson, he believes the new community will be truly new, a new England, in the biblical, baptismal sense of the new Adam, and an exemplar for all other peoples. But beyond that the tone and substance of Winthrop's words are poles apart from Jefferson's. In his concluding paragraphs, he warns of possible failure and goes on:

> Now the only way to avoid this shipwreck and to provide for our posterity is to follow the counsel of Micah: to do justly, to love mercy, to walk humbly with our God. For this end, we must be knit together in this work as one man. We must entertain each other in brotherly affection; we must be willing to abridge ourselves of our superfluities, for the supply of others' necessities; we must uphold a familiar commerce together in all meekness, gentleness, patience and liberality. We must de-

light in each other, make others' conditions our own, rejoice together, mourn together, labor and suffer together: always having before our eyes our commission and community in the work, our community as members of the same body. . . . We shall find that the God of Israel is among us, when ten of us shall be able to resist a thousand of our enemies, when He shall make us a praise and glory, that men shall say of succeeding plantations: "The Lord make it like that of New England."

Compared to this, Jefferson's Declaration reads like a lawyer's brief. Yet it can be questioned how far this puritan ancestor of ours speaks for modern America, how far "generalized Protestantism," as we have termed it here, colors with any degree of significance the fundamentals of the American political system. A careful statement of the argument being advanced combined with the testimony of experts can overcome such doubts.

No one questions the plurality of religious institutions in America or the sharp and copious distinctions that can be drawn between them on matters of liturgy, expressed creed, and preferred organizational structure. What authorities on the subject do suggest, however, is that beneath these cultic differentiations is an extraordinary uniformity, a common core of American religiosity.[19] Moreover, this core religiosity can be seen to be common not only across the Protestant communities, but also to be deeply characteristic of the American Roman Catholic and Jewish communities as well. In America, both these communities, in their congregations if not in their hierarchies, have been significantly "Protestantized," even if to degrees and in ways they have not noticed, much less be willing to admit.

Just as this process has extended throughout the total institutionalized religious life of America, so can it be seen to have extended throughout much of America's extrareligious social life, even as far as the preachments of popular psychology self-help manuals. For all the striking differences in locale and ritual, the contents of a Presbyterian minister's sermon, of an inspirational lecture sponsored by a Reform temple, of the homily at a Roman Catholic wedding, of the luncheon address at an Elks or Rotary meeting, of the report of the president to the members of a Volunteer Fire Department Ladies Auxiliary, not to mention advice columns to the lovelorn in glossy magazines, will all tend in the American manner to urge the same values: personal responsibility and commitment, respect for the worth of others, and, above all, the need to give and receive love, to experience togetherness and fellowship, and to seek personal fulfillment through deep and extended relationships.

There is a ready explanation for the pervasiveness of American Protestantism, especially in its more extended and inevitably more bland forms. What happened to Locke on his way to the American frontier happened also to Luther.[20] The provincialization of Protestantism in America resulted, first, in a radical, protesting religious movement becoming the dominant, conservative outlook by which all else in ambit was measured. It resulted, second, in Protestantism becoming on not a few occasions more than a little "bizarre."

The Bourgeois Ethos

That there is a distinct Bourgeois ethos in America's largely secular domains may be more easily admitted than that generalized Protestantism prevails in its mostly religious sectors. But it is important to be precise about the content of this American secularism. Just as Protestantism stemmed from a recovery of a religiosity centered on the Bible—with all the distinctiveness and particularity involved—so the American Bourgeois ethos stemmed from a highly particularized seventeenth- and eighteenth-century enlightenment rationalism that was profoundly anthropocentric in its fundamental assumptions, scientific in its epistemology, and modern in its outlook and aims. Only assumptions such as these could undergird the vast, sweeping, imperial vision of Jefferson's opening phrases in the Declaration: "We hold these truths to be self-evident, that all men are created equal . . ." The assurance is that the whole universe is ordered and open to rational inspection. This is a world away from Winthrop's little company huddled in love and peering for a light in faith to guide them on their errand into the wilderness.

Nevertheless, as much as Protestantism did for its congregations, so this Bourgeois secularism laid on its witnesses strict imperatives about how to become upstanding members of Jefferson's world. In a political perspective, the first and most obvious of these imperatives, individualism, bears marked resemblance to the first commandment of American Protestantism. Both appear to be insisting on an absolute moral autonomy for each person. Certainly they agree that the individual is energetic and self-directed. But whereas Protestantism put individuals on a path to fellowship with others and an encounter with God, Bourgeois secularism set them on a road to "life, liberty, and the pursuit of happiness," presumably their own. For ethical subjectivism was also a part of this picture. Jefferson was not as clear about this as was Locke, and Locke was not as clear as Thomas

Hobbes before him, but Hobbes had made it plain for them all. In this universe, it is every "man" for himself.[21]

Perhaps all persons were created—whatever that word specifically meant—equal, but they did not stay that way. In the race of life, some forged out ahead. Locke, for one, was not coy about this. He began the *Second Treatise* enunciating the standard, self-evident truth, but some dozens of pages later added this qualification:

> Though I have said above, Chapt. II, *That all Men by Nature are equal*, I cannot be supposed to understand all sorts of *Equality: Age* or *Virtue* may give Men a just Precedency: *Excellency of Parts and Merit* may place others above the Common level: *Birth* may subject some, and *Alliance* or Benefits others, to pay an Observance to those to whom Nature, Gratitude or other Respects may have made it due.[22]

What he really meant to stress, he argues at the end of this paragraph, was "that *equal Right* that every Man hath, *to his Natural Freedom*, without being subjected to the Will or Authority of any other Man."

That is the authentic central note of Bourgeois civilization, that man, being alive and eager, has a claim arising from the simple fact of his existence, to be left alone, to be allowed to get on with whatever he wants "without being subjected to the Will or Authority of any other Man."[23] This is the second imperative of Bourgeois civilization: claim, get, and keep freedom for personal endeavor.

Of course, it can be asked, what would Bourgeois, Lockean, Jeffersonian, secular man do with his personal freedom, what personal endeavors would he undertake? Would he dally about, strum the lute, and read poetry? Occupations of that order did not rank high enough in Bourgeois civilization to capture the attention of its philosophers, although Bentham, one of liberalism's latter-day saints, did argue that if it gave pleasure, poetry was as good as push penny, a silly game British laborers play in pubs. We can press the point. With John Winthrop's civilization nearby, should the Bourgeois man read the Bible—which is no silly game? Jefferson, as we know, thought he might, but hoped he would keep it to himself. In any event, reading the Bible and other similar pastimes had little to do with the necessities of life. Those involved such things as pulling up stakes, going to America, hacking a living out of the woods, and pursuing "happiness." The American dream?

It is instructive in this context to review Locke's chapter on property in the *Second Treatise*.[24] The burden of Locke's argument in this chapter is to establish that our rights to hold property privately and to do with it as we wish are anterior to social relationships. At the dawn of the modern age, this was a new and strange doctrine. Always before, to say something was mine only made sense, it seemed, in a social context where saying it was mine meant mainly that using and caring for it was my responsibility, not yours. Locke wanted to establish matters very differently, and for reasons that will soon become apparent and that are essential to the definition of Bourgeois civilization.

In the beginning, says Locke, all was America. Imagine a savage in the forest, hungry. He finds a nut, eats it. Is it his? Of course. Finders, keepers. But did not God give all to *man in common*? When, then, and how did this nut become the property of that solitary savage? When he began to munch it? When he began to digest it? Locke thinks it was when he picked it up off the forest floor, for otherwise by what authority did he put it in his mouth? But how did it become his as he picked it up? By the assent and acknowledgment of that mankind to whom God gave all in common? A round-robin letter to obtain that consent would consume so much time the savage would have died of starvation before he could legally eat. So, concludes Locke, the nut must have become his when in picking it up he mixed the sweat of his labor with it. This, we must observe, is to rate the anointing and abstracting power of the sweat of the savage palm very high—but no matter. Locke has made his point that things I acquire by my labor are mine without social assent or condition and are therefore mine *absolutely*, to do with as I wish.

Imagine American frontiersmen reading this argument, whether on the actual geographical frontier or on the newly formed American frontiers in commerce, agriculture, or manufacturing. Imagine these pioneers going on to read what Locke says next.

How many nuts can the savage pick up and possess? As many as he can carry, store, and eat before they spoil. If he were collecting strawberries, the number would be much less, unless he sold off what he had beyond his needs. And if he sold that excess for money, he could collect—and sell—all he could, since money, uniquely, does not spoil. Thus, Locke, in a single chapter defined the labor theory of value for all of Western capitalist, Bourgeois civilization and, as significantly, unleashed the law of the unlimited accumulation of wealth. Together these points constitute for Locke and his fellow liberals and descendants the third and last fundamental imperative laid on American, Bourgeois man: work hard and, specifically, make unspoilable money, all you can get; you can pile it up and use it as you please because, since you worked to get it, it is yours absolutely.

The Cloven Consensus

Such, in brief compass, is the heart of the American national consensus, Protestant and Bourgeois. Even in Europe, where these two movements originated in figures as disparate as, on the one hand, Luther, Calvin, and John Huss, and, on the other, Hobbes, Locke, and Adam Smith, they were intimately associated in practice by being adopted as the religious and secular creeds of major segments of the English, German, Dutch, and French middle classes. In America, by their parallel paths of provincialization, they were rammed together.

But there was also the logical connection of their similar first commandments. Both seemed to be saying to the American pioneer: you are the captain of your soul, the master of your fate. In the American environment, those were heady words. They can be said to have broken the dam for the immigrant flood to the New World. In literature, they spawned work as diverse as Jonathan Edwards's sermon "Sinners in the Hand of an Angry God," Benjamin Franklin's *Poor Richard's Almanack,* Emerson's essay "Self-Reliance," and that turn-of-the-century paean to personal responsibility and hard work, Elbert Hubbard's "Message to Garcia."[25] It was as if the ground itself in America preached that the Lord helps those who help themselves—no matter what the line of endeavor.

But this unanimity held only at the most fundamental level. It forced Americans to speak with one voice. But the split in America's individualism between its Protestant and Bourgeois halves ensured that they would speak with different tongues. It ensured that the nation would be schizophrenic, not bipartisan.[26] We were all Protestant/Bourgeois, one people in agony with ourselves.[27]

For that, too, was guaranteed. The agony, the tensions and contradictions between the instructions that the two sides of the American political culture gave to the self-responsible individual were extreme and irreconcilable. There was no way the individual American, on being told on his Protestant side to pursue love in egalitarian fellowship, could instead pursue a Bourgeois life of self-aggrandizement in adversarial competition with his neighbors without experiencing pain and guilt, no matter how flamboyant his triumphs. No matter which way he went, he would be wrong: rapacious if he won, pathetic if he lost. Scores of American novels have been written to this theme, none with more obvious brilliance than Bud Schulberg's *What Makes Sammy Run?* It is the theme, too, of American biographies, such as Garry Wills's biography of Richard Nixon, to which he gave the title *Nixon Agonistes:*

The Crises of the Self-Made Man. It is significant also that Wills put a line from Milton's poem, *Samson Agonistes*, at the front of his book:

O lastly over-strong against thy self![28]

Wills's book makes plain that the principal of the Watergate Crisis (the book was in fact written four years before that crisis broke) was far from being an aberrant figure. Like the heroes of those countless novels, Nixon was centrally an ordinary man, almost the personification of "the average American," at most an extreme of the norm. And the norm in America, once again, is tension, extreme and irreconcilable, between opposed teachings, love thy neighbor, ditch your neighbor. The American, at one and the same time, must be both holy and rich, in church and at work, loving and competitive, generous and greedy.

With tensions and contradictions as great as this and as systemic, it is inevitable that the American political mind should exhibit a perpetual instability. No doubt, by heritage and environment some of us congenitally are more tipped in the Protestant direction, others more to the Bourgeois side. But none of us can escape the double pull and, as occasions suggest, we may drift toward requirements first on one side, then the other. Driven, we will seek to prove ourselves, not only in our own eyes but also in those of people we know to be equally and authentically American but regarding us in an opposite perspective. Once moving in patterns like this, we may in whole groups oscillate between the extremes of the American mind, Protestant judging Bourgeois, Bourgeois judging Protestant.

And there may be reverberating tensions and movements within the two sides. Exposed and vulnerable, Protestants will fall out with Protestants about who is most truly of the essential creed, and Bourgeois with Bourgeois about who is the most "soundly practical." Positions can be staked out, opposing left and right wings on both sides, and these various positions can seek allies. Left-wing Protestants can team up with Bourgeois "liberals," and right-wing Pentecostal with like-minded conservatives.

But there is an overriding fact that must never be left out of account. With these possibilities of movement within the confines of the American political mind, individuals and groups can still move to extremes, to the irrational and even the bizarre, to the limits of that mind. By faith or by greed, Americans have been driven to do many strange things. But seldom if ever does anyone succeed in going beyond the boundaries of the Protestant/Bourgeois individualism of the American political mind. We are caught within that mind. Its

limits are hard. To go beyond those limits we would have to seek out
alternatives to our cloven national consensus. But the American political mind, trapped in the limited vocabularies of its provincialism,
does not provide any alternatives to itself. In the final analysis, even
in our extremities, we are never more—or less—than Protestant/
Bourgeois provincials. This is the ultimate root of our political poverty.

The point can be made in even more negative terms, but perhaps ones with a more obvious relevance to practical politics. Because both aspects of the American political mind at its most profound are essentially individualistic, its Protestant side concerned
with the individual's spiritual welfare, the Bourgeois side with his or
her material welfare, America's consequent political vocabulary is in
its turn essentially privatistic. For politics, it is the reverse of this
point that is important: at the most profound level, America has no
indigenous or autonomous language of the public. This does not
mean that Americans cannot talk in public terms; in fact, their elections and legislative processes reverberate with such talk much of the
time. What the private character of the roots of American politics
means is that all our public talk is either derivative from private concerns, or patently, hypocritically superficial. We argue for public
policies because they can be demonstrated to be instrumentally effective in securing private ends; or because they disguise and misleadingly inflate those ends; or because, for a transitory moment, we
can whip up some genuine patriotism; or because to purify *our* souls,
we need to show love for neighbor. In a more complex cultural environment, gyrating arguments such as these could turn and twist on
tensions between perceptions of personal and social identity. But in
America's provincialized liberal culture, where identity is always personal, discussions of public policy have a perpetual, steep, and morally impoverishing tendency to decline into arguments about personal advantage, whether spiritual or material. For us, the common
good, social justice, the national interest, the public need are not
independently operative conceptions.

3
Ambiguous Democracy

We will now observe how the American people filled up their formal power constructs with a Protestant/Bourgeois content and with what effect, first at the level of general conceptions of democracy, and then, in the next chapter, at the more specific level of institutions and processes.

The thesis to be advanced in this chapter is, first, that from the time of the Revolution forward the Bourgeois element in the American political character had virtually a free hand in designing and stabilizing the content of the ideological side of America's power constructs. On the other hand, more hesitantly at the beginning but, as the nineteenth century progressed, in the end as forcefully and as exclusively, the Protestant element of the American political character took over the definition and articulation of the mythic side of America's power constructs. Second, it will be argued that, given its fundamental biases and inherited intellectual baggage, the Bourgeois ethos in America evolved for its ideological needs a vision of America as a liberal democratic state whose central concerns were elitist claims for personal freedom and sovereignty of the law; meanwhile, the Protestant ethos was evolving for America's mythic self-understanding a vision of itself as a social democratic nation whose primary focus was on an egalitarian national fellowship and the sovereignty of the people.

These two democratic visions are sharply opposed at many points; they require very different political styles and are directed to very different political goals. Nevertheless, these differences in style, substance, and objectives, for all the pain and misunderstanding they have caused, did not obliterate, rather they deeply underlined, the coincidence of the two democratic visions' commitment to the autonomy of the individual—even as they understood that autonomy in very different ways. This common commitment to radical individualism remained the single stem upon which all the division rested. It locked the two democracies in a single embrace. It meant that both could—and in fact did—lay claim to Jefferson's phrase that all men were created equal, although they interpreted its words very differently. It even meant that both could and did lay claim to the French slogan Liberté, Egalité, et Fraternité, although again the words were held to mean very different things and the emphases between the values they denoted were very differently distributed. And what it meant finally and in practice was that actual institutions, events, and personalities were always more or less tangles of the two visions, tangles that only careful analysis can separate.

As often happens in matters of this sort, in the formation of the American nation-state, history reversed logic. In logic, the legitimization of power precedes its exercise. In the course of actual American history, at the state level and then the federal, patterns of governance were carved out, conventionalized, and stabilized in tradition early and quickly. The development of the nation's mythic patterns of legitimization was marked by confusion, false starts, and a need for many reiterations. It was also rent by one colossal failure, the Civil War. Even so, by the time of the Spanish–American War, as the rhetoric and practice of those days vividly illustrated, both sides of the standardized American political dialogue had been so defined and stabilized that their essential outlines were effectively taken for granted.[1]

Liberal Democracy

On the Bourgeois side of that dialogue, the central idea was liberal democracy. America's liberal democratic ideology grew out of an ancient philosophical tradition stretching back to Aristotle. That is not to suggest that this philosophical tradition was itself internally consistent or that liberal democracy was its sole or even, intellectually, its most significant product. What it does suggest is that the Aristotelian philosophical tradition had certain benchmark concerns—most notably for order and rationality—that are important to any full understanding of the political philosophy we know in America as liberal democracy. More particularly, this tradition, from the Greeks forward, had an idealist tendency to understand things in terms of their essences, and, especially, to think of political man in terms of his essential self, his "human nature." By the time of John Locke and the advent of the Bourgeois property holder for whom he spoke in seventeenth-century England, much of the metaphysics required to sustain this idealist approach had been melted away by the ascendancy of modern natural science. But in political science the old verbal habits persisted. In Locke himself and even more in the American founders, John Adams, Thomas Jefferson, and James Madison, the penchant for grounding arguments in suppositions about "human nature," unchanging and timeless, is everywhere apparent. Even more striking is the penchant for clinging to the old vocabularies about the natural order, law, inalienable rights, social tranquillity, and the general welfare.

Nevertheless, *Homo sapiens,* the rock on which these seventeenth- and eighteenth-century Bourgeois ideologists built, was a world away from the natural man in harmonious society that Aristotle had in mind. The new conception of human nature was essentially behavioral, secular, and selfish. For these Bourgeois ideologists, this was not a moral judgment, but a simple, if philosophical, fact. Ordinary people, particularly the lower orders, women, and children, could be superstitious, irrational, and lazy.[2] But "real" men knew what their interests were and, with a prudent rationality, went about getting what they needed by whatever means were indicated. The immediate consequence of this new perception of what constituted real (male) human beings was the further perception that all men were necessarily in a competitive, adversarial relationship with each other. Aristotle's vision of a natural, integrated, harmonious social order was dead, vanished. Instead, Bourgeois ideologists, whether they had actually read it word for word or not, built firmly on this paragraph in Hobbes's *Leviathan:*

> Nature hath made men so equal, in the faculties of the body, and mind; as that though there be found one man sometimes manifestly stronger in body, or of quicker mind than another; yet when all is reckoned together, the difference between man, and man, is not so considerable, as that one man can thereupon claim to himself any benefit, to which another may not pretend, as well as he. For as to the strength of body, the weakest has strength enough to kill the strongest, either by secret machination, or by confederacy with others, that are in the same danger with himself.[3]

It is paragraphs like this that have earned Hobbes the reputation, more than Locke, as the founder of modern liberalism, and of being himself an "impish . . . iconoclastic . . . plebeian."[4]

Especially for Americans, even in the twentieth century, there is something eminently common-sensical about the notion that, when push comes to shove on the bottom line, all men, old or young, big or small, famous and rich or poor and unknown, have more or less equal capacities to kill each other. In a raw civilization on the frontier of chaos, that kind of observation gets confirmed on a daily basis. But notice plainly what Hobbes proposes to do with this "fact." He intends to build a new theory of justice on it, to mount on it a whole new vision of the social and political order. Hobbes is no simple anthropologist reporting the facts. He is a political philosopher. By this paragraph, he has discarded not only Aristotle but also every

principle of social deference and legitimate political authority enshrined by civilizations from the Hebrews, Greeks, and Romans, to
feudalism. In their stead he has laid down simply the raw fact of one
existential natural right to survive against another.

This is where all liberals since Hobbes, implicitly or explicitly,
start their presuppositions as well. This is where Locke's savage, ap-
propriating from God's common gift to mankind as many nuts as he
can use, comes from. And listen to Madison talking about factions,
those combinations of self-centered, selfish interests that abound in
every society.

> The latent causes of faction are . . . sown in the nature of man; . . . It is
> vain to say, that enlightened statesmen will be able to adjust these clash-
> ing interests, and render them all subservient to the public good . . . the
> *causes* of faction cannot be removed . . . relief is only to be sought in the
> means of controlling its *effects* . . . neither moral nor religious motives
> can be relied on as an adequate control.[5]

It is but a step from arguments such as these to the conclusion that
in a properly designed constitutional structure:

> Each department should have a will of its own. . . . the great security
> against a gradual concentration of the several powers in the same de-
> partment, consists in giving to those who administer each department,
> the necessary constitutional means, and personal motives, to resist en-
> croachments of the others. . . . Ambition must be made to counteract
> ambition. *The interest of the man must be connected with the constitutional
> rights of the place.* It may be a reflection on human nature, that such
> devices should be necessary to control the abuses of government. But
> what is government itself, but the greatest of all reflections on human
> nature?[6]

The literalness, the barefacedness of these statements is amazing, or
at least should be for anyone touched with sentiments of affection
for fellow members of the human species. These statements proclaim that the interior logic of Madison's constitution, as much as of
the liberalism it institutionalizes, what makes it tick, and more, is its
appeal to avarice, its unvarnished intent to put the rights of public
office in direct harness to motives of private greed.

This is strong language, but Madison believed, and before him
Locke, and before him Hobbes, that constitutional engineers faced a
monumental problem in a human nature that was at once unalter-
able and also prone absolutely to selfishness, competition, and, no
matter how disguised, a war of all against all.[7] That was a problem
because war was not what these Bourgeois philosophers wanted. Not

for them were dreams of the glorious fury of battle, and the achievements of personal and national honor through adventure and blood. Hobbes himself risked personal ridicule for speaking out against dueling. What these "plebeian" philosophers yearned for, what they hoped government could secure for them and their peers, was, in Hobbes's many times repeated phrases, a "contented" and "delectable" life. Government, of course, could not hand such a life to anyone. Each person had to gain that for themselves. But they would, if given a chance. (The line from Hobbes to the self-centered, hedonism of the readership of *Playboy* magazine is short and direct.)[8] The problem was securing them that chance.

The problem was that men, simply by themselves being avaricious and competitive, tended always to create the chaos that would deny them the opportunity to indulge their desires with an adequate measure of personal safety. In the context of the war of all against all, liberals looked almost with desperation to government to protect each man from his neighbor, to provide them all with a social circumstance in which they could be secure in their possessions and look forward with confidence to enjoying the fruits of their industry. Locke, in these matters following Hobbes step by step, reiterates as his most fundamental principle: "The great and *chief end* therefore, of Mens uniting into Commonwealths, and putting themselves under Government, *is the Preservation of their Property.*"[9] The Preamble of the United States Constitution is no less emphatic:

> We the People of the United States, in Order to form a more perfect Union, establish Justice, insure domestic Tranquility, provide for the common defence, promote the general Welfare, and secure the Blessings of Liberty to ourselves and our Posterity, do ordain and establish this Constitution for the United States of America.

That is why they did it, or, more narrowly, these are the reasons they announced for doing what they did. Either way, it is a Bourgeois world in which government is far more concerned with insuring domestic tranquility and securing the blessing of liberty than it is with building cathedrals, spreading imperial domains, or grooming excellence in virtuous citizens.

Bourgeois government secures its narrow goals by assuming and, to use the patois of contemporary political science, "managing" conflict by moderating the effects of the perpetual war of all against all. To this end, it has two techniques, both of which we will see writ large all across the actual practice of American politics. The first is haggling, or, more politely, mediating. The competing interests are all consulted, and skillful, strenuous efforts are made to harmonize their conflicting claims. Give and take, compromise, balancing hurts against helps, and learning to settle for less are all parts of this approach. And when this process has gone to its practical limit and more remains to be done, the second of liberal Bourgeois governmental techniques is brought to bear: order imposed by a governmental will that is, at once, arbitrary, absolute, and awful.

"Arbitrary," "absolute," and "awful," in this context, are technical terms, derived directly from Hobbesian principles and implicit in all liberal government. The governmental will is arbitrary because, in the liberal world, all willful order is arbitrary. It is simply the imposition of direction by a particular agent. In a world of subjectivities, each automated by a self and its personal perception of its needs, there can be no moral determination of one will and its priorities as intrinsically or even relatively "better" than another. In such a world, the state is but one more will. In a moral sense, before the others, its will is neutral and, therefore, morally arbitrary. However, unlike the will of ordinary mortals, the will of the state must be supposed absolute, that is, final, without allowable appeal beyond it. To have it otherwise is to invite chaos, a return to the state of nature and the unchecked war of all against all. When all the compromising is said and done, the state's solution is simply imposed. But it is imposed awfully. "Covenants," said Hobbes, "without the sword, are but words, and of no strength to secure a man at all."[10] Hence, when the state's will as the final solution is imposed, the sword is raised to seal the bargain with a touch of awe-inspiring terror. By these means, we all will be persuaded to see a personal interest in letting the state's law be final. For these reasons, and these alone, we call it "sovereign."

The sovereign state is thus created, the liberal tradition suggests, because men, "real" men, that is, would be rational enough not to trust themselves or each other to refrain from using their personal swords when it appeared personally advantageous to do so, thereby perpetuating the war of all against all. To limit that war to words, skillful alliances, hidden ploys, and other relatively harmless machinations, all swords and other instruments of violence should be surrendered to the sovereign. Whoever he might be, he would receive a monopoly on the legitimate uses of violence and thereby would be enabled, by the terror of his ways, to hold all the rest of us in awe, that is, more narrowly, to tilt the balance of our self-interested calculations always in the direction of obedience to his arbitrary and absolute commands.

It may be objected that in spelling out this philosophy of Hobbesian liberalism we have gone too far, that what we have spelled out no longer has the look about it of anything recognizably American. That may well be in part because the "look" of American government is largely supplied by its mythic social democratic side, while what we are here analyzing is mostly its interior, liberal democratic logic. But it may still be objected that in raising the specter of the arbitrary, absolute, and awful Hobbesian sovereign we have decisively parted company even on this side of the American political mind with not only Locke and his supplications for a nonarbitrary, carefully limited form of government but also with the whole world of American constitutional regimes and, to be specific, the Bill of Rights.

These external vocabularies of liberalism conceal to a great extent even in our day the tough edge of Hobbes at the core of the Bourgeois mind. To find and acknowledge the essential presence of that Hobbesian toughness is important to even a preliminary understanding of American liberalism. And more is involved in this than rooting American secular individualism in Hobbes's anthropocentric, subjectivistic, radically nominalistic, even hedonistic conceptions of man. The specific connections between American constitutionalism and Hobbes's understanding of law and its relationship to personal freedom must also be spelled out. Let us go over this ground again but with a sharper perspective on the Hobbesian—and liberal—understanding of law.

Like the whole of the liberal tradition of which he was the first and greatest spokesman, Hobbes's first concern was, once again, the personal freedom of the individual. But he believed that there was no freedom worth having if it came without security for life, limb, and property. From these root concerns comes Hobbes's inordinate regard for contracts. Hobbes appears to have believed consistently that men being what they are, contracts are the only reasonable instrument for stabilizing and institutionalizing human relationships. He believed in contracts not only to create government, but also to define the interactions between businessmen, husbands and wives, parents and children, masters and servants. Hobbes's fixation with contracts is reasonable given his prior assumption that all men are, intractably and equally, *persons,* that is to say, morally autonomous, self-directing agents capable of suing and being sued in courts of law, of dealing face to face with each other, and of managing their own lives.[11] In this light, contracts, that is, stabilized relations of quid pro quo, of "I'll scratch your back, you scratch mine," are not only the most likely, they are probably the highest possible form of human intercourse.

These concerns and beliefs surely are immediately recognizable by ordinary Americans as being directly comparable to their own. So is Hobbes's further conviction that the personal advantage and security that contracts bring can only come from a body of law that is known and enforced on all comers. The rub comes when questions are raised about what law is to be enforced and by whom.

On these questions Hobbes's unforgivable audacity lay in being both right, given the generally agreed-on premises of the argument, and being plain about it. Law, he intoned, is command, and, moreover, command backed by sanction. Without practical, meaningful sanction, the most divinely inspired law is worthless. Moreover, the sanction has to be imposed by somebody, like it or not. All the talk in the world about a government by laws, not by men, cannot disguise or alter the fact. The sovereign, says Hobbes, is that person or determinate body of persons from whose sanctions on behalf of the law there is no appeal. When a Hobbesian individual comes up against the sovereign's law, the individual is not going to like it; but that is precisely when the law must be enforced, by somebody, by a designated Hobbesian person, no doubt with a will and a set of concerns of his own, but whose will must be law if there is not to be a return to the state of nature. "But, officer, there's not a soul on this road and I am late to church." "I'm sorry, ma'am, the law is the law. You were doing forty-six miles per hour in a thirty mile an hour speed zone. . . ." You can appeal, and, in the litigious American system, appeal again and again. Until it stops. When it does, the law is, as Justice Hughes said echoing Hobbes, what the judges say it is.[12]

Given the premise of the Bourgeois, Hobbesian man doing his own thing without restraint unless restrained, none of this is disputable. This is the tough edge of Hobbes, and also of all liberalism. It has been much disguised, by talk about natural law, inalienable rights, and the rule of law, in a word, by rhetoric about justice. That kind of talk is meaningful and useful, within limits. The limits were set by Hobbes, by his tough perception that in a liberal world, on the bottom line of push and shove, we are all adversaries with pretty nearly equal capabilities for killing each other. At that point, all philosophical critiques must cease. If there is to be a law, it must be whatever de facto it is.

Translated, what these truths mean is that behind our civilities about justice and limited government, a series of Hobbesian definitions rules our Bourgeois world. His sovereign as a person no longer stalks the land—but his law does. The Bourgeois mind lives and breathes by the hope that all citizens will give the law an automatic obedience, that, on pain of violent death and abject fear of the anarchic state of nature, they will make the law sovereign in Hobbes's terms, absolute, arbitrary, and awful. And for these citizens, too, in the Bourgeois world, freedom, real, practical, operational freedom, at bottom is nothing more than the simple absence of physical impediment, the absence specifically of restraining law. In those areas of life where the law is silent, there I am free. There I can do as I like. Within the limits of the law, I live in my own sphere of "anarchy." As Hobbes said, the law is like a hedge to keep the traveler in his way.[13]

In our complex modern, liberal, Bourgeois world, politicians, lawyers, citizens, and philosophers still tend to think of the sovereign law as a cage. That is the essential image for understanding Madison's contention that in a proper constitution the rights of the office must be connected to the interests of the man. In this light, a public office is for its occupant an opportunity, a free space in which avaricious will with some safety can be allowed to prowl. This is a Bourgeois concept, a tough American ideological reality of government. No number of layers of rhetoric about "public service" and "the will of the people" can conceal either its presence or its primacy in the Bourgeois, liberal democratic concept of effective government.

Of all these points, the most important to remember is that when in the Bourgeois world we talk about the sovereignty of the law, we are not investing law with divine majesty. Instead we are investing it with the tough practical characteristics that Hobbes thought required for any enforced rule. In Hobbes's view the enforced rule must be arbitrary, just as it is, and not dependent on somebody's approval in terms of that person's personal conception of the just and the wise; it must be absolute and not subject to appeal beyond appeal; and it must be awesome and therefore actually effective.

These are the bare bones of American Bourgeois, liberal democracy: personal freedom for acquisitive, adversarial man within the limits of an imposed, sovereign law. More freely, we can give this patter definition: liberal democracy is a framework of absolute law within which individuals can pursue their personal interests with maximum possible freedom. Phrased that way, it is an easy definition to live with—but it must not be taken out of its originating context, the world of adversarial Hobbesian men all of whom, being essentially Bourgeois, want much the same things, they just each want it for themselves.[14]

Social Democracy

It may be with relief that we turn to the opposite pole of the American political mind and talk about social democracy.[15] This is, in terms of human sentiments, altogether a softer, richer world than the Bourgeois world, but it is no less demanding. If it can be said, looking back, that the Bourgeois ethos of liberal democracy came to its fullest—and most directly naive—expression in the opening paragraphs of Jefferson's Declaration of Independence, then it can also be said that social democracy in the American tradition found its finest and fullest expression in Lincoln's Gettysburg Address.[16]

Jefferson in the Declaration sets a tone that is as universalistic as it is rationalistic. The truths he propounds are self-evident to all rational beings, human or angelic, everywhere without regard to time or space. "All men" he should have written as a single word, "allmen," for it is a single concept by which to grasp in aggregate all (male, white, property-owning?) persons in every civilization known and unknown. And all these persons have identical standing, as possible parties under law in any court anywhere, moral agents who can sue and be sued. Jefferson's vision is not just imperial. It is specifically Roman: the free man is a *civis* of the empire; the law is a rule beyond even the *jus gentium,* the law of the nations; it is the *jus naturale*. A more ancient, a nobler disguise for the Bourgeois right to have and to hold could not be conceived.

In contrast, Lincoln's view in the Address is pinched, bound by space and time. Four score and seven years ago, he asks us to remember, our fathers, not men universally, brought forth here, on this continent particularly, not anywhere, a new nation. Lincoln's specificity is as sharp as Jefferson's is loose—Jefferson does not seem to *remember* anything, not even God's proper name. But before that deity, Lincoln stands directly, and before his people, too, and on a battlefield still filled with the stench of death. In the cloth of that moment, Lincoln comes not as a philosopher propounding truths, but as a biblical prophet declaring the meaning of actual history, the history of this, the American people, in this place and time, in Gettysburg, Pennsylvania, in 1863.

The Gettysburg Address is, in literal terms, a covenant renewal ceremony modeled directly, however unconsciously, on the covenant ceremonies of Moses at Sinai, Joshua at Shechem, and Josiah and Ezra in Jerusalem. In its shape and content we can see the lineaments of America's conception of itself as a social democracy, a conception of itself as special and legitimate, a democracy of the ancestors, a nation to stand among the nations in the corridors of biblical time.

Central to any covenant renewal ceremony is the prophet himself, the charismatic hero standing between and yet as one with both God and people, the link in life between them.[17] And in this link, the prophet's words, his address, are an act by which he brings God and people into one focus in both time and space. Technically, his words are an act of congregation. In space, by the power of his words, by the force of his soul flowing through his words, he summons the people before him into one body, one life, one enterprise of souls come together before their god, so that, in the Bible's repeated phrasing, they may go out as one man and speak with one voice. In time, the prophet's address brings history into focus, the people's history as they are lead to understand it. This understanding begins with consciousness of the present ("Now we are engaged in a great civil war . . ."), framed between a specific past consciously recalled, and an equally specific future consciously anticipated. To interpret the present thus framed in its historical context is the prophetic function. But the interpretation of the moment in which we stand is not exhausted by its announcement. The prophet presses his interpretation on us as a choice, as a flash of freedom to begin again. "Therefore," said John Winthrop in the last lines of his sermon, "let us choose life, that we, and our seed, may live" (Deut. 30:19). "Now therefore," said Joshua to all the people assembled at Shechem, "choose this day whom you will serve" (Josh. 24:14–15). And so Lincoln at Gettysburg put it to the American people: "It is for us the living, rather, to be dedicated here to the unfinished work which they who fought here have thus far so nobly advanced."

The prophet puts the moment of choice to his people in an interpretation of history that is through and through redemptive. The formal elements of that history, the saga recalled, the crisis now perceived, the mission foreseen, are filled and connected by a redeeming thread of promise. A covenant between people and god, between nation and destiny, has been made, broken, and renewed, and in the context of it the people find, lose, and recover their identity and legitimacy.

This sense of a people tested on the anvil of history, of terrible trial and as terrible triumph barely won is the motif of the Address, but it is expressed even more literally in the Second Inaugural:

> Fondly do we hope, fervently do we pray, that this mighty scourge of war may speedily pass away. Yet, if God wills that it continue, until all the wealth piled by the bond-man's two hundred and fifty years of unrequited toil shall be sunk, and until every drop of blood drawn with the lash shall be paid by another drawn with the sword, as was said three thousand years ago, so still it must be said, "the judgments of the Lord, are true and righteous altogether."

Politically, what comes out of this prophetic understanding of American nationalism is, most obviously, the role of the prophetic leader, the charismatic hero who by words acts to congregate the people. Without him, the people would have no recollection of themselves, no understanding of their crisis, no sense of direction and commitment, in sum, no identity and no legitimacy. The significance of this leadership role for the development of the modern American presidency can hardly be underestimated. At the theoretical level, American, biblical-style nationalism has two other implications as well.

The first of these has to do with the notion of the sovereignty of the people. The phrase slides easily off the tongue and seems to be a commonplace of all democratic theories. Even Hobbes may be thought to have subscribed to it. Did not his sovereign, for all of being arbitrary, absolute, and awful, derive his power, just or otherwise, from the consent of the governed? Certainly he could not retain it without that consent. But the second implication of America's biblical nationalism is that sovereignty of the people has a particular meaning that is at once as individualistic as anything in Hobbes and yet profoundly communitarian as well.

The communitarian element in it is immediately apparent in the profundity of the nationalism that this tradition's biblical language is able to summon up. The weight of it is, emotionally, overwhelming. What American cannot feel a wrench on the heart from the closing words, the summons, of the Second Inaugural:

> With malice toward none, with charity for all, with firmness in the right, as God gives us to see the right, let us strive on to finish the work we are in, to bind up the nation's wounds, to care for him who shall have borne the battle, and for his widow, and his orphan, to do all which may achieve and cherish a just and lasting peace, among ourselves and with all nations.

The social power of this nationalism, the sense of pull into the vortex of its moral endeavors, has a double source. One is its capacity to invoke not just the divine but the divine located in the whole sweep of history. To claim that America has a rendezvous with destiny is for many people as powerful an invocation to join God's work as is a personal theophany. At the same time, there is the imagery of the people massively assembled. In this tradition, the will of the sovereign people is not well determined by a random sample of house-to-house polling. The people must be assembled by their leaders, in convocation with each other, in the presence of their history. They must be imbued with a deliberate consciousness of themselves as a people summoned to decide and to speak. This is what gives such a sense of power to general elections, not just the voting, but the long campaigns leading up to the voting. In some ways, the campaigns are more politically significant than the voting, however that turns out. For in the campaigns, by every available symbol, song, and story, by words and signs, the people are addressed, aroused, informed, challenged, in a word, assembled. And it is with the weight of their full assembly that they then speak as a sovereign people.

There is a real sense that, in the light of this kind of analysis, the result of any full and healthy general election is unanimous. All participate in and vote for the result, those who voted against the prevailing outcome as much as those who voted for it. What truly wins and lives is the process in which and through which the sovereign people assembled find their will, no matter whether this way or that.

This highly communal understanding of the sovereignty of the people colors deeply the latent individualism inherent in it. However communal it may become, American social democracy remains an effusion of the nation's Protestant, evangelical heritage; and that heritage never wavers in its conviction that every soul, man or woman, young or old, rich or poor, mighty or lowly, must make the decision, the commitment, to life on a personal basis. This understanding of personal commitment is indigenous to the biblical tradition and was one of those elements in it that became exaggerated to an extreme in the American provincial environment.

The immediate consequence of placing these radical demands on the individual in the highly communitarian environment of American nationalism was the development of an equally radical egalitarianism. Equality in the act of commitment overrides all other possible distinctions, and breeds, absolutely, an equality of membership, an equal standing for every person in the common fellowship. The American social democratic tradition is decisively animated by Paul's statement to the Galatians: "There is neither Jew nor Greek, there is neither slave nor free, there is neither male nor female; for you are all one in Christ Jesus" (3:28). Both sides of this statement are essential to its meaning: all earthly distinctions are but naught; in community we achieve wholeness, oneness.

The totality of the American social democratic tradition, its language so steeped in biblical phrasings and allusions, the startling clarity of its representation of the nation's need for a prophetic hero to bring it together, the warmth of its invocation of egalitarian fellowship, and its proud assurance that these people assembled speak as the nation's true sovereign, has been a fountain of aspiration for the American people. This has been our standard. Over the decades, from all corners of the country, politicians and parsons have used it to solve the problems of our identity, to tell us in all our pluralism who we legitimately are. Again and again, they have told our story. (Often it was told quite inaccurately, and with major omissions, such as, how did the blacks get here? And whatever happened to Abigail Adams's plea to her Constitution-defending husband, John, for respect for women? But no matter. The rhetoric flowed on.)

From all parts of the globe, in exodus across the raging seas, came all kinds to found here the first "new" nation, born in freedom to guarantee freedom for all. These are the aspirations by which, as a nation, we ask to be judged.

We ask to be judged a social democracy, because that, in the legitimacy of our aspirations, is what we truly are. And again the patter definition flows easily: a social democracy is a community, an egalitarian, fraternal people congregated in history by a charismatic leader in full-throated pursuit of—usually rather distant—goals of social justice. That is America's myth, the vision of itself by which it measures its legitimacy as a people.

The Myth/Ideology Cycle

We have presented in fundamental terms the visions America has of itself as, in practical, operative ideology, a liberal democracy, and, in aspiring myth, a social democracy. We should review their formal points of congruence and opposition.

Their most basic point of formal congruence is in their individualism, their agreement on the moral autonomy of the individual. But immediately they divide. The social democratic vision summons the individual to obey God—or whatever "other" (history, honor, social hope) to whom he or she feels obligated. Meanwhile, the liberal democratic vision summons the same individual to a life of self-aggrandizement. Hence, the fundamental collision, the norm of tension, is between the urge to become a good citizen in neighborly fellowship with others in our shared community, and the contradictory urge to use freedom to become successful entrepreneurs on our own behalf and for snatching whatever public largess might be inveigled to come our way.

Of course, this central tension in American political life is rarely exposed in terms as sharp as these. This is in large part because in its initial terms the dialogue between the poles of this opposition is interior to each of us. No matter how predominately we, as individuals, may find ourselves near one or the other of these poles, we all experience their double pull. In consequence, we all can honestly pro-

claim our allegiance to Liberté, Egalité, et Fraternité and thereby
mostly conceal the contradictory definitions that our cloven tradition
gives to the political meanings of these terms: freedom with others
versus freedom from others; equality in membership versus equality
in opportunity; community of neighborhoods versus aggregations of
crosscutting interests.

Thus concealed at their base, when these contradictions reappear at the overtly political level, they often go blithely unnoticed.
Textbooks often list as the fundamental principles of American government sovereignty of the people and sovereignty of the law, and
leave it at that. But, logically, can our nation-state afford two sover-
eigns? Substantively, if the people are sovereign, does not the law,
and more especially the law of our Madisonian constitution, which so
effectively and systematically disperses any massed power the people
might accumulate, become an unpardonable yoke on the expression
of their will? On the other hand, if the law is king, are not the people "a great beast," in Hamilton's phrase, whose anarchic desires
must be tamed and caged by the law?[18] In these terms, social democracy is a democracy of the sovereign people, and liberal democracy is
a constitutional democracy, a democracy in which the law is sovereign.[19]

In the American political tradition, the dynamics of these oppositions are supplied by the near exclusiveness with which these two
democratic visions perform their distinct functions for the political
system as a whole. Systematically, the one legitimizes us, the other
teaches us how in politics to get things done. In consequence, in
actual historical contexts, the two meet only from time to time in
head-to-head collision. Often their contact is tangential, and there is
room for slippage, drift, and long-after-the-fact mortification. But,
within the shallow limits of America's provincialized political culture,
the drift apart can never extend to the point of permanent disas-
sociation.

It is possible within tolerable limits of simplification to construct
a pattern or cycle of the interactions between the social democratic
myth and the liberal democratic ideology of the American political
system.[20] What might be called the normal, or first stage, relationship
between them is one of more or less remote tension. The nation
legitimizes itself happily with Fourth of July parades, pledges of allegiance in the schools, and presidential proclamations and addresses.
The people—or at least those segments of them capable of significant political action—are more or less well mythed. Meanwhile, the
operatives of the state's machinery, at the federal, state, and local
levels, go about their business with genial proficiency. The major

established interests cut their deals and get enough of what they want, so that their unhappiness is precluded from becoming a danger to the political order. Costs are concealed, euphemisms abound, and unexamined paradoxical statements proliferate. America, the world's most humanitarian and richest nation is, with some discomfort, happy. More or less easily, when things pinch, we change gears: that is all right in theory, we will say, but in practice . . . Or, alternatively, we will say, practical necessities to one side, America is not like other nations, we have no territorial ambitions, we seek nothing for ourselves . . .

But internal contradictions are never far from the surface. When unattended problems, by our own standards, multiply and fester, almost any incident can bring one or more of the underlying contradictions of the political system to the nation's excited attention. This is the second stage, the intensity stage, in the nation's myth/ideology cycle. It is most marked by the discrepancy between the demands of myth for solutions to the problems it has exposed and the capacities of ideology to generate suitable responses. Myth's social democratic traditions speak in terms of moral absolutes and demand programmatic, long-term solutions. Ideology is not designed in those terms. Its proficiencies are in terms of negotiation and mediation between competing interests before whose standings in moral terms it is merely neutral. Or, when the proverbial bottom line threatens, it can propose arbitrary solutions imposed, if necessary, by force—always a costly prospect. Negotiations to negotiate the nonnegotiable may in fact be enough to deflect the intensity of the problem, and under the appearance of beginning solutions, there may be a return to the condition of normal tension.

But often enough this does not happen, and the cycle of myth/ideology interaction moves to a third stage, the crisis stage. The contradictions between the demands of social democracy and liberal democratic performances now do go head to head and become everywhere evident. Outrage is expressed. Bungling performances by operatives desperately trying to go two ways at once are exposed for the wonder of the whole world. Euphemisms are abandoned, and moral and constitutional principles are set out with clarity and profundity. Comprehensive solutions are formulated, detailed, and exactly proposed. Studies and reports follow, and perhaps also prosecutions and sentences if criminal action has been found. And, of course, all too often, violence.

That violence is as predictable a part of the workings of the American political system as it is of American Hollywood productions and TV police dramas is amply affirmed simply by the frequency of its occurrence. But it should also be noted that American political violence takes many forms, some of them oblique. Presidential assassinations are part of this picture, as are street riots and strikes, and ethnic and racial violence on both an individual and mob scale. So too are America's various wars of suppression, the Civil War, the Indian Wars, and the military actions in the Philippines, Latin America, Korea, and Vietnam. It should be noted, too, that in many of these cases, violence initially employed in professional and restrained ways became uncontrolled and spent its final outbursts with total abandon.

The general significance of this catalogue of American political violence should not be lost. It is a commentary on American political capacities. Violence, it has been well said, is, in political terms, weakness. It is crucially important evidence of an inability to find and utilize political solutions to problems. It represents, in short, political breakdown.

As the standard pattern of myth/ideology interaction proceeds, in the fourth stage, the crisis part of the cycle eventually subsides, often enough from defeat, abject surrender, exhaustion, or a simple return to apathy—in other words, without solution. The standoff between mythic, moral, absolutist demands and ideological maneuvering among competing interests just collapses. Ringing declarations of principle are forgotten. Euphemisms return in all their original abundance, and paradoxes are lightly tolerated. In the popular phrase, the times come when we must put matters behind us. To forgive and forget, with occasional hesitations, becomes the order of the day, and there is a more or less gradual return to the condition of normal strain. The recovery stage of the cycle thus leaves America in position to repeat its habitual myth/ideology cycle on another issue.

This formal, four-stage cycle of myth/ideology interaction in American politics can be described as a process of neutral equilibrium, as in the spin of a cone lying on its side free to roll only in a circle, or like a marble that circles wildly inside a cup whenever the cup is jiggled even slightly. For once again, what sets up the original tension on which the cycle is based, what kicks it off into the intensity stage and then shoves it into the crisis stage and on through recovery and return, are permanent limitations in the American political mind, its lack of alternatives to the irreconcilable tensions within itself, and, most important of all, the fundamental discrepancy between the absolutist demands of myth and the compromising capacities of ideology.

That the contradictions between myth and ideology in America are extreme may be admitted. That they have these radically limiting and frustrating consequences in practical political and historical terms has yet to be established. Analytically, that will be the task of the balance of this book. Here the case may be illustrated by examples.

Admittedly, there are many incidents and other actualities of American political life that do not fit the myth/ideology cycle we have been describing, either because they are incomplete, do not follow the outlined sequence, or follow some completely different pattern. On the other hand, there are an ample number of incidents that do fit the described cycle, and with such precision and significance that they fully demonstrate the cycle's explanatory power. The Spanish–American War, the American response to both World War I and World War II, the New Deal as a response to the depression of 1929, the various red scares and McCarthyism, the Vietnam War, and, more compactly, the Watergate affair, President Carter's aborted effort to rescue the Iranian hostages, and the Iran–Contra scandals of the Reagan administration, President Bush's Persian Gulf War, all fit in this category and will be referred to many times over in the subsequent chapters of this book. But the most important incident in this group is the Civil War, the most serious crisis by far that the American political system has faced.

To see this, we must first sketch again the national and historical context in which that war was fought. To a remarkable degree, we Americans are what we think—albeit, because of fundamental contradictions in our traditional thought patterns, ambiguously. Not failed democrats, or partial democrats, we are and have long been successful democrats, successful social democrats and successful liberal democrats, simultaneously in often painful contradiction. This has produced many paradoxes.

The most extended and fundamental paradox in American politics is that involving our national unity. In the celebrations of our self-legitimizing, Protestant-tinctured, biblically oriented, social democratic myth, we are a people bound by a common faith and a shared historical experience. Yet, at another level of political reality, the level of our Bourgeois liberal democratic ideology, our national unity is very nearly a sham. As a nation in this perspective, we are barely an aggregation of individuals and corporate persons each pursuing singular interests in personal ways for private satisfactions. In this perspective, we are at most a state, a single legal frame that holds us all uneasily.

That Americans hold these two understandings of their unity

simultaneously is a true case of cognitive dissonance in which, in tumbling confusion, we understand ourselves first one way and then the other. And there can be no resolving the contradictions between these views. If we are to be mythically legitimate, we must be one. If we are to be ideologically free, we must be many. History, making us both Protestant and Bourgeois but no more and no less, allows us no alternatives.

In this national, historical context, the Civil War was a breakdown, but only in the consensus that there was a consensus.[21] The substantive consensus to Protestant/Bourgeois, liberal/social, democratic values remained, but, for a catastrophic moment, neither North nor South believed that it did. They were led to this disbelief in part by their conduct toward each other, but also in larger part, by self-doubt. On both sides, there were persistent practical uncertainties about noble causes, and, even more, gnawing moral questioning about courses of practical action. The result, predictably, was an explosion.

The focal point of the war, in a political sense, was indeed the issue of slavery. That slavery was an evil had been acknowledged from the beginning, but ambiguously. Jefferson had included in the Declaration a philippic against the institution in which he personally had some participation—only to have Congress strike it out as unnecessarily provocative to the southern colonies.[22] The question turned not on its merits, but on who was to determine those merits and who would pay for such determinations as were made. Could the sovereign people impose their absolutist moral aspirations? Or could men be left to indulge compromisingly their interests?

The issue had been there from the beginning; the abolitionists fanned the burning coals into bursting flame at Harper's Ferry. The nation's institutions, lead by some of the country's most distinguished and astute politicians, sought bravely to manage the growing conflict by compromise piled on compromise. But when Lincoln's election elicited a radically disproportionate—perhaps even "bizarre"—response, the crisis erupted. Negotiation, mediation, and conflict management had failed.

And so, at terrible cost, a "solution" was imposed, arbitrarily, absolutely, and awfully. Surrender was unconditional, but the terms at Appomattox were charitable beyond credibility. However lauded still, they rendered the war meaningless. The nation's catastrophe was solved by a policy of forgive and forget. Everybody went home. The legal status of blacks had been changed from "slave" to "second-class citizen," a condition that was sealed by the Supreme Court decision of *Plessy v. Ferguson* (1896). With that decision, the South won what it had fought and bled for almost to death: the right to determine for itself its own destiny—and the relations between the races.

More seriously even than that, the war and its aftermath left intact the structural incongruities of the American political system that spun the problem out of hand in the first place. No more terrible example could have been given the American people of the incapacity of their political system to solve its internal contradictions—or of the price that would have to be paid for that failure to achieve resolution. Yet, despite advances here and there, the major outlines of the problem, the place of the black community in white America, remain essentially unresolved. As much as ever, ideology cannot respond to the challenges of myth: liberal democracy cannot instrument solutions to social democratic aspirations.

A structural/institutional explanation for these failures is the work of the next chapter.

4

Ambivalent Government

The presence in the American political system as a whole of two sharply differing democratic traditions requires that we make a systematic effort to determine their differing institutional needs. We will also want to characterize the success they have had in getting these institutional needs met in the actual daily practice of American politics.

The main contention of this chapter is that both of America's conflicting theories of democracy have had remarkable success at shaping the nation's practical political institutions to their particular requirements. These practical institutions (the various governments, federal, state, and local; and their respective branches, executive, legislative, and judicial; as well as their various bureaucratic units) all came into existence with the nation's adoption of its federal and state constitutions and the statutes creating local government systems. That was the easy part. Defining and sustaining understandings of the powers and responsibilities of all these bodies and of their multifarious relationships in an ongoing life of political practice was a vastly more complicated business. And it took time. The whole of it can be termed a process of institutional articulation and development. Some parts of it, necessarily, were completed almost immediately, others were delayed, and preliminary answers to certain questions were often subject to much subsequent modification.

As a total historical process, America's development of its institutional arrangements closely paralleled and was intimately integrated into the historical process by which America developed its general conceptions of social and liberal democracy. This was so much so that by the time the process of institutional articulation was completed, roughly by the end of the nineteenth century, virtually all of these practical political institutions had been given two, conflicting as it were, bifocal understandings of themselves. In each case, from the president in Washington to the local sheriff, from the national Congress to the local council, from the Supreme Court to a neighborhood justice of the peace, there was a social democratic understanding largely for purposes of mythic legitimization and a liberal democratic understanding for ideological purposes. And across the board, all down one side the understandings were essentially Protestant, while all down the other side the understandings were essentially Bourgeois.

The specific task of this chapter is to show how all this was achieved at the level of principles for establishing, organizing, and functioning governmental institutions.

Practical institutional patterns for a modern nation-state must answer three basic questions:

1. What is to be the ground, in law or tradition, on which the various *governments are established* and on which they are to be related one to another?

2. What essential patterns will be used in designing the *internal organizations* of these various governments and for relating the powers and responsibilities of their various departments?

3. What *process patterns* should prevail in the operations of these various departments and in their relationships with each other in the ongoing political process?

We have seen that America's general democratic conceptions gave flatly contradictory answers to the most fundamental political question: who (or what) is to be sovereign in the community. Mythic social democracy said the people were sovereign. Ideological liberal democracy said the law was sovereign. What we will now see is that these democratic visions followed through systematically and gave equally contradictory answers to these more practical questions about institutional design.

Federalism/Confederalism

There is one political system in America, but within that system there are many governments. A government is an independently situated public authority having a significant assignment of powers and responsibilities in a defined jurisdiction and, crucially, independent sources of financial support for its operations. That is to say, a government is a public authority that can do its job pretty much on its own, however much it may from time to time seek the support and cooperation of other bodies. In this sense, there are more than eighty thousand governments in the United States, counting the federal government in Washington; the fifty state governments; all the cities, towns, counties, townships; and, finally, the very large number of what are called special-purpose governments, mostly school districts. The first question that arises at the institutional level is whether there are patterns by which all these largely independent governmental entities in America can go about their work in their frequently overlapping jurisdictions without devouring each other or going to war with each other (as, once, they did).

The formal answer to this question is that especially the fifty-one most significant of these governments, the federal and state governments, are related by the federal principle, and all the rest are no more than legal creatures of the state governments. But this nicely clear-cut answer is almost always fudged with qualifications. Federalism is a difficult concept to define and apply with precision; moreover, to say that especially major city governments are no more than "creatures" of the state governments is greatly to misstate the case, at least politically.

It will be contended here, first, that when law, politics, and the practice of public administration are all added together, there is not a great deal of significant difference between how any of these governments relate to each other, federal to state or local, state to local or federal, local to state or federal. They are all nearly constantly into each others' pockets and offices, and, except for differences of scale (which, of course, are often vast), in much the same ways. But it will also be contended here, second, that when all these intergovernmental interactions are viewed in a suitably broad perspective, two patterns emerge that, when disentangled, can be shown to be respectively federal, in a quite precise sense, and, with equal precision, confederal.

Moreover, the federal pattern in these intergovernmental relations can be shown not only to be congruent with liberal democracy but also to presume necessarily that form of democracy's primary commitments to constitutionalism and sovereignty of the law. Equally, the confederal pattern can be shown to be not only congruent with social democracy but also to presume that form of democracy's commitments to sovereignty of the people.

Federalism is a system for establishing and relating governments. In it a fundamental *law* divides power between one central government and two or more provincial governments. What is crucial here is that the fundamental law is logically prior to the governments that it creates, recognizes, and empowers. It is in this sense that, for a federal system, the law is and must be sovereign. As such, in a federal system, the law not only assigns some powers to the central government and others to the state or provincial governments; it also doles out some powers for concurrent exercise and withholds other powers from being exercised by any government.

Confederal systems reverse all these emphases. A confederation is a system of governmental establishment in which a community of *governments* decides collectively to charter a central agency to perform certain functions for them all in their name. It is a league of states, like the United Nations, in which the existence of the states and their governments are presumed to be logically prior and superior to any collective law by which they charter their central agency.

It was in terms of these understandings of federalism and confederalism that the North and South conducted their debate about the legal and logical status of the Constitution. The North held that the document was, in the language of the document's own Article VI, "the supreme Law of the Land" and counted in support of this view the clear implications of especially Article IV and its clauses about full faith and credit being given in each state for the legal acts of the others and about how each state should honor the privileges and immunities of the citizens of all the other states. On this view the Constitution establishes a vast legal frame that charters, contains, and relates all governments at all levels into one lawful whole, a single union from which no one could be allowed to escape without gravest cost to the integrity of the sovereign law of the whole.

On the other hand, the South held that the Constitution was a compact between the states. There was much real history in support of this view. The Articles of Confederation had been clearly confederal in substance as well as name, and the delegates to the Philadelphia Convention had no mandate to change that. Moreover, the convention itself was conducted, especially in its voting procedures, as a conference of states seeking a compact through their delegates. And the constitution they drafted prescribed that its adoption would be by ratification by the states acting as such. It was only later that spokesmen for northern interests began to invoke the Constitution as the sovereign law of the Union and to elevate statutes enacted in its name above the will of the individual states.

The North had the language of *McCulloch v. Maryland* (1819) and other Supreme Court decisions on its side, but the South persisted with positions it had taken from the start. Slavery was the South's "peculiar institution" and defined its civilization. In entering the union, the southern states had sought to advance certain specified and limited interests, and these did not include putting their identity on the block. Against all claims for the supremacy of federal law, they invoked an alternative principle, the sovereignty of the people in their states assembled. This principle, the right of the people assembled in their natal communities to define their primal identity against all outsiders and moral absolutists, confederalism not only recognized; it stood foursquare upon it and was a direct expression of it. As much as federalism enshrines the law, so confederalism enshrines sovereignty of the people.

The North won the argument, but only by force of arms: in law, the United States of America is a federation. But as in so many other ways, the Civil War was inconclusive on this issue. It may be that when it comes to getting things done by use of law, that is, ideologically, America is a liberal democratic federation. In that perspective, the United States is a huge legal structure within which the government in Washington is by far the biggest player. Especially since the passage of the income tax amendment, its vast financial resources funneled through grant-in-aid programs and other means have enabled it to develop, direct, or operate nationwide schemes of welfare benefits, road-building programs, and a host of other activities that have the effect of not just dwarfing, but of positively shackling the individual states. This is a nationalizing federalism with a vengeance.

But it is also only part of the story. Truism or not, it is important to include in any perspective on the Civil War and the debates and tensions leading up to it that the South's arguments were and very much still are an integral element in the totality of the American experience. In its defense, the South appealed in an American style to principles and values that are profoundly American. And to this day, systematically, when Americans put on their self-legitimizing mythic guise, those appeals are still heard, and not just from the South. Most dramatically, during presidential elections, confederal understandings of the American union are dominant. Party leaders, TV commentators and the media generally, to say nothing of ordinary citizens, all appear to assume that the individual states are discrete, sovereign entities, each endowed with distinct political and cultural identities. "Madam Secretary," intones the voice over the loudspeaker from somewhere on the vast floor of the nominating convention, but in accents selected we must presume by central casting to preserve that authentic down-east twang, "the proud state of Maine, home of the finest potatoes in the Union, casts its votes . . ." Candidates brandish their local origins, "distance" themselves from their national parties, and even brag of their inexperience in Washington politics. Contributing powerfully to these atmospherics is continuing talk about "states' rights" and opposition to federal government interference in local affairs.

The issue between the two views of America's intergovernmental relations is not one of centralization versus fragmentation. Federalism and confederalism are nearly equally susceptible to both tendencies, sometimes simultaneously. Grant-in-aid programs cultivate both bureaucratic centralism and local government fragmentation; presidential campaigns encourage both national unity and local particularism. The issue, the ambivalence, is rather that when American political actors have to think of their governments as organized for practical political action, they go for a vocabulary that presupposes these governments relating within a legal (federal) frame; when these same actors have to think mythically, of a morally legitimized America on the march in history, they go for a vocabulary that presupposes these governments rooted in their local communities and surging together through shared (confederal) patterns of patriotic love and commitment to the national heritage and mission.

It is important, as we conclude this discussion, not to appear to be resolving the debate over whether America is truly a federation or a confederation by suggesting it is some kind of hybrid of the two, a conceptual mush halfway between the poles of tight federal union and loose confederal union. What we are suggesting instead is that Americans oscillate between two vocabularies, each of which is employed with some conceptual precision. This was evident even in the pre–Civil War debates. For analytic purposes, we presented those debates only in their initial terms where they appeared to be relatively clear cut. But in fact, as the debates extended, both sides contributed to their confusion. The South frequently sounded as if it were defending an "interest" sanctioned by law, never mind its morality. Slaves were property, legal chattel, to have and to hold. Even more resoundingly, the North claimed the legitimacy of the American people assembled in a national union. The result is not a hybrid, but a logical tangle of two vocabularies, the disentanglement of which is always a considerable analytical challenge.

"Separation of Powers" and "Checks and Balances"

This same kind of ambivalence between contradictory vocabularies bedevils the concepts by which Americans seek to understand the internal organization of their governments. The American doctrine of "separation of powers" and its attendant complexities have been represented by national myth as a straightforward business of an assignment of powers to three "coequal" branches that is then "modified" by "checks and balances." Analysis can show that this traditional presentation conceals substantial confusion.

In logic, separation of powers achieves its differentiation between the branches of the government by functional distinctions, one branch to legislate, one to execute, and one to adjudicate. These distinctions in logic are reinforced by the Constitution's organization into Articles I, II, and III; by its language ("All legislative Powers herein granted shall be vested in a Congress . . . ," etc.); by the city of Washington's layout and architecture; and, very significantly, by the facts that the Congress is constituted as a relatively large, deliberative body as befits an organ charged with legislating, that the president is a single figure as befits an executive charged with acting with dispatch, and that the Supreme Court gives every appearance of being exactly that, a court of judges serving *en banc*. Into this well-developed pattern of clearly delineated and separated powers, so called modifications by "checks and balances" cannot intrude without massive contradiction. Checks and balances mix precisely what the doctrine of separation of powers meant to keep separate: functions and assignments of power. It must not be forgotten that the separation of powers doctrine, as popularized by Montesquieu in the century just before the founders of the American republic put it to use, was designed specifically to prevent executive tyranny by stripping the king of quite precisely his legislative and judicial powers and by lodging them elsewhere in the governmental structure, where he would be unable to get them back.[1]

What, then, is the commentator to make of the fact that in the document of 1787, clear adulterations of the distinctions necessary to maintain the orderly identity and separation of the branches takes place? Specifically, what are we to make of the grant, in the form of the veto power, of very significant legislative powers to the president? What are we to make of the fact that this grant, along with other factors, has led some of the most widely quoted commentators on the American presidency to insist that of the many functions assigned to that office perhaps the most important are those that make the nation's chief executive the nation's "chief legislator"?[2] How in the logic of separation of powers can he be both?

These may be thought just expositional difficulties, but there are practical implications of considerable magnitude as well. Since *Marbury v. Madison* (1803), the Supreme Court has held the power of constitutional review. That it has held this power and used it, with increasing frequency, cannot be denied. Whether it should have this power is, however, for many persons still an open question, and some of them have held that its having it has come about only through an act of usurpation. In light of any principled understanding of the doctrine of separation of powers, that characterization, so far as the legislative power is concerned, cannot be denied. What was the Court doing in *Brown v. Board of Education* (1954) if not bringing the law of practice into conformity with not the law of constitutional precedent (which was crystal clear that "separate" could be "equal"), but the evolving aspirations of the American people about the status of blacks in their shared community? Questions about this kind of deliberative "legislation" coming out of the Court are by no means moot. Every time a new judge needs confirmation to the Court, a clamor develops over not just his or her qualifications but also over the criteria to be used in evaluating those qualifications. Is the person to be selected simply on the basis of competence as a legal technician (and "judicial restraint")—because we presume the Court to be simply that, a court of law? Or do we see the Court as, effectively, a legislative bastion of last resort for the defense of personal privacy, the rights of women, the status of blacks and other racial and ethnic minorities, and of freedoms for the politically unpopular against, specifically, the dominance of majorities in the nation's legislative bodies? In this case, the Court should be staffed not by legal technicians, but by judges selected for their courage, maturity, and wisdom, their powers of perception for the enduring values of the American tradition, for their sense of "justice" beyond the law.

Or, on another issue of this same sort, does the president have, inherently from the nature of his executive office, "executive privilege" to justify withholding from the other branches information about what has gone on in the White House? Many presidents have claimed this privilege, arguing that without it they could not truly be the nation's chief executive as required by the doctrine of separation of powers. In *United States v. Nixon* (1974), the Supreme Court held, even while ruling against Richard Nixon's specific claims, that the presidential office could sustain a general claim to this privilege—within limits. But how can an office have a right more or less? By what doctrine are those limits to be determined in each case? By what doctrine, philosophy, or set of principles can the president's privileges be determined? Without rules to set those limits in practice, questions about them will remain perpetually open, to be closed if at all only by emotional appeals to the personal trustworthiness of particular persons.

So long as easy talk goes on about checks and balances "modifying" the government's system of separation of powers, there can be no end to questions of this sort. Claims of independence and charges of dependence can all be made equally plausible and, more important, equally beyond principled resolution.

The idea of checks and balances "modifying" separation of powers also fails to provide any explanation for the Constitution's bicameralism. There is nothing in the doctrine of separation of powers that requires two houses of Congress, and it is hard to see how any modification of that doctrine by checks and balances would require it either. Madison, in *Federalist* No. 51, argues initially that a division of the legislature into two houses is necessary, practically, to weaken it in the face of the other two branches. But the dominant line of his argument ends with the famous assertion that ambition must be made to counter ambition. That would seem to suggest that the center of his attention had shifted from questions about the relation between the branches to the problem of the check and balance between the two houses. What then has become of the doctrine of separation of powers between the branches?

This kind of confusion is so impenetrable that it is no wonder that many of the textbooks, when listing for learning by rote the checks and balances in the federal government, notice exclusively the checks the branches have on each other, and omit the situation between the two houses altogether. But this, in the end, is doubly odd. It is odd, first, by the simple omission of what is, from the point of view of the ongoing political process, unquestionably the most significant source of check and balance in the Washington "merry-go-round." It is also theoretically odd, because the check and balance in the legislative process is the one true check and balance in the whole system in the sense of a head-to-head confrontation between identically constituted powers.

Beyond this inability to explain some of the most obvious features of the Constitution, the traditional theory that what we have in Washington is a simple system of separated powers modified by checks and balances also more generally fails to account for the persistent appearance of paradox that runs right through the whole of Washington's operations. In all three branches, there are persistent ambiguities about what law and tradition expect of them. It is not just that the Court does on occasion act like a legislative body; obdurately, by solid tradition, it is expected to act like one even while, just as obdurately, it is expected to restrain itself and act simply like a court. The same kind of driven contrariness seems to afflict the other two branches. It is clearly possible to interpret Article II of the Constitution as an imperative instructing the president to confine himself to taking care that the laws be faithfully executed. But are there not equally enshrined in the American political tradition a host of precedents and imperatives that instruct him to mount the vastly larger role of trumpeting the nation forward on its historical missions? Equally, if there is in law and tradition an imperative that calls for judicial restraint, then why is there not in the same law and tradition—with all its citations to constitutionalism, theories of limited government, and careful assignments of specific powers—an imperative calling for legislative restraint? What is it in our whole body of constitutional law that impels legislators—often to the consternation of presidents—to immerse themselves, individually, by committee, and collectively, in details of budget making, policy implementation, and bureaucratic administration?

The inadequacies of the traditional explanation that what we have in Washington is a government organized by separation of powers "modified" by checks and balances compel us to think of alternatives to it. As we proceed to do this, we should note that the primary methodological difficulty with the traditional explanation is its parsimony about theory. It holds that the founders used one theory for defining and relating the branches of government, which they then for practical reasons modified in various ways.[3] The gap in this approach is in the failure to note that calling reasons "practical" is no explanation for their presence, that modifications do not spring out of the air of mere common sense, that, in short, methodologically we must presume that the founders must have had theoretical reasons for their modifications of separation of powers theory. All of this is to say simply that the founders must have been working with more than one theory about governmental organization, that in more or less inexplicit ways they were working with at least two theories that, logic to one side, they somehow imposed upon each other.[4]

Once this possibility is admitted, the authorities on the intellectual milieu of eighteenth-century colonial America will suggest immediately a second theory of governmental organization that was easily available to the founders, namely Aristotle's theory of mixed or "balanced" government.[5] What has restrained the authorities from forcefully advancing this second theory as also operative in the minds of the founders is mostly a reluctance to depict the founders as philosophically confused. But the founders were confused, as confused as other members of their intellectual generation, whether in America or in Europe. The founders used separation of powers doctrines, largely derived from their readings in Montesquieu, to set up the appearances of their constitution; they then, in confused and often quite hidden ways, slipped into their work mixed government theory, which they derived not only from Aristotle but also from Polybius and Cicero, and also, indeed, Montesquieu, who was in fact almost as confused about these matters as they were.

It will take some analysis to sort all this out. We will address first the separation of powers doctrine in what might be called its "pure" form, then mixed government theory, and then both as they generally operate in the American constitutional structure.

Pure Separation of Powers

The pure doctrine of the separation of powers can be presented simply. Its tripartite division of governmental powers, so often di-

agramed in the textbooks as a kind of inverted devil's fork, is familiar to us all. So also is the requirement that persons serving in one of
the branches should not be permitted to serve at the same time in
either of the other two, to ensure, in Madison's words, "that each
department should have a will of its own."[6] As familiar as these
points is the fundamental problem the separation of powers was—
and still is—thought to solve, the problem of tyranny. Power, it is
said, corrupts; absolute power corrupts absolutely. The concentra-
tion of all power in one set of hands is the very definition of tyranny.
But the very familiarity of these points may conceal from us both
their originality and their particularity. It is not immediately obvious
that the functions of government, its range of public services, could
or, alternatively, should be split up—exhaustively—between the legislative, executive, and judicial branches. Few from Aristotle through
St. Thomas thought in those terms. It is no more innate that these
branches should be constituted in independence of each other. What
we, in the Anglo-American world, now call the judicial system clearly
originated in a service offered by the king, in defense of his peace,
in competition with the older manorial courts. And the separation of
legislative functions from the executive remains a radical—and
mostly not pursued—suggestion even in the modern world. Finally,
the notion that power corrupts—and that absolute power corrupts
absolutely—is original only in its phrasing. The substance of the lesson is as old as Plato. But it flies nonetheless in the face of another
lesson as easily preached and learned, even if not much in America,
that without power, chaos reigns, that the creation and massing of
power may be necessary to stabilize, ennoble, liberate a community
and its citizens.

Montesquieu did not in fact originate the doctrine of separation
of powers. That was the work mostly of a scattering of public officials working in the century before him to bring a host of new governmental conceptions into being as feudal forms of government
eroded. Montesquieu's genius was to attempt to state systematically
this whole process.[7] His clumsiness and frequent contradictions are
in fact a tribute to his efforts to achieve comprehensiveness. Nevertheless, key paragraphs in his work define with surprising simplicity and freshness the rudiments of a new doctrine.

> In every government there are three sorts of power: . . . By virtue of
> the first, the prince or magistrate enacts temporary or perpetual laws,
> and amends or abrogates those that have been already enacted. By the
> second he makes peace or war, sends or receives embassies, establishes
> the public security, and provides against invasions. By the third, he

> punishes crimes, or determines the disputes that arise between individuals.[8]

These spare definitions still speak imperatives to which our modern institutions listen. So do they also hear these admonitions.

> When the legislative and executive powers are united in the same person, or in the same body of magistracy, there can be then no liberty; because apprehensions may arise, lest the same monarch or senate should enact tyrannical laws, to execute them in a tyrannical manner.
>
> Again, there is no liberty, if the power of judging be not separated from the legislative and executive powers. Were it joined with the legislative, the life and liberty of the subject would be exposed to arbitrary control; for the judge would be then the legislator. Were it joined to the executive power, the judge might behave with all the violence of an oppressor.
>
> Miserable indeed would be the case, were the same man, or the same body whether of the nobles or of the people, to exercise those three powers, that of enacting laws, that of executing the public resolutions, and that of judging the crimes or differences of individuals.[9]

These simple, eighteenth-century phrasings do more than remind us of the principal points of separation of powers; they also are emphatic in their reminder that the goal of the doctrine was not just the prevention of tyranny, but also, beyond that, the preservation of "the life and liberty of the subject" from "arbitrary control." But, having said that, it is important to know how Montesquieu defined liberty. He insists that liberty is not simply being able to do as we please. On the contrary, he states, "in societies directed by laws, liberty can consist only in the power of doing what we ought to will, and in not being constrained to do what we ought not to will."[10]

Montesquieu is, decisively, a modern political philosopher. His essential concern is not with determining the meaning and character of a rational and just order immanent in Nature; it is in finding ways and means to liberate the will of man. But "man," for Montesquieu, is not man alone, as he was for Hobbes and even for Locke. Man, for Montesquieu, is man the citizen, man caught up in community where he finds membership and fulfillment beyond mere self. The history of political philosophy goes forward from Montesquieu to Rousseau, not Hobbes. The will of man emerges truly for Montesquieu as it does for Rousseau only in the general will, the life and law and spirit of the community, the sovereignty of the nation and its people.

If we are, thus, to comprehend in some fullness the doctrine of the separation of powers, we must set it in the context of Montesquieu's book *L'Esprit des Lois.* It is, at bottom, essentially a communitarian doctrine. Its focus, obviously, is on tyranny, an evil in government, but the purging of this evil is meant to release the spirit of the people, the sovereign will of the nation. In this light, the executive, the original monarch stripped of his legislative and judicial powers, remains the supreme voice of the people, their commander in war, their representative in peace, the source of their tranquillity in domestic affairs. The legislative body is the articulator of their sovereign will, the embodiment of themselves in law. And the courts are the receptacle of their wisdom and sense of justice. In a properly constituted government, there may or may not be a formal constitution, a written instrument. However that may be, the institutions of government are not finally grounded in law, but in the will of the people. In Montesquieu's world, the people, not the law, are sovereign.

Two other principles of particular importance to the American experience flow from this understanding of the doctrine of the separation of powers. The first is that, in this communitarian perspective, the relations between the branches should be governed not by a spirit of hostility and competition but rather by feelings of mutual regard and trust, by cooperation within patterns of rationally arranged divisions of labor. Second, all the powers of government should be understood to be responsible, in a quite technical sense, to the people. This must be thought to be the case even in the absence of any system of elections or other formal institutional apparatus for holding government responsible. Executives, legislators, and even judges legitimately can possess power only as they hold it in specific obedience to the people's will. This means both that they can, in one way or another, be held answerable and accountable to the people, and also that they should find direction in all that they do from the will of the people. In a powerful and profound sense, through his understanding and expression of the doctrine of separation of powers, Montesquieu was a spokesman not only for a rising surge of social democratic feeling in the northwest Europe of his day but also, more specifically, for the tradition of responsible government. Lincoln would call it government by, for, and of the people.

Mixed Government

As the rarefied statement of the doctrine of the separation of powers focuses on Montesquieu, so the rarefied statement of mixed government theory must focus on Aristotle. The institutional expression of this theory in a bicameral legislature is the theory's distinguishing feature but does not speak for its essence, for its essential understanding of the nature and purposes of political life. For that, something of the full length of Aristotle's political philosophy must be laid out.

In his more sanguine moods, Aristotle, like Plato before him, preached a civic idealism that has contributed powerfully to Western traditions of participatory citizenship and communal life. But Aristotle had his gloomy moments, and it was from these that he made his contributions to mixed government theory.

His approach is deceptive. It begins with what appears to be a straightforward and empirical attempt to analyze and categorize the various kinds of governments he observed in the city-states of his day. What followed became a catechism of political science down to modern times (which has now largely discarded it). Governments can be by one man, the few, or the many. If sovereignty is vested in one man, Aristotle implied (the text of the *Politics* is sketchy on this point), he would probably be some kind of hero and very rich. If it is vested in the few, Aristotle held they would definitely be men of the better sort and relatively rich. If the many hold the reins of government, they would constitute what some of Aristotle's students had no reluctance identifying as "the uncultivated herd" and Aristotle himself called the poor. This numerate/socioeconomic analysis is then carried to the level of political institutions, or, more precisely, to the level of political essences, because Aristotle, as a Greek idealist philosopher, believed that if government was exercised through an institution that was essentially characteristic of a particular class, then that government would be almost necessarily in the interest of that class. Thus, a government by a large assembly, the political institution most associated with the poor masses, would nearly inevitably be a government that would represent and be largely on behalf of the interests of the poor, even though the assembly for all its size might not include more than a fraction of the total poor population. Similarly, according to this line of argument, a small council would speak for the rich classes, and a king would speak for himself.

Aristotle did not deny that a king might, at least for a time, govern beneficently—in which case his government could be classed a monarchy—but he thought it highly probable that such a government would soon degenerate into a tyranny. Similarly, a council might constitute true aristocracy, again at least for a time, but oligarchy would always threaten. Lastly, the poor's massive assembly might, with proper leadership, constitute a genuine polity, but demagogic leaders were bound in time to sway it into rabid democracy, a government Aristotle understood to be by, for, and in the interest of the mob. Moreover, Aristotle hypothesized that these patterns of degeneracy might slide into and out of each other, so that as monarchy degenerated into tyranny, it might be rescued by aristocracy, which, in turn, as it degenerated into oligarchy, might be rescued by polity before collapsing into mobocracy, the whole revolutionary cycle of civil strife and turmoil revolving back to begin again with monarchy.[11]

Aristotle was emphatic that the primary engine driving this revolutionary cycle was class war and, more particularly, the greed and paranoia of the rich confronting the hunger and envy of the poor. That is an important point, one that Madison, among the Americans, would be at the greatest pains to note. But of greater importance for political science is the fact that Aristotle, by this kind of socioeconomic political analysis, has laid down the fundamental principles of what can be properly called representative government. Aristotle is presupposing that society—any society—is more or less permanently divided into competing classes, factions, interests, call them what you will, and that each of these can design and seek to create a characteristic political institution that, once established, will speak for and assiduously represent its needs.

Aristotle now becomes a constitutional engineer and lays down the principles of mixed government. The problem is turmoil in society: its causes cannot be eradicated; society is permanently divided into competing factions. But a shrewdly designed, skillfully balanced constitution can contain and moderate the excess of civil strife by mixing into one encaging legal structure all the institutions representative of the society's major factions: crown, council, and assembly. The result is a bicameral system—or even a tricameral system if included in the total constitutional structure was an executive figure playing a moderating, interventional role between the council and the assembly.[12]

Three aspects of this system are of special concern to Americans. First, the system is absolutely dependent on the rigidity of the encaging constitutional law. In any practical situation, the task of determining, case by case, the requirements and limits set by that law will have to be assigned to some body or person who can be depended on to be impartial, fair, and final. In America, that role would ultimately be assigned to the courts. But there can be no disputing that the system requires such a role and that it must be assigned somewhere other than to the monarchical, council, and assembly aspects. They must be excluded because, by definition, they are interested parties who by their nature must be disciplined to stay inside the system.

Second, this system represents the major interests into which the society is divided.[13] Aristotle on this matter had a binary, or, at most, a trinary focus. But even he, if pressed, would have surely admitted that on occasion the rich, for instance, could be divided among themselves and their council would have to represent a double interest. No matter. The principle of the system, of representative government in this context,[14] is that all major interests in the society should receive distinct, direct representation, and know with assurance that should they seek it, they would get it, whether the interests are binary, trinary, or an extended pluralism.[15]

But what of those groups or elements in the community too weak, too scattered, too unorganized, too simply "poor" (women, children, slaves, aliens, the chronically ill, the old, the "truly needy") to constitute an "interest" capable of seeking and getting representation in the system? They are, from the point of view of the system, politically invisible, and are left out. Representative government is, in this tradition, essentially elitist, a politics exclusively for those politically capable of and "interested" in being represented in the political process.

Third, the system is, by essential constitution, a system of checks and balances. Note that all its elements are seen performing without distinction the same functions. All the system requires is that whatever is done can only be done with the concurrence of all elements. Perfectly, at this level, apples check and balance apples, which check and balance apples. The difference between the elements, crown, council, and large assembly, arises not from the requirements inherent in discharging distinct functions, but from the characteristic differences between the groups being represented. The assumption, once again, is that every society will contain aspiring heroes, snobs, and clods. The task of politics is not to point the way forward into history, or to fathom the enduring will of the people in their nationhood; it is instead to manage conflict, to harmonize, in one way or another, perhaps by doing nothing at all, the diverse claims of the competing interests. Expand the number of interests claiming attention, preserve only the guarantee that all will be heard, and it is revealed that the true name of "checks and balances" is, indeed, representative government.

Responsible Government/Representative Government

That both these theories of governmental organization, the doctrine of the separation of powers and the theory of mixed government, are present in the Constitution composed by the Philadelphia

Convention should be obvious simply from our definitional discussion of them. The most explicit evidence of their combined presence is that first sentence of Article I:

> Section 1 All legislative Powers herein granted shall be vested in a Congress of the United States, which shall consist of a Senate and House of Representatives.

The comma in that sentence carries the heavy load of linking what comes before it, which is pure separation of powers, with what comes after it, which is pure mixed government.

Of the more subtle evidence, note especially the prolix language assigning the president his veto power in Section 7 of the same article. That verbosity is cast in terms that are transparently those not of the people's hero but of the *deus ex machina* supposed by mixed government theory to be capable, in the collective interest of the whole, of moderating between the partial interests represented in the two houses. On the other hand, what are the presuppositions of Section 3 of Article II, which call upon the president to keep the Congress informed of the state of the Union and to recommend to it such measures, bills, and programs as he thinks are required? In the first case, the president speaks within the context of civil strife rending the community; in the second, he articulates the will of the whole people.

The confusion of the two theories extends even to the most important of the commentaries of the Constitution. We all remember the gist of the definition of tyranny given by Madison in *Federalist* No. 47, that it is too much power in one set of hands. But notice his exact words:

> The accumulation of all powers, legislative, executive, and judiciary [pax Montesquieu], in the same hands, whether of one, a few, or many [pax Aristotle], and whether hereditary, self-appointed, or elective [pax the British model involuting both], may justly be pronounced the very definition of tyranny.

The only way Madison could have bettered this statement for our illustrative purposes would have been for him to have tacked on to the end of it the phrase, "and the source of perpetual civil strife." That phrase would have completed the confusion in his thought, for just as he had two theories, one from Montesquieu, the other from Aristotle, so he had two problems, one corruption in government, the other corruption in the community. So why not throw logic to the winds and use two complete vocabularies of politics simultaneously?

This, so the argument of this chapter runs, is what the American people, following Madison's confusing lead, proceeded to do. They combined the vocabularies of federalism and mixed government theory to produce a language of liberal democratic, representative government for ideological purposes; and they combined the vocabularies of confederalism and separation of powers to produce a language of social democratic, responsible government for mythic purposes.[16] In this way, they mixed both their Protestant and their Bourgeois heritages into the central fiber of their politics and destined themselves perpetually to acting out the tensions between them.

The congruence, on each side of these equations, of the various principles involved must be underlined. The core of the liberal democratic theory is sovereignty of law in the face of a multiplicity of individualized actors. The central drift of federalism, as so emphatically stated in Madison's exposition of it, is to institutionalize in law a nation's territorial fragmentation, in patterns that follow with remarkable precision the institutional recognition of social-interest fragmentation granted by mixed government theory. This kind of fit between different levels of principle is equally achieved on the social democratic side of American politics. The core of American social democracy is its reverence, beyond all law and formal institutions, for the enthusiasms of the historically focused people. Confederalism's loose structures and its emphasis on the natal roots of actual neighborhoods answers to these social democratic assumptions, as does separation of powers doctrine. The whole motif of that doctrine is to allow the free enthusiasms of the people to flood upward and through especially the executive but also the legislature and even the courts. What we are confronted with, then, in the American political system as a functioning whole is two complete democratic theories, each internally coherent and each comprehensively providing answers to questions ranging from the basic concerns of political life to patterns of established political institutions.

We are also confronted with the polarities of a spectrum on which we can do, as it were, a prismatic analysis of American politics. Just as any beam of light is a complex of colors that when refracted through a prism can be seen individually, so any event, personality, program, or institution of American politics is a complex of elements. On first appearance, this complex of elements appears confused, contradictory, even paradoxical. But when such a complex is placed between the definitional poles of myth and ideology, the differing elements in that complex can be shaken out and identified, and the tensions between them then understood.

The chapters still to come will spell out all these assertions step by step, covering all the major institutions of the American political system, from president and Congress down to interested "client" and participant "citizen" (for these too are "institutions" in the sense of traditionalized and legalized patterns of roles and expectations to be played out by specified categories of parties). In anticipation of that survey, it may be useful to summarize briefly the two political styles Americans developed and how these styles apply to each of the system's major institutions. The key to the whole of it is that each of these institutions must be looked at if not through a prism then through bifocal glasses.

The central—and powerfully centralizing—figure in America's Protestant-tinctured social democratic vision of itself as a living political process is the president, and his primary responsibility in office is to promulgate the American myth. He shoulders this responsibility directly from the imperatives of the pure doctrine of separation of powers as set in the context of America's confederal union of sovereign peoples assembled in their natal communities. He discharges this responsibility by the words he speaks, the proclamations he issues (or that are issued in his name), and the images he projects. And in this process, he summons up our past, he understands our present, and, nobly, he anticipates our national future. It must be emphasized that this is an intensely personal role played out day in and day out, and individual presidents have proved variously good at it.[17]

The president is accompanied in his execution of this role by candidates seeking to succeed him, by other executives in the system (especially governors of major states and mayors of large cities), and occasionally and to a lesser degree by sundry legislators and other public figures. All are more or less burdened to carry the mantle of America's mythic legitimization.

Also central to the mythic, social democratic vision of America are political parties. These are conceived as massed armies of aroused citizens mobilized in support of their leaders. They thrust before the whole nation, it is supposed, alternative formulations of the people's sovereign will. In elections, the people choose between these formulations, and the sponsors of the chosen program then swarm into the nation's executive offices in particular to implement what the voice of the people has decreed. But woe to those victors if, at the next elections, they are found to have been false to their promises or sorry in their performance of them, for then they will be held responsible to their electorates and called to account.

In this vision, bureaucracies play indispensable and much-emphasized parts. They are the professionalized receptacles of the people's will. From the secretaries of the great departments to the ordinary police officer on the beat, America's public servants are understood to be agents of the people's will pushing forward the nation's historical advance. The courts are similarly understood but seen as playing a less significant role. They are mostly valued for their ability to establish, in wisdom and justice, the guilt or innocence of persons charged with crimes. Only from time to time do they play larger roles, but those times can be highly charged with drama.

Finally in this social democratic vision is the citizen, the ordinary, the "real" American, on whom all else in this vision rests. He or she is expected to be hard working, honest, simple, alert, and, above all, a participant. His or her ballot is sovereign. That, in the social democratic vision, is where it all begins.

When the vision is shifted to the Bourgeois liberal democratic perspective of the system's operative ideology, and we move, as it were, to a close-up focus on its elements, all is transformed. Now the Congress—not the president—is the premier American political institution. It is largely staffed by soft-spoken, genial, highly competent, and patient operatives, many of the most important of whom have very little general public recognition. Their primary responsibility is to be accessible to the organized interests in the community, to represent those interests faithfully, and to harmonize their conflicting claims. Congress comes to this role directly from the imperatives of mixed government theory set in the tight legal frame of American federalism. And it executes it by a continuous process of negotiations, linked compromise, ad hoc solutions, and, of course, checks and balances.

The proficiency, the nationally visible modes, and the manners of members of Congress in Washington have made them role models for virtually every other politician in America. Even the heroes of the system, from the president on down, have to learn something of how to play the game of American ideological politics, the process of give and take, of going along to get along, even if they despise it, play it badly, or only play it intermittently. All must learn that what makes American politics tick on its ideological side is a process of avaricious transactionalism, a politics of who gets what, why, and from whom. That is not "human nature." It is a specific style of politics that, however covertly, was built into the American political system by Madison (who then made it perfectly explicit in the *Federalist Papers* that he had done so).[18]

Central to this ideological process of American politics are the lobbyists, lawyers, and other agents of the major interest groups and

private corporations who feed on or otherwise benefit from governmental activities. These hard-working, infinitely knowledgeable, and
highly professional individuals work closely with members of the
federal, state, and local legislative councils and must be considered
partners with them in the ongoing political process. There is a third
group that also belongs in this process, the heads, deputy heads, and
bureau chiefs of all the bureaucracies at all levels of the political
system. They, too, are partners in the process of policy formulation
and execution that gets things done in American politics.

Major operatives of this ideological side of American politics are
the judges, but, decisively, they are not "partners" in the process.
Rather it is for them to enforce and conserve the law, in all kinds of
cases, civil and criminal, to maintain the legal frame, the cage, within
which all others ply their trades.

Where do ordinary American citizens fit into this Bourgeois, liberal democratic, ideological picture? Hardly at all. On its ideological
side, American politics draws a sharp line between the powerful and
the powerless, between those who have the resources and the interest to find and use access to the policy process and those who do not.
This is not to suggest that American politics is dominated by a single
elite. American politics in fact exhibits an extraordinary pluralism of
elites. It is rather to suggest that in America on its ideological side,
most of us are at the bottom of the system. We rarely even know
who is getting what from whom at the top and would not be able to
do very much about it even if we did. We, the ordinaries of the
system, are politically invisible.

Of course, back on the other, the mythic side of American politics we are visible indeed, and that is the larger point of the matter.
In the full picture of American politics as an ongoing process, its two
styles tangle and retangle nearly constantly, often quietly and merely
misleadingly, but sometimes fiercely with results that can be exciting,
embarrassing, bizarre, tragic, or all these in combination.

II

INSTITUTIONS AND OFFICERS

The American political system's broad theoretical characteristics achieve their practical reality in the system's diversity of political institutions and offices. Moreover, the contradictions and tensions in the general patterns of the system all find reflection in its particular offices and their occupants. These officeholders all become, in a phrase, "adaptively schizophrenic." They parallel both in their understandings of their responsibilities and in their individual personalities the divisions in the system as a whole. Nevertheless, they create these characteristics in widely contrasting ways and with sharp differences of emphasis.

The primary task of the judges is to stabilize the system as a whole by concentrating the work of the courts on the ideological role of conserving established law, the legal cage. Their mythic role, although important, is relatively subdued.

The nation's chief executive, the president, in contrast, is essentially a mythic figure charged with proclaiming America's legitimacy. His ideological role is relatively minor.

Congress, in further contrast, wears its mythic colors with considerable discomfort. Its primary responsibility is ideological: to harmonize the conflicting claims of the competing interests, national, state, and local, foreign and domestic, that feed off the government in Washington.

With suitable variation arising mostly from differences of scale, much the same kind of observations can be made about local government leaders and their offices.

Into this world of the system's dominant constitutional structures and personalities, the civil and uniformed servants of the nation's bureaucratic structures fit with a systemic awkwardness. The reasons are fundamental, theoretical, and irresolvable. The nation's bureaucrats constitute a massive, indispensable, but never fully absorbable "third term" caught between the dominant elements of the political system. As such, for all the hugely necessary and mostly good work they do, their standing in the system is a perpetual source of unhappiness to themselves, to the system, and to the public.

5

The Courts and the Constitution

Americans are a litigious people. In terms of sheer volume, the law contained in books housed on American library and law-office shelves that is to be enforced, abided by, broken, neglected, cited, deciphered, and, above all, learned, sets world records. The same is true with the number of lawyers practicing and employed, both absolutely and relatively, the number of cases brought to court, and the amount of time spent processing these cases. And Americans are a litigious people not just quantitatively. They also attach an extraordinary qualitative significance to what they do with the law, lawyers, and the courts. Americans believe—and are endlessly taught by their school textbooks to believe—that major social and political changes can be effected by working through the law with lawyers in court, far beyond the settlement of this or that dispute between particular parties. Minority groups, especially, but also other politically disadvantaged groups, such as women's groups, frequently make conscious decisions not to take their appeals through legislative bodies and other popularly elected bodies, but to work through the courts instead. And major corporations and other similar well-established institutions, including on occasion even government units, invest from time to time their legal struggles with this kind of higher, longer-term value.

Why do Americans attach so much significance to the law and the work of lawyers and the courts? The quick answer is that ours is a constitutional republic in which the written constitution, through its own restrictions, permissions, and empowerments, and through a host of subsidiary laws and institutions created pursuant to its terms, has come to affect virtually every aspect of our lives, both individually and socially. This quick answer makes an important point. To an extraordinary degree, the Constitution, written in 1787 and amended only marginally since, constitutes the American community, socially, politically, and in other ways as well. Moreover, in our history the courts have claimed to an extraordinary degree the power of determining what the Constitution means and how it will be applied. No wonder therefore that in the American political system judges are extraordinarily important people, as are also the people who work around and with them.

But this quick answer also conceals almost as much as it reveals. It leaves unsaid that the law, especially in the Anglo-American tradition, has definable characteristics that quite rigidly come to define and restrict its social and political operations and effects. These definitions and restrictions in turn severely limit the possibilities and goals that the courts can be expected to achieve. More important, the quick answer about the relationship of the Constitution and American life conceals fundamental ambiguities about the work of lawyers and the courts.

In popular imagination, in the symbols engraved in the façades over the entrances of public buildings, in the rhetoric of lawyers, judges, and politicians, American courts are portrayed consistently as sources of justice, wisdom, and mercy; fair, firm and impartial. That is the judicial myth. As a real, functional element in the American political system, this myth generates and gives meaning and purpose to much political behavior. Judges are accorded great respect personally, and their decisions are accepted as binding within the limits set by law. Moreover, people sometimes do get from the courts settlements of their disputes that at least approach abstract standards of justice, wisdom, and mercy. But it can be sharply questioned how far justice, wisdom, and mercy as administered by American courts can go in effecting real social change.

In the perspective of the political system as a whole, the mythic role of the courts is a useful, even a necessary role, but it is not the primary function they perform. Their ideological role is both more generally significant and far more of a determinant of how judges and other court personnel habitually understand and go about their work. In the tradition of politics that was first articulated by Hobbes and Locke and that developed into the patterns of liberal democracy, government by law is the central value. Specifically, government by law is the foundational value for both federalism and mixed government theory. Neither can be implemented without it. In the English liberal tradition, and in American practical experience decisively, it is the courts who protect this value and make it operational. In the light of this tradition, the first responsibility of the courts is to conserve not justice, not wisdom, not mercy, but the law, actual, positive, and known. All in all, American courts do this work of conserving the established law tolerably well. But the social effects of their doing this work—and the restrictions that flow from their in fact doing it well—require careful evaluation. In the first half of this chapter, we will examine the abstract, philosophical character of this understanding of the work of the courts and then its operationalization in American practice. In the second half we will examine the special case of the Supreme Court in both its ideological and mythic aspects.

The Judicial Act

In the liberal democratic tradition, the judicial act, the work judges do in court, is grounded purely and plainly in the ideas of Thomas Hobbes.[1] There are a number of steps involved in this process.

Before a court can hear a case, there must be a dispute to be settled. It must be settled because otherwise, so the Hobbesian assumption goes, it will threaten to spill first its participants and then the whole of society back into the state of nature, where life beyond the pacification of the law is, "solitary, poor, nasty, brutish, and short."[2] Anarchists and other communitarians do not make this assumption. They assume that quarrels, especially in the absence of threats of compulsion, will subside of themselves and leave no lingering hostilities. The dominant human impulses, they think, are those promoting fellowship, not competition. Hobbesians regard such views as pathetically unrealistic, whether the dispute is a lovers' tiff or a titanic struggle between two international corporations over the assets of a third. Obviously, most disputes in any society never reach the courts, and even of those that threaten to do so, many achieve out of court settlements and never go to trial. But there is a perpetual and substantial margin of socially threatening disputes, Hobbesians argue, that are not self-resolving. It is these which, if not resolved by the courts, will turn the whole of society into their battleground.

Nevertheless, there are restrictions on the kinds of disputes Hobbesian, liberal democratic courts will undertake to settle. For one thing, these courts are not very good at settling philosophical disputes. For such disputes to be held justiciable, the parties in them would have to become so hot that one or the other of them did somebody "harm," that is to say, in Hobbesian terms, violated, curbed, or otherwise diminished the "interest" (life, limb, liberty, or property) of another. The harm must be definable, perceptible, in some sense, measurable. Otherwise the dispute is not a dispute of a sort that, if not resolved, would threaten the common peace and security—so the Hobbesian assumption runs.

Moreover, not only does the dispute have to be real, in the sense defined, but it has to be between real, discrete, definable, and distinguishable "persons." The courts determined long ago that persons do not necessarily have to be human beings and that not all human beings are persons (such as infants and the mentally incompetent). In the eyes of the (Hobbesian, Anglo-American) law, business corporations and estates are persons in the sense that they can be parties to disputes, have standing in court, and be held responsible for the conduct of their affairs. They can sue and be sued, can legally hurt and be hurt. This is to say, what finally defines a person in this Hobbesian view is that a person can be held to have an "interest," and it is to protect or advance their interests that brings persons into court.

Governments, it must be especially noted, are held in this Hobbesian universe to be persons and to have "interests." In the most general sense, a criminal act is one that hurts a government, its peace and public law, its particular interest, its, effectively, private interest. When even the sovereign's interest is effectively private, government, and its presumed concern with the public good, is belittled. That, once again, is the Hobbesian rub. The Hobbesian imagination sees all persons whatsoever as private.

Anglo-American, liberal democratic courtrooms see society as an aggregation of parties, every one of whom is pursuing its private interest. When in pursuit of their interests parties collide, a dispute may emerge that will threaten the general conditions of peace and security. If these disputes are serious, the courts may be able to resolve them. Disputes that do not arise in terms of these formulas, or that, arising differently, cannot be twisted into the required shape so as to appear as if they so arose, do not constitute ground for a "case."

With such a vision of civil reality, it is understandable that trials in liberal democratic courts should be handled as "adversary proceedings." In a Hobbesian court, a trial is seen as a moment in an ongoing relationship of essential hostility and competitiveness, a moment when the basic relationship has broken into the open to the point of threatening the civil peace. Court action is an effort to corral this outbreak into the framework of proceedings that can be observed and monitored by an impartial judge. The adversaries ("parties") are expected to go at it full tilt but with argument and maneuver rather than with tooth and fang. Counsel for the parties, not only out of respect for their clients but also as officers of the court, is expected to represent the interests of those clients to the limits of counsel's talents and of restrictions imposed by law. Should counsel show traces of compassion or altruism, the whole process effectively would begin to break down.

What is the role of the judge in all this? Obviously, he or she must maintain outward decorum or peace in the court. Everything must be kept within limits, the limits that separate civilization from barbarism, limits that are more quantitative than qualitative. When both sides have had their say within those limits, the judge, guiding and guided by the jury, if there is one, proposes a resolution. And what is thus proposed is effectively imposed (even if it is appealed to more august courts above).

Hobbesian presuppositions dictate one final restriction to the work of Anglo-American liberal democratic courts. The solutions proposed by the judges in these courts must be within the terms of their understanding of the law. The law here is not the law of nature, or God's law, or the law of pure reason and wisdom, and it certainly is not the law of common sense or even Athena's justice. The law to be imposed is the law of the state. In the phrase we used before, it is the law actual, positive, and known. It is the existing law, positively promulgated by the duly authorized authorities, published and known by the public, or at least by their attorneys. Judges, in this tradition, are not supposed to be wise, creative, or judicious. They are expected to be learned or, failing that, teachable by counsel.[3] Beyond that, they are expected only to be skilled at taking the known law and applying its general principles and particular requirements to specific cases. "Judicial activism," as it has been termed, is no part of this game as defined by Hobbes and the liberal democratic tradition.

Why not? Why should not judges be wise and just? The arguments, once their premises have been granted, are persuasive. The appeal to wisdom, justice, in a word, to heaven, is always an appeal to how particular individuals understand these things. Such an appeal is therefore inevitably, people being as they self-centeredly are, an appeal to their self-interested understandings, that is, to what individuals take to be heaven's mandate. The appeal to heaven, therefore, is in the end also an appeal to violence, the only way to resolve the different interpretations, so the Hobbesian argument runs, of what heaven says. Far better, in this imperfect world, to bar the appeal to heaven, and appeal instead to the existent law of the state, actual, positive and known.

Of course, even the actual law as positively promulgated may be subject to dispute. The words may be there in black and white, but their meaning and application may be ambiguous; sometimes even the exactly relevant words may be missing. To guard against the dangerous implications of these possibilities, judges in this liberal democratic tradition are rendered as disinterested as practice will permit. All ordinary men and women, Hobbesians assume, are interested, and their interests twist and turn and pull their words and actions in whatever directions interests go. Certainly this is assumed true of parties and counsel appearing before judges. But judges, it is hoped, can be different. They can be conditioned and trained to be interested only in the interest of the law.

Judges should be elected by special kinds of elections or appointed by special processes that regularly include disinterested evaluations by the legal fraternity. Such evaluations should address only issues of character, learning, and competence. Once elevated to the bench, the judges' terms of office should be long. And while in office, judges should be isolated from other streams of political life. Administratively, financially, and politically, the "independence" of the judiciary should be to a perceptible degree guaranteed.

Courts are to be housed in special buildings (that as often as not look like Greek temples). There, the judges sit high above everyone else and are treated with elaborate protocol. Even the fact that they wear robes is significant: in them, judges do not even look like ordinary mortals.

Most important, judges are trained. They are trained to know the actual laws that apply in the jurisdictions of their courts and to be skilled in the application of that law's principles, rules, and procedures. More than that, judges are trained in the traditions of law, so to acquire certain characteristic habits of thought, to have "legal minds." Competent, clear, rational, professional, disinterested, and lacking in sentimentality, these are the first characteristics of the legal mind. But this is also a mind that thinks habitually and virtually unquestioningly in terms of all those Hobbesian presuppositions about parties and disputes and the law being a hedge between civil disputation and the war of all against all. More specifically, the judicial version of the legal mind is trained to think conclusively, to strive to settle the disputes that come before them finally, "absolutely." That is the Hobbesian objective: to end the argument. No judge wants to be overturned on appeal. When appeals are made and finally go to the Supreme Court of the United States, the trained judicial mind instinctively will seek to halt in final terms the threat to the established order, to the framework of law that encages us all. It was in the context of this kind of trained, habituated thinking that one of the nation's most revered judges made the remark that the law is what the judges say it is.[4]

The judicial act, as we have been describing it—learned, skilled, disinterested, and always in defense of actual, positive, and known law—is only part of the story of judicial life. But in the American tradition, it is clearly the predominate part. Moreover, it is comprehensively developed and fully idealized. It has its own philosophic foundation and appears to be free of internal contradictions. Its vision is limited, and our account of it has been at pains to emphasize especially those restrictions arising from its concern to perceive disputes as hurts between parties. This is a legal tradition that will have difficulty recognizing the real issues in, for example, matrimonial cases; it will be clumsy beyond bearing in child-abuse cases; it will be cruel in its handling of rape cases and uncomprehending in cases involving racial, gender, and age bias. But the purpose of our account so far has been simply to reveal this Hobbesian, liberal democratic understanding of the judicial act as a distinguishable, definable, and predominate element in the American judicial tradition.

The Judicial Process

On television, courtroom scenes mean drama. Spectators pack the benches; all eyes are focused on the unfolding spectacle of the contest between counsel played out before the implacably stern judge and the determinedly impassive jurors. There are moments when a pin could be heard to drop; at other times, rhetoric will shake the walls.

There are cases in actual American courts that approach the drama of the TV picture. These are "important" cases, because of the persons involved, because of the nature of the material at issue, or because the decisions are thought to have broad social implications. For the vast majority of more ordinary cases, however, the actual courtroom scene is very different. Tedium is the principal hallmark. Most of the people involved in actual courtrooms and routine cases wait for hours for their cases to be called. Most of the actions taken when cases are finally called are brief, perfunctory, and swift. The Supreme Court in Washington, in an average year, may process close to two hundred cases, many of them comparatively minor. But an actual municipal court in a busy session may process half again that number of cases in a single day.[5]

One factor dictating this kind of rapidity is court overload. In a major city, court calendars are jammed with both civil and criminal cases. Another factor is that, while the personal dimensions of cases may be significant and painful, the legal issues are often so routine as to be humdrum. A third factor allowing for rapid processing is that courts have developed the shortcuts for handling even complicated cases quickly. For our purposes, the most challenging of these shortcuts is plea bargaining in criminal cases.

When a crime has been committed, an arrest made, evidence assembled, and a decision to prosecute determined, a calendar date for a trial will be sought. At this point, both the prosecution and the defense know fairly exactly what evidence has been assembled, and counsel for both sides, presumably experienced in these matters, can make educated guesses about how it will stand up in court. It is now, on the basis of these considerations, that a deal with the opposing counsel may be sought and struck. In exchange for a guilty plea from the defendant—who often plays no more than a passive role in these proceedings—the prosecution will reduce the charges or promise to request a reduced sentence. It has been estimated that up to 90 percent of criminal cases involving charges of prostitution, drug abuse and trafficking, assault, robbery, and so forth, are handled this way in American courts.[6]

The prevalence of plea bargaining makes it an integral part of the American criminal-justice system, but in a strict, liberal democratic perspective (not to mention the perspectives of social democracy), it can be nothing but offensive. If the defendant is poor, if counsel is a court-appointed attorney or a legal-aid society representative harried by too many assignments, if the police work on the case has been heavy handed, and if the district attorney's office in charge of the case is anxious to rack up a record of convictions—all of which conditions are only too frequently met—then factually innocent people can be persuaded simply to knuckle under and go to jail. On the other hand, if the defendant is well connected, if the defense lawyer is well paid, energetic, and smart, if the police and the district attorney are overworked and anxious to get on to other things, then factually guilty people can get off virtually scot free. In either event, what the process yields is not "justice," proven and clean, but a deal heavily influenced by who has what kind of leverage over whom.

But in a larger ideological perspective that takes into consideration the needs of the political system as a whole, the plea-bargaining system is clearly defensible. It goes a long way toward clearing dockets, and it does so with a semblance of respect—not for justice—but for the law. A law is broken, an arrest is made, a plea of guilty is entered, a sentence is handed down. The formula for Hobbesian sovereignty is preserved: awful, absolute, and arbitrary. De facto security, stability, peace is preserved. Next case. Rough justice? The state of nature is rougher still.

It is in this perspective of guarding and sustaining positive law and de facto peace that the American court system has earned a justified reputation for getting a job done. This is especially true at the federal level, but, even if unevenly, it is also true in many state and local courts. Nevertheless, even in this larger perspective, there are serious problems with the American court system on the ideological side of its work.

The laws the courts are to enforce come to them from a variety of sources and in great quantity: statutes from Congress and state and municipal legislative bodies, the great mass of regulations and rules issued by government departments and agencies, remnants of the old English common law, and the court system's own precedents and rulings. Finally, there is the Constitution itself, as well as the constitutions of the states, municipal charters, and so on. The sheer bulk of all this law, the bones and bars of the legal cage enclosing us all, combined with its often uncommon intricacy and detail ensures that even quite ordinary cases coming before courts can require the extended services of highly trained specialists, that is, expensive lawyers.

The cost of legal cases, in money, of course, but also in time, energy, and psychic welfare, become exorbitant. In cases where shortcuts are not taken, where one or another of the parties decides to make a fight for it, trials can drag on for years. Case preparation is a major source of delay, but so also, where juries are involved, can be jury selection. In fact, the modes of jury impanelment can themselves be subjected to sharp criticism both because of the kinds of people they tend to favor and because of the enormous waste of time for persons summoned for jury duty but never used.[7] The conduct of trials can also be criticized as tedious and clumsy. Adversary proceedings require time and expertise to extract evidence and present it in an orderly way and on occasion, for example in rape cases, can result in the humiliation of witnesses to the point that, despite recent efforts to curb this result, the victim is more on trial than the defendant. If the result of the trial is a string of appeals, whether based on claims of substantive miscarriage of justice or on technicalities, what has already taken months stretching into years can now extend into decades with proportional increases in costs. On all these counts, some variation on the French system of inquisitorial proceedings dominated by professionally recruited, trained, and appointed judges would, on the face of it, be preferable. However, the American adversary tradition is not only so hallowed by time but also so rooted directly in the nation's liberal democratic presuppositions that any change to those kinds of arrangements is out of the question.

These same Hobbesian, liberal democratic presuppositions are the source of what some believe is the most serious problem posed by the American court system, its inability to grasp and deal with the social context in which the disputes it is called on to resolve appear.[8] Once again, deliberately and directly, the courts by their traditions are compelled to understand and treat all parties appearing before them as essentially private persons. What is lost in this vision is any kind of informed understanding or compassionate interest courts might have about why and in what social circumstances the criminal events being investigated took place. Trial procedures are bound to reduce all such questions to judgments about individual motives and personal actions directed to private ends.

A well-known American sociologist, in a different context, defined what he termed "sociological imagination" as the capacity to perceive private troubles as public problems.[9] In these terms, a single black man's death at the hands of a gang of white youths should be set in the context of worsening race relations. Unless the social problem of race relations is addressed, charging the white youths with manslaughter would do little to prevent recurrence of racial violence. Yet, given the presuppositions of their procedures, American courts, whether knowingly or not, are compelled to shed any tendencies they might have toward sociological imagination. More important, by these same presuppositions they are compelled to enforce a general unconcern for whatever social problems might show up in their deliberations.[10] Guilt and loss must be held to be private, individual, even merely personal by the courts. Social guilt, social cause, social cost, collective concern, and collective responsibility are not comprehensible concepts in the Anglo-American legal tradition.

The Special Case of the Supreme Court

The characteristics of courts and judges in the American tradition come together with a special prominence in the work of the Supreme Court. The primary emphasis in this court is still on the ideological business of maintaining the legal cage, conserving the law. Mythic concerns are more prominent than in the lesser courts, but still secondary. To see all this, let us review three cases that virtually all observers would include in any short list of the court's most important.

The first is the 1803 case of *Marbury v. Madison*. The case was fraught with political overtones. Before the case was brought to the Court, the chief justice, John Marshall, then as secretary of state, had himself played a role in the preliminary moves that brought the dispute to a head. Moreover, both the reasoning and the effects of the decision can be regarded—and were at the time—as masterpieces not of judicial reasoning but of political tactical skill. In his decision, Marshall denied Marbury, a nominal political ally, the minor judicial commission Marbury had been seeking, but claimed he was compelled to do so because the law that might have permitted him to grant the commission was, he declared, unconstitutional.

Marshall thus gave a minor victory to his political opponents, Madison and his fellow Jeffersonians, but at the enormous price of claiming for the Court the power to declare acts of Congress unconstitutional. It was a classic case of losing a battle to win a war.

Marshall had to stretch to reach his conclusions. He could have simply said that the act in question was defective insofar as it applied to the powers of the Court; in so doing, he could have sidestepped the larger issue of constitutional review. But Marshall argued broadly, claiming that the Constitution is law and that therefore it is for courts to interpret and apply it. When modern judges make the claim that the law is what the judges say it is, Marshall is their approving ancestor.

It is this claim that makes all judges very special people in the American political system, and Supreme Court judges the most special of all. By it, judges are thus the ultimate arbiters of the rules that constitute society. Is this view defensible in a democracy? Certainly the Jeffersonians thought not. Even today, in admittedly somewhat arcane circles, the debate still rages.[11]

In a mythic, social democratic view, the people are sovereign, not the law. Their will should prevail. Before the people, courts and the law should give way. John Taylor of Caroline, Jefferson's earliest intellectual surrogate in these matters, argued both that judges should be immediately responsive and responsible to the people and that constitutional review was a responsibility of the citizen and to be exercised through the ballot.[12]

But in a liberal democratic perspective, Marshall's view is not only defensible; it is overwhelmingly persuasive. In a perspective that holds that the extant law, actual, positive, and known, is all that stands between civilization and barbarism, preserving that law, interpreting it and applying it with finality is a task that must be done by someone. Once that is admitted, the case for giving this task to judges, on the ground that no one else in the political system is as comparably trained and disinterested, can hardly be disputed.

The core concept in this argument is the notion that the Constitution is law, not policy; that it defines the rules of the game, not winners and losers; that it shapes the contours of politics, not the content. Judges, even when most clearly winging their way through broad silences in the Constitution's provisions, are thought to be interpreting the law, not making it.[13]

This notion that the Constitution is a cage containing actors and interests, a cage that disinterested judges must maintain, was much reinforced by the Court's second most famous case, *McCulloch v. Maryland* (1819), a case that again put Marshall in the forefront.

Congress, in pursuit of certain national objectives, had established a bank of the United States. The state of Maryland, not liking that bank, put a tax on it that threatened to put it out of business. James McCulloch, cashier for the Baltimore branch of the national bank, refused to pay. Maryland sued.

There were two principal issues: did the national government have the right to charter a bank even though nothing to that effect was directly listed in the powers of Congress in the Constitution? If it did, could a state frustrate that national government's will by putting an onerous tax on one of its instrumentalities? Marshall and his brethren decided both issues in the national government's favor.

Marshall argued first that the constitutional clause giving Congress the right to make all laws "necessary and proper for carrying into Execution" its listed powers clearly gave it the right to do things like chartering banks. More important, he argued in the oft-quoted sentence: "If the right of the states to tax the means employed by the general government be conceded, the declaration that the Constitution, and the laws made in pursuance thereof, shall be the supreme law of the land, is empty and unmeaning declamation."

The effect of the first of these arguments was to underline Washington's claim to be a national government with broad prerogatives to carry out its assigned responsibilities. The effect of Marshall's second argument was double. On the one hand, it resolutely established the federal government as a powerful and independent entity, not a by-your-leave creature of the several states. As interesting, especially from the point of view of the Court itself, Marshall's argument lent powerful substance to the concept that the Constitution was truly a national document, that the framework of law it created encompassed the whole of the American experience in one legally comprehensive unity. The judges of the Supreme Court were now effectively proclaimed cage keepers for the nation, coast to coast, border to border.

It is in this context that the third case we will review takes on its major interest for us. This case, *United States v. Nixon* (1974), tested the Court's power to bring even the nation's most powerful (mythically) actor to heel.[14]

As the investigations of the Watergate scandal moved toward their climax in the summer of 1974, it became clear to prosecutors that tapes the White House had routinely made of conversations between President Nixon and various of his personal assistants might supply crucial evidence of criminal intent and action. When their requests for these tapes were denied by President Nixon, they issued subpoenas. Nixon resisted, citing executive privilege, a claim that independence of the executive branch under the doctrine of the separation of powers would be compromised by violations of the confidentiality of its proceedings. The dispute went to the Supreme Court, where four of the sitting justices, including the chief justice, were Nixon appointees.

The chief prosecutor in the case, Leon Jaworski, argued forcefully:

> The President may be right in how he reads the Constitution, but he may also be wrong. And if he is wrong, who is there to tell him so? . . . this nation's constitutional form of government is in serious jeopardy if the President, any President, is to say that the Constitution means what he says it does, and that there is no one, not even the Supreme Court, to tell him otherwise.[15]

Swayed by these arguments, the Court issued a unanimous decision. It admitted that the president could claim executive privilege but held even so that this generalized claim did not extend to withholding specifically identified materials wanted in a criminal investigation. More significantly, the Court reasserted with sharp emphasis its claim to be the final interpreter of the Constitution. It went back to *Marbury v. Madison* to quote the words, "It is emphatically the province and duty of the judicial department to say what the law is." It quoted subsequent decisions that denoted "this Court as ultimate interpreter of the Constitution"[16] and added its own argument that "notwithstanding the deference each branch must accord the others, the 'judicial power of the United States' vested in the federal courts by Art. III sect. 1 of the Constitution," cannot be shared with or devolved on any other branch or body. When all is said and done by everybody else, the Court—speaking for the sovereignty of the law—has the last word.

In general terms, it is vitally important to keep the status thus claimed for the Supreme Court in perspective. It is only a court. Specifically, it is not a council of revision of a sort employed in other countries and even discussed at the Constitutional Convention in 1787. That is to say, the Court does not stand at the shoulder of Congress to check each law as it comes through the legislative process for constitutionality, nor does it inspect every executive act and decree as they emerge from the White House. Like all the courts in the Anglo-American tradition, it is essentially passive. It cannot issue hypothetical opinions. It must wait until disputes on particular issues are brought before it in justiciable form. Even then, tradition compels the Court to resolve those issues on the narrowest available grounds. In consequence, the keeper of the last word often does not get to speak as soon as it might like. Sometimes, it cannot speak at all on major issues of the day.

Moreover, when it speaks, the Court is confined by the presuppositions of the legal system it is bound to conserve to thinking in terms mostly of the rights and counterrights, claims and counterclaims of effectively private parties, even when some of those parties claim to be speaking for the public interest. This is not an intellectual universe that is open to broad strokes of social creativity. Again and again, the Court's opportunities for freewheeling legislative policy making in the clear absence of actual law are reduced to balancing the respective private interests of the competing parties.[17] This is not to undervalue the seemingly public role of the courts in preserving the rule of law. It is in fact to underline that role—even as it is stressed that the role is in most fundamental terms a narrow one restricted to defining and conserving a system of law that is itself socially narrowing and restrictive. This is the American political system's clearest example of a public function's being derivative from and instrumental to private ends.

The Mythic Role of the Courts

All of these observations are drawn from the perspective that sees the judicial system in essentially ideological terms, in its role as guardian of liberal democracy, and more particularly, in its role under mixed government theory of ensuring the encagement in the framework of positive law of all the ordinary political actors with their inevitably self-centered Bourgeois interests. In this role the judicial branch is the total political system's primary source of stability, and this, as we have said, is its predominate function by a wide margin. But the judicial system, like all other aspects of the political order in America, has a mythic side, and this side is routinely of some importance and, on occasion, especially in the work of the Supreme Court, can rise to a special prominence.

As always, we must emphasize that the switch to mythic perspectives is not achieved by fine-tuning the ideological side. A change in intellectual gears is required. In myth as opposed to ideology, the courts are performing qualitatively different roles for qualitatively different goals. The paradigm now is not *Marbury v. Madison,* but something more on the order of the decision of Solomon resolving the dispute between two women over the baby they both claimed (1 Kings 3:16–28). The king's suggestion that the baby be cut in half and divided between the disputants had nothing to do with the law. It was a shrewd trick that manipulated the truth out of the real mother. It earned the king the respect of the people not because they saw him as learned and skilled in the law, but because "they perceived that the wisdom of God was in him, to render justice."

All courts must appear to render justice wisely to receive a general social legitimization. They must do this, too, to preserve the reputation of the political system as a whole. It is a question of trust. Again and again, we see defendants go to trial proclaiming not only their own innocence but also their faith in the American system of justice. But to do justice requires something special from judges. It requires that they not only know the actual law, established by due authority of the state, but that they be prepared to stand in judgment on that actual law, and, if it be defective, amend it, fill in its gaps, or even rewrite it.

All judges find themselves from time to time called on to do something like this kind of work, and for most of them it goes against the grain. But the imperatives calling for it are powerful. The Constitution and much of the law growing out of it are grounded in eighteenth-century understandings of technology, economics, and cultural mores. The Constitution assumed the institution of slavery for blacks and gave not a thought to the subjugation of women. The notion that judges can be guided simply by the "original intent" of the framers in interpreting and applying the law in late twentieth-century circumstances and in the context of a great bulk of recent legislation flies in the face of both reason and reality.[18]

But judges, especially many Supreme Court justices, have many times tried to do just that, and with paradoxical results. From the Civil War until well into Franklin Roosevelt's New Deal era, a Supreme Court majority consistently attempted to keep the law in conformity to its earliest eighteenth-century foundations, especially in economic matters.[19] They defended the institution of private property against all comers, they foreclosed the possibility of an income tax, they stymied efforts to bar child labor, they narrowed the interpretation of the commerce clause virtually precluding national government regulation and management of the emerging national economy, and they pitted triumphantly the doctrine of "substantive due process" in the name of individual rights over the social claims and obligations of government police powers.[20] In consequence, transparently, they were not "interpreting the law," but reading into it their personal—and largely archaic—economic philosophy. In so doing, in case after case they transformed the Court into effectively a third house of the legislature, unelected, reactionarily conservative, and fully capable of vetoing the best-laid plans of the other branches of the government.

This was more than frustrating. It was paradoxical. In these cases, the Court was going toe to toe with the other branches at policy making, at defining and proclaiming what kind of nation America would be, at, in short, myth making. But the content that the Court wanted to give the myth was not the largely Protestant, socially conscious, and egalitarian content traditional for American myth, but an extreme version of those essentially Hobbesian, liberal democratic, capitalist values with which the Court is most comfortable.

This was an error on the Court's part, even if an understandable one, and the nation's social democratic ire was kindled against it. By the 1930s the Court was the object of considerable ridicule, and a crisis of legitimacy was averted only by the accident that through a spate of deaths and resignations there was a relatively rapid and complete turnover of justices.[21]

A much more serious example of the entanglement of the Court with mythic problems—one with truly tragic implications—was the case of *Brown v. Board of Education* (1954). The parents of a black girl in Topeka wanted her to go to a nearby school rather than to one comparatively far away. The difficulty was that the city's board of education, following the dictates of a local option law, had decided that the nearby school was reserved for white children and the faraway school for black children. On behalf of their daughter the parents sued, and the case wended its way to the Supreme Court. In a carefully crafted unanimous opinion, led by Chief Justice Earl Warren, the Court held that the old doctrine of "separate but equal" was wrong, that separate was inherently unequal and a denial to minorities of the Fourteenth Amendment's requirement of equal protection of the laws. Desegregation of public school systems would now be required everywhere.

It is important to put this case in its context. The National Association for the Advancement of Colored People (NAACP), which was the principal backer of the parents in the case (who financially could never have carried the case on appeal to Washington by themselves), had been preparing to argue a case like this for some time, some could say virtually from its founding half a century before. Moreover, the NAACP had already won, in the decade before *Brown* went to trial, a string of victories gaining admission for blacks in law schools, graduate schools, and undergraduate programs all across the South.[22] In addition, the Court itself cooperated by treating the *Brown* case and its associated actions as class actions with the broadest possible implications. The Court has sustained these interpretations in such subsequent opinions as *Cooper v. Aaron* (1958). Most important, in subsequent decisions, the Court held that desegregation was to proceed in school systems all across the country "with all deliberate speed" and propelled local courts and judges into the work of seeing that it did.[23] They even broadened the scope of the original decision so that it included the abolition of not only de jure segregation but de facto segregation as well.[24] Busing programs to achieve racially mixed and balanced school populations administered under the approval of judges are a measure of the heroic efforts the courts have made in this regard, efforts that continue today.

In this context, *Brown v. Board of Education* is a milestone victory in an upward march, its language noble and inspiring. But in a larger context, that same language seems quaint and self-defeating. This case and its companions were all preceded by the desegregation of the armed forces that began in the Korean War as a military necessity and then proceeded as a matter of principle. The Court cases were followed by the civil rights legislation of the 1960s, the desegregation of public facilities all across the country, and the notable increase in the black presence in commercial sports, universities, and professions, and to a lesser but still significant degree, among elected officials. Whatever *Brown v. Board of Education* did, it did not do it alone.[25] Even the urban riots of 1967 should be included in the overall picture.

But what did all this activity achieve? The specific achievements cannot be denied. Black faces now appear where they never did before. Certainly some attitudes have been challenged and changed. But the general conditions of the black community as a whole across the nation as measured by a wide variety of statistics are deeply disturbing. Welfare rates relative to the total number of blacks, as compared to the situation with other social groups; educational achievement rates; unemployment rates; black/white ratios in prison populations; family stability statistics; mental and chronic disease rates; crime rates, especially of certain kinds of crime associated with despair and anomie, all paint an increasingly bleak picture.[26] Major segments of the black community now appear to constitute a virtually permanent underclass excluded from the mainstream of American social life. Particularly disturbing are the conditions of young black males. Their unemployment statistics alone are deeply disturbing; these statistics are persistently so high as to be almost meaningless beyond indicating that very large numbers of them have never had jobs, do not now have jobs, and have no prospects of ever having jobs.[27] Such armies of the permanently unemployed, marked by race and gender, are a waste, a tragedy, a grave injustice; they are also socially dangerous. Furthermore, this is a danger that all indicators tell us grows worse day by day.

What, in this larger context, are we to say now about *Brown v. Board of Education?* In intent, this case was pure myth. This time, the Court got the myth right. It understood that blacks wanted equality of social membership. This was the meaning packed in their perception that "separate" is inherently unequal. This is John Winthrop's ideal that we can make ourselves a loving fellowship in which we can mourn together, laugh together, work together in one common life. But when the judges came to make their ideal operational, when they tried to find constitutional language in which to ground their hopes, they fell back on the Fourteenth Amendment. They tried to equate equality of social membership in a loving fellowship with "equal protection of the laws." That cannot be done. Winthrop and Hobbes, for all their having been born in the same land and year, were not talking in the same worlds.

The tragedy is not that in *Brown v. Board of Education* the Court was compelled to propose means radically disproportionate to its goals—although this is true. There was no way a mere court could change the social status of the black community in America. But the real tragedy is that the means the Court sought to use were completely disconnected from its goals. To reach its decision, the Court assumed a mythic stance. It overturned *Plessy v. Ferguson* (1896); it stood in judgment on the law, actual, positive, and known, and sought to bring that law into conformity not with some higher law but with the real historical aspirations of the American people. But in doing all this, it remained faithful nevertheless to its Hobbesian presuppositions. On those presuppositions, it is the function of the Court to stabilize the nation within the limits of liberal, not social, democracy, so much so that it may be said to have locked us in liberal democracy's frame. But it locked itself in there, too. It could lift its vision no higher than the claim to have guaranteed blacks equal protection of the laws. Can that kind of language change long-entrenched social patterns of racial distrust and division? Can granting rights alter the fundamental patterns of a way of life?

Blacks, as the saying goes, are "tired of being left out," and well they might be. The failure of the Court in considering this problem lay in its (Hobbesian) congenital inability to conceptualize even the meaning of membership in community. Their granting of rights to blacks amounted to letting them sit on the doorstep of a house whose doors remained firmly shut. It was a failure of ideas.

6
Presidential Greatness

The American presidency is, by the common consent, the focal point of the American political system. In this office the contradictions and tensions, the hopes and fears, the creative possibilities and crippling limitations of the whole system seem to come together. In consequence, the analysis of this office, of its powers and responsibilities, both explicit and implied, of its modern institutional articulations, of its full panoply of emotion-engendering symbols, and to some extent its actual record of success and failure, must have a high priority in any survey of practical American institutional theory.

Our analysis of the presidency in this chapter can be built around the issue of whether, for all its central position on the American political stage, the presidency is a strong office or a weak one. This is by no means the only significant issue generated by the presidency. For instance, the problem of its accountability is also a major concern. But for expository purposes, the question of what the office can do practically has major advantages, for it goes to the heart of the concerns—and hopes—of most citizens.

The answer to the question of the president's power, so our analysis will hold, turns on which level of political reality is considered: at the mythic level, the president must be understood as hugely powerful; at the ideological level, he is surprisingly weak. More specifically, the ongoing dynamic pattern is of national myth heaping up power after power upon the presidential office and its occupant, and then of ideological processes steadily draining all that away, leaving the occupant, in regular practice, isolated, frustrated, and lonely.

Contrasting Images of the Presidency

Woodrow Wilson, our most intellectual president, remarked in an often-quoted passage, "The office will be as big and influential as the man who occupies it."[1] There are important elements of truth in this observation. It emphasizes the personal character of the office, and it, implicitly, underlines the source of this feature in the fact that the presidential office has only a narrow base in constitutional law.[2] Wilson's remark therefore points us squarely toward a difficulty that has confronted all analysts of the American presidency: how to disentangle the permanent institutional, theoretical character of the office from the biographical facts of the men who have occupied it. We can begin not just with fact but with anecdote, a series of contrasting anecdotes.

In 1972, at Christmastime, President Richard Nixon ordered and with some fanfare announced his decision to undertake the systematic "carpet bombing" by American B-52's of Hanoi, the capital of North Vietnam. The unilateral quality of this decision outranked in the minds of outraged critics even its strange combination of audacity and desperation. Some cited the quotation from Secretary of State Seward that Edward S. Corwin, still the dean of constitutional scholars of the presidency, had put across the title page of his book *The President: Office and Powers:* "We elect a king for four years, and give him absolute power within certain limits, which after all he can interpret for himself."[3]

Arthur Schlesinger, Jr., went further. In an article published in the *New York Times*, he began by quoting from an old letter by Abraham Lincoln, "See if you can fix *any limit* to his power," and then went on to declare that Nixon, by greatly extending a long-term trend among activist presidents, had "by 1973 made the American President on issues of war and peace the most absolute monarch (with the possible exception of Mao Zedong of China) among the great powers of the world."[4]

Lest it be thought that this is an example of a single scholar losing his objectivity to the partisan heat of the moment, it may be noted that the same crisis prompted David Apter and Robert Dahl, two of the most respected names in American political science at the time, to comment in a jointly signed public letter that President Nixon's ordering out the bombers

> reveals more starkly than ever before the complete breakdown of the American constitutional system in the domain of foreign policies involving the employment of military forces.
>
> In this domain the arbitrary power of the President has over three decades swelled to a magnitude flatly inconsistent with both the intentions of the Founders and the requirements of a democratic order.[5]

In all this commentary it was not soon noticed that the bombing, in political terms, in its sheer violence spoke more of diplomatic weakness than strength, and that it was soon stopped because it proved, militarily, to be considerably less than "cost-effective."

Then there is the story of the president's mouse. It was 1977. President Carter saw a mouse running across the floor of his study one evening. The next morning the General Services Administration, charged with the care of government buildings, was summoned to find and eradicate the mouse. It did that. But then a second mouse was detected, by its smell, because it was dead in the wall of the Oval Office. Again the General Services Administration was summoned, but this time they claimed they had done their job; the dead mouse must have come from the White House lawns and was therefore the responsibility of the Interior Department. The Interior Department demurred. Regardless of where it might have come from, the dead mouse was undeniably now *inside* the White House. The president exploded, claiming that he could not "even get a damn mouse out of my office." Concluding this tale of bureaucratic inertia in the face of presidential fulminations is the fact that an interagency task force was then created to decide what to do. The bureaucratic officers involved had a point: what precedents with what budgetary implications would be set by deciding who would dig open a White House wall? Congress could be counted on to take an interest in how that decision went.[6]

As shopworn or more is the story of President Harry S Truman's comment about the advent of the Eisenhower presidency. Important to the telling of this story is the change that has come over Truman's reputation in the scholarly community. During his tenure, he was widely thought too small a man to fill even the shadow of his predecessor, Franklin Roosevelt. But in the wake of a succession of failed presidencies since his time, scholars have radically revised their opinions of Truman. It is not only the plain-spoken, clear decency of the man that now captures admiration; it is also the fact that in the perspective of time it is now obvious that Truman was one of our more competent presidents. He knew how to do the job. It is in the perspective of this new view of Truman that Richard Neustadt, who actually worked on Truman's White House staff for a number of years, can now be seen spinning his famous tale, in his book *Presidential Power*:

> In the early summer of 1952, before the heat of the campaign, President Truman [who was retiring from office] used to contemplate the problems of the General-become-President should Eisenhower win the forthcoming election. "He'll sit here," Truman would remark (tapping his desk for emphasis), "and he'll say, 'Do this! Do that!' *And nothing will happen.* Poor Ike—it won't be a bit like the Army. He'll find it very frustrating."[7]

Eisenhower did find being president frustrating. Neustadt, immediately after this story, quotes a commentator on Eisenhower's first term saying, "In the face of the continuing dissidence and disunity, the President sometimes simply exploded with exasperation."

Anecdotes prove little. Even as illustrations, much depends on their careful selection. But the point of those just told—that behind the appearance of vast power in the presidential office there is much frustrating weakness, and that this holds on matters large and small and across time—is also a point rooted in the literature on the presidency.

Neustadt published *Presidential Power* in 1960. In set appearance, it is a simple, how-to-do-it book, a how-to-win-friends-and-be-a-successful-president book written by the consummate insider. The book's publication caused a sensation: it was both widely praised and widely denounced. Some decried the book as blatantly Machiavellian. In fact, by connecting so directly the powers of the office to the interests of its occupant, it was purely Madisonian. Its central theme was established not only by the anecdote just told, but also by its opening sentences:

> When we inaugurate a President of the United States we give a man the powers of our highest public office. From the moment he is sworn the man confronts a personal problem: how to make those powers work for *him.* . . . My theme is personal power and its politics: what it is, how to get it, how to keep it, how to use it.[8]

Neustadt's whole thesis can be seen as compressed into these sentences. His argument presupposes that the American political community is permanently fragmented into a great pluralism of interests each led by its own elite. It presupposes further that the constitutional system has dispersed power so effectively that virtually every one of the interest elites has some kind of access to one or another lever of political manipulation. In such a world, no one, not even the grandest of presidents, can rule the whole roost. Authority structures are effectively flat. The one constant will be a political process of many actors, variously sized and positioned but all sufficiently independently situated to meet with others and negotiate, compromise, and cooperate—or hold out for better terms. To survive, presidents must learn this lesson in American political geography. Each one will have to learn as he takes up office that he is but one actor in a world of many actors, and that all those other actors are as stubbornly self-centered as himself.

By coincidence, only a few years before Neustadt's book came out, another classic on the American presidency had appeared, Clinton Rossiter's *The American Presidency*.[9] This book was not so well received as was Neustadt's. It was thought too flamboyant and insufficiently grounded in the facts of the presidential office. But it was a popular success and far more influential on general opinion. Rossiter established the tradition of thinking of the presidential office as a connected series of roles in each of which the president was a "chief": chief of state, commander in chief, chief executive, chief legislator, and so on, through a list of ten or more roles. Rossiter's book is thus diametrically opposed in substance to Neustadt's. For Rossiter, the president is the supreme commander of just about everything. For Neustadt, ever the minimalist, the president's primary power is no more than the "power to persuade."

Much has been written on the presidency since Neustadt and Rossiter published their works.[10] But Rossiter's book, better than any other, got the myth right; Neustadt caught with exactness the ideology of the office. Moreover, Rossiter's flamboyant language demonstrates that the American president's first responsibility and primary power is to proclaim American political myths generally and also specifically the myth of his own greatness. In proclaiming these myths, the president masks, often with great success, his actual operative weakness in the ideological go-around of Washington politics, the weakness revealed, again with considerable precision, by Neustadt's analysis.

Before examining this thesis in detail, it may be well to put it into historical context. Lincoln, arguably, was America's greatest president. His words, his actions, his character were all cut to a heroic scale. But what, overall, can be said of his achievement? He preserved the Union, no mean success, to be sure, but at terrible cost and with a result that at most can be said to be a restoration of the status quo ante bellum. It is this minimal record, even more than the manner of his death, that makes him so essentially a haunted, tragic figure. Franklin Roosevelt, again beyond much argument, was our most proficient president. Why? Because he possessed to such a high degree an extraordinary combination and range of competencies. No president more successfully stilled the people's fears ("We have nothing to fear but fear itself"), or raised its hopes ("America has a rendezvous with destiny"), or made it laugh ("but when they pick on my dog . . . "). Equally, on the other side, no president more successfully and with such sustained competence played the game of Washington politics—or enjoyed it as much. Stories of his tricks and ploys are Washington legends. It is no wonder, then, that Roosevelt's leading biographer subtitled his volume "The Lion and the Fox."[11] But what do summations of this sort of the careers of our greatest presidents mean? What do they say implicitly about the capacities and limits of the American political system in general and of the presidential office in particular? How much can a figure compelled to be both lion and fox accomplish in the actual course of history?

The Myth of Greatness

The powers that America's social democratic mythic tradition, with all its Protestant/biblical richness, heaps on the presidency inspired Rossiter and fired his imagination. "The Presidency . . . unites power, drama, and prestige as does no other office in the world," is one of his more moderate statements.[12] Here are three others that go somewhat farther:

> The President, in short, is the one-man distillation of the American people.[13]

> The final greatness of the Presidency lies in the truth that it is not just an office of incredible power but a breeding ground of indestructible myth.[14]

> It is a priceless symbol of our continuity and destiny as a people. Few nations have solved so simply and yet so grandly the problem of finding and maintaining an office of state that embodies their majesty and reflects their character.[15]

Language such as this, it may be argued, is more descriptive of what people think, and, specifically, what Rossiter personally thought, the presidency ought to be than of what it objectively is. There are certainly no objective grounds for determining one way or the other whether this or that president was or might have been a "one-man distillation of the American people." But we dismiss this language only at our peril. The general popularity of Rossiter's book and his categories indicates that he spoke for many Americans, indeed, was almost a champion of their views. His enthusiasm is infectious. With a childlike faith, he is telling us what we already know, that this is the way we would like things to be, this is the kind of president we would like to have. In this light, Rossiter's words take on a kind of scholarly precision: he is representing with some exactness our national myth of the presidential office, of the heroic leader who will distill our disparities into one life, one hope, one identity, one nation. That surely *is* the American president—in the perspective of a future gazing myth. He is our hope.

However narrow the actual constitutional base of the presidency, it is wide enough to support this crystal-ball vision of the office. The long first section of Article II has only two operative phrases: "The executive Power shall be vested in a President of the United States of America," and, in the prescribed oath, "I will faithfully execute the Office of the President of the United States." None of these terms is self-defining, nor are there universally agreed definitions of them. But certainly the words "executive," "power," and "office" all bespeak authority, dispatch, control, and, above all, a sense of direction.

Sections 2 and 3 of Article II are somewhat more specific. So far as the duties of the president are concerned, their provisions can be summarized:

1. He is to be "Commander in Chief" of the nation's armed forces;

2. By and with advice and consent of the Senate, he can make treaties with foreign governments and appoint and receive ambassadors;

3. By and with advice and consent of the Senate, he appoints the heads of various executive departments, and he can require their reports in writing; he is to take care the laws be faithfully executed;

4. He can convene the houses of Congress, give them information, and recommend measures to them (this power is greatly enlarged by the veto given the president in Section 7 of Article I).

These are the bare bones of the president's constitutional grants of executive, military, diplomatic, administrative, and legislative powers. Rossiter pumps them up. Without specifying whether he means the word "chief" in the sense of most important or, alternatively, the person in charge, he proclaims that these constitutional grants alone make the president lawfully "Chief Executive," "Chief Legislator," "Chief Diplomat," "Chief of State," as well as "Commander in Chief," both successively and cumulatively, in the sense that he brings to the exercise of any one of them the prestige of having all the others as well. The president, Rossiter says, wears all his hats at once.

Rossiter can justify this kind of inflation by arguing that the American people have swelled the constitutional mandate with what might be called the mandate of tradition and election. This has been a two-way process. Especially the great presidents—beginning with Washington, but extending through Adams, Jefferson, Jackson, Polk

(a Rossiter favorite), Lincoln (of course), Cleveland (maybe), Theodore Roosevelt, Wilson, and Franklin Roosevelt—have each left the
imprint of their personal style, ambitions, and achievements on the
office. And again this is a cumulative process. Lincoln's understanding of the responsibilities of the president as commander in chief of
the armed forces no doubt grew out of the experience of Washington and Jackson but was nevertheless a permanent expansion of the
role, an expansion that made way for the experience of Wilson and
Roosevelt in World War I and World War II. Equally, what Wilson
did for the president's role as "Chief Legislator" presaged Roosevelt's leadership of Congress during the early New Deal days—and
also left a record that assigns responsibility in this area that no subsequent president has even attempted to evade.

At the same time, the American people responded to these great
presidents, both as personalities and as actors on the political stage.
They reelected them—Roosevelt three times over—and, as important, recorded and remembered their achievements in books,
speeches, schoolhouse lessons, and monuments. The record is thus
rendered continuous, self-perpetuating, and constantly enriching.

The consequence of this double process of actual presidential
leadership paired to great popular acceptance and response is a permanent and substantial expansion of the president's powers and responsibilities. As a result, above and beyond the roles prescribed for
the presidency in the Constitution, and mostly in language unknown
to it, he has become "Chief of [his] Party," "Voice of the People,"
"Protector of the Peace" (in times of crisis), "Manager of Prosperity,"
and "President of the West." These are, once again, Rossiter's in-
flated terms, but, as mentioned before, they clearly speak to widely
felt hopes and expectations in the American people for the modern
presidential office. How much they do can be seen best not by looking up Rossiter's expansive and imprecise definitions of these titles
but by examining two other processes independent of his text.

The first of these is the wide assortment of powerfully evocative
symbols that have clustered around the presidential office and its
occupant. The most obvious and in some ways still the most impressive of these is the White House building itself, a veritable shrine
mantling the current occupant with the whole of the tradition he
inherits. Then there are the "libraries" that modern presidents have
taken to creating in their names after they leave office. These affairs
are combinations of museums, monuments, and archives, and the
prototype of them all, Roosevelt's library at Hyde Park, New York,
has now been dwarfed by such large structures as the Lyndon John-

son Library in Austin, Texas. All these buildings transmit a message
to their visitors that the men whose memory they preserve and celebrate were not only heroes in their own times, but are still factors in
the national consciousness.

As vivid as this architectural symbolism are the immediate trap-
pings draped around the current occupant of the office, the endless
photographs of him seated in the Oval Office, or striding to open a
press conference, or climbing aboard a helicopter to fly off from the
Rose Garden to a weekend at Camp David, or greeting the members
of a winning football team. There are the Marine Guards who mark
his entrances and exits, the bands striking up "Columbia, Gem of the
Ocean," or "Hail! to the Chief." There is Air Force One to wing him
as in a chariot across the sky to distant lands. And so numerous and
significant as to make up a class by themselves are all the symbols
invoked in presidential election campaigns, the razzle-dazzle and
hucksterism of the national nominating conventions, the ballyhoo,
balloons, parades, and speeches on the campaign trail, the election
night excitement, and TV broadcasts of victory celebrations. Above
all, there is the solemnity of the inauguration ceremony and its all-
important address. On occasion, there is the presidential funeral, a
national day of mourning in which the whole nation weeps, as in the
wake and interment of John F. Kennedy following his assassination.

Much more specific in spelling out the meaning of the American
presidential tradition than these symbols is the second process, one
widely called the institutionalization of the presidency. This is a process by which the president's staff has grown from the proverbial
single secretary George Washington employed, paid out of pocket,
through the formal creation of the Executive Office of the President
in 1939 (on the recommendation of a famed Committee on Administrative Management formed by President Franklin Roosevelt and
chaired by his predecessor Herbert Hoover), to the point where that
office contained close to five thousand persons.[16] All these persons
on the president's staff are dedicated, so the theory (myth) runs, to
helping the president carry out his multitude of responsibilities, to
being, as the popular metaphor goes, his eyes, ears, and hands. They
are there, hard working and loyal, to ensure that the president truly
is president. In consequence, the list of their offices and assignments
becomes an important guide to what specifically the president in
modern times is expected to accomplish.

The list is long, complicated, and changes from year to year. It is
enough for our purposes to pick out the major items. The first of
these is the White House Office, the president's inner circle of im-

mediate advisors and assistants. Although the organization of this group varies with the vagaries of presidential style and with the talents and proclivities of available personnel, it almost invariably includes a press secretary, legal counsel, an appointments secretary, a speech-writing staff, and a team of senior advisors with variable assignments ranging from congressional liaison to summit conference preparation. The whole is headed, at least in time, by a chief of staff, and supported by assorted assistants, secretaries, and the like. The number of people involved is between three hundred and four hundred.[17] It is also worth noting that a high proportion of the people in this group are young or known to be personally attached to the president through long service elsewhere. Few have an independent stature, especially in politics, and their standard of competence varies widely. It is finally worth noting that in the basement of the west wing of the White House, just steps away from the Oval Office and the president's living quarters, there is what is known as the Situation Room, a kind of combat-conference-command-and-information center continuously manned to ensure instant communications with American forces and representatives throughout the world, including, as required, outer space.

The image projected by the White House Office, its staff and equipment, is of an immensely burdened chief executive but with unrivaled information and analysis resources. Above all, it is an image of a decision maker and direction indicator who, by simply spinning his chair, can turn to address directly this or that audience or summon into the aura of his office this or that collection of interested parties. This is an impression much reinforced by the habit presidents have of tucking into the White House Office on a temporary basis particular commissions or agencies tackling special problems in which they have developed a personal interest. They want it known that they have taken direct charge of the "war" on whatever, be it drug-law enforcement, a breakdown in government somewhere, a crisis overseas, a natural disaster at home.

The other units in the Executive Office of the President give even more specificity to this overall impression. Of these, the most important are the Office of Management and Budget, the National Security Council, the Council of Economic Advisors, and, to a lesser degree, the Office of (domestic) Policy Development. Other units have titles like Office of Science and Technology Policy, Council on Environmental Quality, and Office of U.S. Trade Representative.

The Office of Management and Budget has a long history. It was first established after World War I when that experience suggested strongly that the federal government should have a single, comprehensive budget.[18] Modeled after British practice, what was called the Bureau of the Budget was first installed in the Treasury and then moved, to give it more prestige, into the then recently created Executive Office of the President in 1939. Its name and mandate were changed to its present title under President Nixon, who took a considerable interest in its work. It is now charged not only with the yearlong effort to develop an annual Executive Budget covering the whole of the executive branch, but also with ensuring that all agencies conform to presidential policies as each fiscal year progresses. It is particularly charged with monitoring departmental and agency proposals to Congress and the administrative rules and regulations they may issue to the public.[19] No agency, in image, in the Executive Office of the President more confirms the Rossiterian notion that the president is in personal charge of the whole of the executive branch, that he is its "Chief Administrator."

The National Security Council was established in 1947 at the same time that the three armed forces were chartered as separate agencies under civilian leadership in the Department of Defense. The formal council, composed of the president, vice-president, secretaries of state and defense, chairman of the Joint Chiefs of Staff, and other officials, is supposed to meet, develop, and advise the president on a coordinated and cooperative national security policy combining diplomatic, military, and other resources. In short, it is supposed to ensure that Pearl Harbor does not happen ever again. Over time, interest has focused not on the council, but on its director, the president's national security advisor, and on the increasingly active and sizable staff he heads. In this connection, it is also to be noted that the Central Intelligence Agency and the National Security Agency report to the president through the national security advisor, and that this was designed to ensure that the president would have access to high-quality foreign intelligence uncontaminated by the departmental biases of the State Department and the Pentagon. The net effect of all this apparatus is to underline powerfully the notion that the president of the United States is personally charged with not only securing the defense of the nation, but also with the leadership of the free world.

The Council of Economic Advisors and the Office of Policy Development carry forward and develop this kind of responsibility into the areas of economic management and domestic policy concerns. The overall effect of all these agencies is to articulate with considerable, specific definition the range of expectations that the American people have for presidential leadership, expectations that, while not firmly lodged in law, are clearly so in tradition and practical institutions. Rossiter, for all his flamboyance, was talking about something real in the American political system, as real as anything else in it, the range of actual institutionalized hope the American people have for their president as symbolized by the mere existence of his Executive Office in all its complexities.

Beyond the Executive Office of the President are ranged the major departments of the federal government, not only State and Defense, but also Agriculture, Commerce, Labor, Transportation, Health and Human Services, Education, Justice, Energy, Interior, Treasury, and Housing and Urban Development, and Veterans Affairs. All, in national myth, are expected to hew to the line of presidential leadership. And they, too, although less directly than the units of the Executive Office, are by their names and responsibilities definers of presidential power. So also are, if in a still more distant way, the independent agencies, such as the Tennessee Valley Authority and the U.S. Postal Service, and the multifarious independent regulatory commissions.

Nor is this the end of the matter. In myth, perhaps the president's finest hour is the State of the Union Address. He is brought to this occasion by constitutional mandate as elaborated by the example of President Wilson and the practice of every president since. As he speaks, it is clear that the TV and radio networks that carry his word and image across the globe think him a cross between Tribune of the American people, Chief Legislator of Washington politics, and Leader of the Free World. Arrayed before him in their party ranks are not only the members of the American Congress, the members of the Supreme Court, leading figures in the president's own executive administration and of his personal entourage, but also the ambassadors and other representatives of every significant power in the world. His speech is regularly punctuated by outbursts of applause, even cheers, so much so that media representatives keep count of how often these interruptions occur. The general impression is of massed cooperation, of forces of every sort coming centripetally together in the president's very person from every corner of the government, the nation, and even the world. It is an impression of such resurgent might that there can be no wonder that Rossiter closed his book with the confident assurance, "There is a Presidency in our future. . . ."[20]

The Ideology of Weakness

It is fashionable, in discussions of the American presidency, after presenting the kind of picture just drawn, to then go on and admit

that all that massed power is subject to various and serious constraints and can be exercised only within, as it is said, "limits."[21] It
will be argued here that this is a serious misstatement of the president's situation. In terms of our analysis, myth, at the ideological
level, fundamentally misconstrues presidential power. The case is
not that Rossiter is generally right but has to be "modified" by Neustadt's insights. The case is that, at the level of political analysis with
which he was concerned, Rossiter's propositions, without undue exaggeration, are highly accurate, but they provide few clues for the
president's activities and capacities at the level at which Neustadt
worked. We cannot simply slide down a scale to get from Rossiter to
Neustadt; we have to change political worlds, to change the name of
the game, to go from social democratic myth to liberal democratic
ideology.

In the liberal democratic framework, in which American government tries to get on with doing the actual work of governance, the
president is a surprisingly weak player. This is not to say that he is
helpless. If he is smart, patient, and knowing, there are things he
can do and games he can win. But relative to the expectations generated by myth about his massive, across-the-board responsibilities, he
is across-the-board weak to a degree that has often surprised most
particularly occupants of the office. In consequence, of the many
functions of presidential myth, one of the most insidious is the way it
masks presidential operative weakness from his cohorts, from the
American people, from, sometimes, the world and foreign leaders,
and, finally, from the president himself.

The truly fundamental point to be made about the president's
situation when he turns from mythic proclamations to the day-to-day
toil of carrying out programs and managing the bureaucracy is that
he leaves a world of cooperation and centripetal forces for a world
of competition and centrifugal forces. In an often-used phrase,
there is an ongoing "guerrilla war" between the president and Congress, between the departments, within the departments, even within
the president's own Executive Office. This is not simply the unfortunate consequence of personality defects in government operatives
high and low. It is rooted in the logic of Madisonian/Aristotelian
mixed government theory that would pit throughout the government ambition against ambition. More deeply, it is the Lockean/
Hobbesian war of all against all, caged within the sovereign limits of
the law. It is in this world that Neustadt tells the president to make
the powers of his office work for *him*. It is in this world that the
president is like Ishmael, "his hand against every man and every
man's hand against him" (Gen. 16:12).

It is important to keep our balance on these matters. The president's primary roles are all mythic, and certainly all recent presidents and their assorted staffs have been both preoccupied by and virtually shameless in their attempts to sustain and project through every conceivable travail the right mythic images. They know well the rules of that game. What we are now detecting is that behind and beneath all this mythic activity is an undercurrent that flows, decisively, in an opposite direction, that discolors the mythic gestures and hopes in contrasting hues, and that steadily drains away their power and possibilities.

This is most obviously true in the president's dealing with Congress. To use a familiar metaphor, the president will march to the bridge of the ship of state and chart a course for the nation, saying, "Take it over there!" Pursuant to these commands, he will recommend to Congress legislative measures, including, most importantly, a budget, the Executive Budget that his Office of Management and Budget has labored for over a year to craft and bring forth on time in January with much fanfare. But Congress is a labyrinth of committees, subcommittees, and individual members and their staffs. It moves slowly. More important, in contrast to the president, it is primarily an arena of ideological politics in which questions of national policy get individualized into questions of who gets what. Congress is dotted with members of long service who have built up over the decades their own personal patterns of allegiances and alliances. At best, they will one by one have to be bought into the president's program. The usual pattern is for the president's proposal to be simply received and absorbed. Months later, president and Congress will dicker over a budget plan of quite different composition. It will be months after that before actual appropriation measures begin to emerge one by one from the congressional mill. By this time, the details of the president's original proposals will have been simply forgotten by the press and public; and, while he may still be championing his essential philosophical commitments, there may be little in the actual legislation being drawn together by Congress that he can claim as his and can fight to save by threats of veto and the like.[22]

It is essential to any understanding of this process by which Congress disintegrates presidential, broad-scale initiatives that it is not caused by accident, by character defects in the members of Congress, or by some secret cabal of nefarious "interests." The mixed government theory built into the Constitution constitutes the two houses as independent bodies and fills them with individually situated political actors every one of whom has long since learned, on pain of political suicide, Neustadt's lesson: to make the powers of their offices work for them, collectively, in loose coalitions or, as the case may often be, individually.[23] As much as the president and his staff know the rules of the mythic game, these members of Congress know the rules of the ideological game and play it for keeps.

Much the same dynamic can be observed in the president's relations to the departmental secretaries. The heads of the major departments are all nominated by the president. Although they are subject to confirmation by the Senate, that body generally gives him a free hand to pick whom he wants. As with his own staff, the president mostly avoids picking people with substantial political standing who might be able to challenge his primacy.[24] New administrations, especially, resound with talk about how this administration will be marked by collegiality and openness. The president proudly poses with his "cabinet" and announces that it will meet regularly. These are standard mythic hopes for a government that can govern in terms of a cohesive, comprehensive, and cooperative national policy effort.

But departmental secretaries quickly learn Washington's mixed government ways. Cabinet meetings are soon dispensed with. Few of the secretaries have time to become immersed in problems outside their own concerns and resent however well-intentioned incursions by others into their own jurisdictions. More important, each department secretary is from the outset powerfully pulled away even from the White House by the need to cultivate the support and loyalty of his or her subordinates and of the permanent staff of the department's bureaucratic structures. Moreover, they will do this best if they assiduously court the clientele groups their departments individually service, even if this brings them into conflict with presidentially preferred policies and pronouncements. Finally, there is Congress. Secretaries know where, in the end, their departmental bread gets buttered, and they will often seek congressional support through back channels even while appearing to bow to the dictates of the president and his Office of Management and Budget.

Not surprisingly, the president for his part also can draw away from his secretaries, if only by simply leaving them alone to get on with whatever they can. He, too, will find cabinet meetings dispensable, and some presidents have found it useful to dispense as well with meetings of the full, secretary-laden membership of the National Security Council. Instead, such presidents have found it preferable to deal with their own staff through their national security advisors and with relevant secretaries individually. Those secretaries are most importantly the secretaries of state and defense, and even these enormously important individuals can find themselves being left out of White House consultations about their jurisdictions and responsibilities. They even can be found on occasion to be somewhat content with this state of affairs.

The net effect of all these goings-on is to leave the president, ideologically, increasingly isolated. Even as myth heaps power on him and calls up patterns of interaction and cooperation all across Washington, the ideological undercurrents of the city promote suspicions, competitions, recriminations, and divisions of effort.[25] On occasion, some of these rivalries can be offset by temporary, ad hoc agreements between sometimes oddly juxtaposed parties brought together by a shared need or a crosscutting interest. Such coalitions can be relatively broad and long term or merely be a momentary agreement between two prominent, sharply antagonistic individuals not to create "unnecessary" difficulties for each other. But, no more than the effusions of myth, can such self-interested agreements conceal the underlying facts that, at the ideological level, Washington relationships are essentially adversarial.

The disintegration and disconnection of mythically supposed patterns of cooperation and discipline can extend into the president's own Executive Office. Even with the White House Office itself, paranoia-inducing pressures can reach hothouse levels, and the temptations to manipulate facts and persons, to search for allies wherever they might be found, and to propound one-sided theories and recommendations for personal advantage in the name of higher causes (or vice versa), all are as overwhelming here as anywhere else in Washington. A half dozen years before the Iran–Contra affair investigations of the Reagan era documented how far this kind of backbiting, infighting, concealment, and quasi conspiracies can go, two veterans of the relatively benign Carter administration's highest levels recorded this comment of their experiences. The Executive Office of the President, they said, had grown into a "bloated and disorderly grab bag of separate and mutually suspicious staffs, units, councils, boards, and groups with strikingly different histories, purposes and problems."[26]

There are identifiable casualties in this process by which myth heaps up impossible expectations on the presidency only to have ideological undercurrents disconnect them and seep them all away. The first thing to go is all hope for coherent, cohesive national government. In the first flush of a new administration, the urge everywhere is to confront national problems with comprehensive, integrated, and articulated responses. Backed by his mandate from the people, the freshly elected and triumphant president promises to implement his philosophy, broadly conceived and fully developed.

He promises a "revolution." For a while, backed by much media hyperbole, it will seem that the president has launched something that merits those terms. He will send Congress a full calendar of proposals. As important, he will use all his powers to root out several thousands of holdover political appointees in the higher reaches of the bureaucracy and to replace them with people of his own stripe. Only gradually will it become apparent that, for each bureaucratic and legislative success, prices have been paid, concessions have been made, compromises have been exacted.

As these are coming to light, the president will be seen to have lowered his sights. He will begin to be selective in his objectives. While stonewalling against the unwanted initiatives of others, he will confine his own to a single Supreme Court appointment, one major piece of domestic legislation, or a single foreign-policy question.[27] When a counterproposal begins to develop widespread support, he may suddenly switch fields and adopt it and push it as if it were his own. State of the Union and other addresses will often accurately reflect this process. The broad strokes invoking traditional values and national objectives will still be there in all their fullness, but the concrete list of practical policy suggestions will look more and more like a patchwork of what is politically feasible and less and less like the coherent steps of a policy revolution.

The progress of the administration will become episodic. The unceasing calls to mythic greatness will prompt it to skip reactively from crisis to crisis as they arise or can be contrived. A great president acting "presidential" must move or at least appear to be on the move. Increasingly, the president and his cohorts will focus on events whose course they think they can control to their advantage. To do this, they sometimes go to bizarre lengths. During the Carter administration, the Iranian hostage crisis dragged on from weeks and weeks into months and months. Both the public and the president himself became impatient for a solution, and the image of presidential greatness suffered measurably. Finally, the president and his advisors in the White House settled on a plan to rescue the hostages by having helicopters snatch them out. The plan, in concept, was indeed bizarre, and the secretary of state resigned in protest over its implementation. Its diplomatic and military consequences, if it had succeeded, were wildly unpredictable. As it turned out, the plan had to be aborted because of accidents early in the attempt to bring it off. The hostages were not rescued; neither was the Carter presidency.

Under increasing pressures, these processes can go considerably further and have, as the revelations of the Watergate and Iran–Contra affairs showed. In the exposés of both of these contretemps, two powerful tendencies were shown to have been at work. One was a sense of exceptionalism. The president or his immediate associates were revealed to have fallen victim to feelings that they were called to undertake such high missions that ordinary moral limitations and the usual strictures of the law did not apply. As one of them said, sometimes you have to go beyond the law.[28] With this "work-of-God" mentality, as it might be called, the people involved in these affairs were prepared to, and in fact did, lie to the public, to the press, to Congress, to investigators, and, most importantly, and perhaps most frequently, to each other. They were also guilty of assorted crimes and conspiracies to commit crimes, the most important of which was probably sustained efforts to obstruct justice, but also included a wide assortment of efforts ranging from burglary, violation of the neutrality acts, arms export control acts, various restrictions placed on foreign-policy activities by special congressional legislation, as well as various standard rules of international law respecting the rights of sovereign powers, and, finally and simply, fraud.

That is a remarkable list. It bespeaks a comprehensive lawlessness in the White House, the shrine of American constitutionalism and democracy. The president's defense, especially President Reagan's, was that he was not himself involved in these activities and, more particularly, remained entirely ignorant of certain key elements in them. It was thought that this was a credible hypothesis, in the light of Reagan's well-known "hands-off" managerial style. As credible, if not more so, is the alternative hypothesis, that the president was in fact fully informed at every juncture in these affairs, but that he and his subordinates systematically destroyed all evidence of this and also systematically lied about it all in response to their higher, exceptional, mythic calling to protect the presidency.

The second tendency, at work alongside the sense of moral exceptionalism, was a profound belief that to pursue his higher calling the president and his White House staff would have to go it alone or, in the phrase of the day, go solo. Obsessed with mythic callings, feelings of isolation, the obduracy of the regular bureaucracy, and the obstinacy of Congress, the presidents in these affairs turned to a few intimates and self-reliantly undertook to do things their own way. To call the results bizarre is to understate the case. In both affairs, Watergate as much as Iran–Contra, well-established public policies and valued political traditions, including some actively enunciated and defended by the president himself, were turned topsy-turvy. As important, for the point of view of public administration experts, were the violations of essential principles of executive management. Established bureaucratic capacities and expertise were by-passed and ignored. Instead, staff officers, with minimum skills and certainly no expertise, undertook line operations of the greatest deli-cacy and danger. From this point of view, the most lasting impres-sion of the Watergate affair and even more so of the Iran–Contra affair is of unprincipled, lawless managerial incompetence, to a scale for which it is difficult to find parallels, public or private.

In thinking about these affairs and how they occurred in Amer-ica, it is important not to write them off as accidents of history, per-sonality defects, or flawed judgments—even though they involved such things. At bottom, both Watergate and the Iran–Contra affair are mostly examples of standard American political patterns gone to extremes. Both are extremes of well-established institutional norms. In both cases, the norm is of operatives reacting to imperatives to make their offices work for their own interests, albeit in contexts of ever-exaggerating myth. How far this process might go can be seen in the emphasis on military adventurism that would have to be in-cluded in any full accounting of President Reagan's invasion of Gre-nada or of President Bush's excursions into Panama and the Persian Gulf.

What Do the American People Want?

We can put the analysis of this chapter into a slightly different perspective by asking, as Freud did so plaintively of women, what do the American people want of their president?

Polls by the score show that the first quality voters expect in a presidential candidate is honesty, integrity, personal character.[29] They want a man they can trust. It was claimed by one pollster in 1984 that the only way President Reagan could lose his bid for re-election was if it was shown he dyed his hair.[30]

The analysis of this chapter argues that, before presidents pick policy options and start governing, they are expected to promulgate believably the national myth. This has been a feature of the presi-dency from George Washington on down, and it has gathered strength with every crisis the national consciousness has had to ab-sorb and endure. It is characteristic of myth that it not only is widely believed, but that it must be believed. Myth is necessary belief. With-out it, national legitimacy and hence also national community col-lapses. In a society such as the United States where the national ide-ology constantly is disintegrating our sense of community into a ubiquitous, rapacious individualism, believing the national myth be-comes a daily crisis, a routine anxiety, a national hunger.

The myth America wants its president to promulgate is, as these things go, relatively specific. The first element is that we are a people full of love and fellowship for each other, that we have a history in which our failures are amply recorded but recorded meaningfully, because we are dedicated to achieving definable ideals of social justice, liberty, equality, and fraternity. A second element in the national myth is that through our system of popular democracy, this president, backed by his triumphant party, has come to power to set us on a new road to national achievement. And the final element in the national myth the president asks us to believe is to believe in him, that he is a great president, that he is master of his administration, Office of Management and Budget and all, and will lead us forward. All this is trust, trust in ourselves, trust in democracy, trust in him. Obviously, we further hope that the particular policies he chooses to support and recommend to Congress will be congruent with that trust, but that is a secondary matter. Polls regularly reveal that presidents are personally more popular by far than their particular policies.[31]

In sum, we ask our presidents to give us believably a historic identity. But there is a problem here. Sometimes, in fact often, presidents fail. Then what do we do? The myth of popular government teaches that we can—or should be able to—hold our governors responsible for their conduct in office. But our political system in fact gives us few instrumentalities for doing this. Congressional oversight is inconstant, piecemeal, and clumsy; moreover, it has its own concerns and distractions. Press conferences can bring and have brought presidents to bay, but only extraconstitutionally and mostly only on the president's own terms. Elections are a formal option but come at fixed times. By the time the next election comes around, much has been forgotten or confused with other issues and memories. The failed president may not be running for reelection anyway. Impeachment, the major reserve option, is a blunderbuss that can only be invoked against provable "High Crimes and Misdemeanors," not for policy failures and misjudgments.[32] It can also be ducked. When it became clear that Nixon would be impeached for his Watergate involvements, he simply resigned—and then was granted a pardon by his successor, a man in whose selection he had had the major part. When the congressional committees investigating the Iran–Contra affair issued their final report after nearly a year of intensive, large-scale work, Reagan dismissed it, saying that the committee had labored to bring forth a mountain but had produced only a mouse. His spokesman was equally dismissive. He said the report, which in fact detailed meticulously and voluminously specific charges including many laid directly to the president, contained nothing new, that the American people were tired of all the talk, and that it was time to move on.[33]

There is a lack of resolution in all this. It suggests a kind of moral bankruptcy. Myth, in all its exaggeration, condemns ideology but cannot bring it to account. Myth goes on, but tattered. A failed president may not be a criminal, but he can be a cause of deep popular alienation. Is this what we mean when we say he must be both lion and fox?

7

Legislative Supremacy

The thesis of this chapter can be put in challenging terms: Congress is a legislative body—but only in myth. In ideology, its essential function is very different. In ideology, Congress is the nation's primary and paradigmatic instrument for harmonizing the conflicting claims of the competing interests, and this, in fact, is its primary role.

We can put this thesis in institutionally more dramatic terms. The president's State of the Union Address is his finest—mythic— hour. It is so for the Congress, too. In myth, the first function of Congress is to sustain the president, Tribune of the People, Leader of his Party, Chief Legislator. In this role, Congress hears the president's address, punctuates it with applause, and, afterward, dutifully comments on it. It also, rapidly, forgets it. Congress has more pressing matters on its mind.

Or we could begin by revising a famous statement about Congress. "Congress in its committee rooms," said Woodrow Wilson long ago, "is Congress at work."[1] Revised to bring it up to date, the statement should read: "Congress in subcommittee is Congress at work."[2]

The Mythic Legislature

Convened in the Capitol, Congress looks like a legislative body. These looks do not deceive. Congress really is a legislative body—in myth (for myth is real, too). It is situated like a legislative body; it is organized like a legislative body; it makes laws like a legislative body. Most important, in the context of the whole of the American political system, Congress lays claim to the title of being the nations's supreme legislative body. That title was effectively laid down by Montesquieu, but it had been defined in more explicit terms by Locke before him (note the Hobbesian premises of the argument).

> The great end of Mens entering into Society, being the enjoyment of their Properties in Peace and Safety, and the great instrument and means of that being the Laws establish'd in that Society; the *first and fundamental positive* Law of all Commonwealths, *is the establishing of the Legislative* Power; . . .This *Legislative* is unalterable in the hands where

126

the Community have once placed it; nor can any Edict of any Body else, in what Form soever conceived, or by what Power soever backed, have the force and obligation of a *Law*, which has not its *Sanction from* that *Legislative*, which the publick has chosen and appointed.[3]

This is straight, pure separation of powers theory: the vox populi wells up and speaks through the duly constituted and authoritatively assembled legislative body of the representatives of the people. By the legislative body, and only in, by, and through it, does the will of the people become the law of the land. This not only gives Congress its title and authority, it gives Congress an essence, purpose, and identity: to issue the law of the land.

It was this identity of Congress that the president and his associates in the Iran–Contra affair most affronted. The White House was determined by congressional investigators to have failed to keep Congress informed, to have raised monies and spent monies without Congress' authorization, and to have engaged in activities during periods of time when Congress had said plainly that they were not to be done.

The president and his men violated other principles during the course of this affair, most notably the principle of the rule of law. They did this most egregiously in the degree to which certain of their efforts "privatized" government. They set up, equipped, and operated an "agency" that had no basis in law and for which they secured funding from outside sources. Congress, obviously, had an interest in such extralegal goings-on and condemned them. But the rule of law is a liberal democratic value of the nation's operative ideology. It was violated in the course of carrying out an operation. The initial and fundamental insult to Congress was to its mythic status, to its authority and standing before the people, to its title as the people's supreme lawgiver, and only secondarily to the laws that it had in fact given.

Congress, in its consciousness of itself as the nation's supreme legislature, has housed itself accordingly. The Capitol, with its imposing dome, façades, and long, rising steps to its entrance, is more symbolic monument than usable building. The slope on which it is placed, in the long perspective of the mall stretched out before it, becomes, Olympuslike, "the Hill." The chambers where the Senate and House meet are shaped like amphitheaters, a form more conducive to flights of oratory than the kinds of conversational, cut-and-thrust debate encouraged by the oblong shape of the British House of Commons. In the array of mythic symbols that make up the

Washington scene, Congress comes close to preeminence, over-shadowing at times even the White House.

To all mythic appearances, Congress is organized like a legislative body, that is to say, along party lines. In the myth of social democratic, popular government, come election time, the parties battle it out for the right to represent the people's will in the government. For Congress, this means the parties vie to see which of them can win the most seats in the Senate or House, because winning these contests means "taking control" and "getting to organize" the won chamber. So the media and the textbooks uniformly inform us. But what does "taking control" and "getting to organize" a chamber of Congress mean? In mythic image, controlling a chamber means setting the agenda of bills to be discussed and determining which of them will be passed into law; organizing a chamber means putting party members into all its leadership positions so that they will be able cooperatively to control the chamber's work. In sum, so the image suggests, having a "Democratic Congress" (or, alternatively, a "Republican Congress") means that this party's "program" will be enacted into law as mandated by the will of the people. Is all this too obvious to be so painstakingly spelled out? Not if it is recalled that, in an ideological perspective focusing on actual congressional operations, "winning Congress," as we shall see in a moment, means something so different—and less—that the difference between the two meanings is startling and needs to be explained. For now, it is enough to say that, in myth, image is what matters, and that in this perspective, party victory in Congress is an eagerly sought and apparently meaningful feature of any comprehensive view of that body.

In the House, it means that the winning party gets to name and elect the speaker of that body, who acts as both the chamber's presiding officer and leader of his party. In the Senate, the comparable figure is the majority leader. In both houses, these leaders are backed by an assortment of officially designated deputies and assistants (called "whips," because of their supposed capacity for getting party stragglers into line). The majority party also gets to name all the chairmen of the committees and subcommittees of the two houses. Backing this display of comprehensively organized leadership is a regularly organized set of meetings of the majority party membership in each house. These meetings elect that leadership and discuss and settle official party positions on upcoming legislation.

All this conveys an impression of party doctrinal coherence, and organizational cohesion, an impression that is enhanced by the fact that the majority party's efforts are exactly imitated on a lesser scale

by the minority party. It too has leaders and whips and party meetings. Even on the official Senate and House committees and subcommittees, where party memberships are assigned in roughly the same
proportions as in the houses as a whole, the minority memberships
are led officially by their ranking member. As is the majority party,
so shadows the minority party.

Are experts, people who really know about how Congress works,
now anxiously signaling us from the wings of our argument that
things do not really go the way this party picture suggests? Never
mind them now. We are focused on the myth.

In myth, Congress makes laws like any self-respecting legislative
body would. That is to say, it has formal procedures for introducing
legislation, debating it, amending it, passing it, and calendars for
processing bills one after another in an orderly way. This is important because modern legislatures, especially at the national level, are
inundated with legislative proposals, their time for discussions of
these is limited, and proceeding in formal, organized ways is a necessity if anything is to be accomplished.

The world standard for procedures of this sort was evolved and
set by the British House of Commons. The American Senate and
House of Representatives have largely accepted this standard even
if, as we will see, their qualifications of it rob it of much of its meaning. Nevertheless, for mythic purposes, it is important to spell out
the obvious and see clearly what it is that the American chambers
were trying to accept.

The British procedure goes like this:

First reading. A proposed bill is received by the chamber's secre-
tarial staff, printed, and distributed to the membership so that they
may study it, and, on an individual and party collective basis, discuss
it with such friends, experts, and interested parties as they may care
to reach.

Second reading. Time is found in the chamber's calendar for a
general discussion of the proposed bill. Its main principles are identified and debated. Possible amendments may also be discussed but
may not be formally proposed for adoption. The question before the
house at this stage is simply, do we wish to have a bill of this sort, as
developed along these general lines? If that question is answered
affirmatively, the bill is sent to committee.

Committee stage. Committees, relative to the size of the house as a
whole, are small. They can call in experts and interested groups to
testify about aspects of the proposed bill. The aim of a committee's
discussions of a proposed bill, in the light of the action of the house
at the second reading, must be exclusively to improve the bill, by

amending it in detail, or perhaps more substantively in the light of such major amendments as might have been discussed at the second reading.

Report stage. Led by the committee chairman, the amended bill is reintroduced to the house as a whole. All changes from the original bill have to be debated and accepted, and amendments that lost in committee may be brought up again. Chambers going through this stage often will adopt special rules that by being informal, facilitate this process. They may also empower their presiding officer to exercise firm control over frivolous, repetitious, picayune, or dilatory amendments and debate.

Third reading. The bill as now amended is debated in its final, full form. Individual members state their considered views and party positions are staked out. If the bill passes this stage, it goes out of the house and to such other steps as may be required for it to become law.

These are only the bare outlines of the British standard legislative procedure. It can be and regularly is elaborated on in intricate detail. It can be stretched or compressed to accommodate various kinds of legislation. But even in bare outline, this procedure can be seen to follow a clear logic. Every step is designed to serve a serious purpose, and the whole is supposed to achieve comprehensive and fair debate for every bill. By following this procedure, a legislative body can do what it is supposed to do: make law.

The clue to the whole is the second reading, both in respect to when it occurs and to what it is supposed to accomplish: the decision to have a bill of a certain sort. That the American practice reverses the second reading and the committee stage, so that one or another committee gets hold of a bill before any general discussion and may kill it before it goes any further in the legislative mill, is, once again, something to which we will have to return. For now, let it simply be noted that, in the *main*, the American practice follows the British, including specifically its nomenclature, and that shows at least intent to be "legislative" in a proper sense.

All this legislative organization, procedure, and intent comes to a climax annually when the president appears before Congress in joint session of the two houses to deliver the State of the Union Address. He appears as spokesman of the people to list their needs for legislation as he understands them. This amounts to his proposing to Congress a legislative agenda. The comparison to the queen's speech (actually written for her by the cabinet) on the opening of the British Parliament's annual session is inviting and apparently exact. In each case, before this commanding figure of the supreme executive are arrayed the whole body of the legislature and, more particularly, its majority party controlling leadership. To this leadership element, the speech of the sovereign executive must appear to be so many detailed requests for legislative action, to be heard, received and debated by the legislature, and with all deliberate speed to be enacted by the legislature. In this sense, the House of Commons, which does indeed almost always enact the program laid down in the queen's speech, embodies the full nature of the modern legislature. It is, in the last analysis, an "assenting chamber." If the commons does not assent to the executive's legislative requests, everything stops, and a new government must be found that can command that assent.

It is important to the complete description of the myth that Congress is a legislative body to note that Congress, on hearing the president's State of the Union Address, goes through the motions of being an assenting chamber, of being, therefore, a true and complete legislative body. No State of the Union Address has been greeted with hisses and boos, and no president, no matter how unpopular, has ever suffered the indignity of being confronted with an organized walkout. On the contrary, every such address is not only dutifully applauded, but thoughtfully analyzed and evaluated by senators and representatives of every stripe for an expectant public, and all of them dutifully promise to give the president's proposals the most careful attention.

Through this point we have the myth complete, and it can be said that, ostensively, at every major turn, Congress is a legislative body. But it must also be said that myth wears very thin, and nowhere more so than with respect to the State of the Union Address. Battle as they may, few presidents get more than a fraction of what they ask for. Certainly also, as the months slide by, it is readily apparent that Congress is not apt to use the address as an actual legislative agenda.[4] And to mention just one other point: the notion that Congress is "controlled" and "organized" by coherent, cohesive, disciplined parties who could respond as such to the president's address is nothing less than a charade.[5]

So why is the charade played out, at such cost in time and effort, at the risk of exposing all concerned to charges of hypocrisy? There are various minor reasons, including a number of practical conveniences one of the most important of which is the way it makes Congress an endlessly available butt of presidential frustration. But the major reason is plain: by playing out as best it can the myth of being a legislative body, Congress buys into the nation's general social democratic myth and thereby establishes its legitimacy. In short, it plays out its myth because it must. And it may be added that the notion that the American Congress is a party-run, dutifully deliberate legislative body is no more extravagant than the Rossiter version of the presidency.

Ideological Harmonization

Because it falls in daily practice so far short of its mythic ideals, Congress is widely thought both by commentators and the public to be a failure. Harry Truman is not the only president to have filled the airways with cries against what he called "a do-nothing Congress." Congress is routinely berated for being clumsy, tardy, insufficient, tangled, dominated by vested interests, and so forth.[6] But Congress is a failure only in myth. In ideology, the Civil War breakdown to one side, it has proved to be something of a success.

Myth fundamentally misconstrues what Congress, in ideology, is actually doing. Thus misjudging Congress, myth thinks Congress a disaster. This is serious. Most citizens and commentators tend to judge Congress in mythic terms, because myth is what both identifies and legitimizes Congress. There is a powerful element of social necessity in so judging Congress. Even senators and representatives fall prey to this necessity, at least from time to time.[7] But senators and representatives, on pain of political survival, are subject to another set of imperatives, the imperatives that direct them to quite different tasks. Put, they are told, the business of legislating laws in the name of the sovereign people to one side; instead, heed the claims of your supporters. That way you will be a real "pro," successful and respected. Make the powers of your office work for you—and your clients.

It is essential once again to notice that these alternative imperatives do not arise from petty selfishness in the members of Congress or from the overweening importuning of vested interests. They arise from the constitutional principles that define Congress' operational essence and structure its relationships to the political system as a whole. We have said with such emphasis that Congress is a legislative body only in myth so that we can say with the same emphasis that it is, in ideology, the political system's primary and paradigmatic instrument for harmonizing the diverse claims of the competing interests. It is the system that decrees that Congress, in ideology, has work to do very different from its mythic functions, that this work must be done, and that members of Congress, collectively and individually, can take a professional pride in doing it well and consistently.

The work assignment that comes to Congress ideologically stems from mixed government theory. This theory, in essence, holds that the tripartite division of power between the chief magistrate, the upper house of the legislature, and the lower house should ensure the representation in the governing process of the interests respectively of the community as a whole, the "rich," and the "poor." But Aristotle in America was read by Hobbesians wearing glasses ground by Locke. The result was not just Madison. More specifically, as these matters pertain to Congress and its procedures and assignments, the result was John C. Calhoun and his doctrine of "concurrent majority." The essence of Aristotle was retained: "governments" "represent" "interests," in a phrase, "representative government." But, in America, all this is, in a word, pluralized. Representative government becomes a complicated business in which the widest assortment of interests get represented through a myriad of institutional devices.

Calhoun, with good reason, is usually thought of as a spokesman for the South, or, more narrowly, for the interests of South Carolina with respect to questions about tariffs and slavery. But his genius was that in doing this work he uncovered principles essential to the operation of American politics generally, and of Congress particularly, principles that are as valid in our day as they were in his. Of all he wrote, this is his key paragraph:

> To prevent any one interest or combination of interests from using the powers of government to aggrandize itself at the expense of the others . . . [there must be adopted] . . . some restriction or limitation which shall so effectually prevent any one interest or combination of interests from obtaining the exclusive control of the government as to render hopeless all attempts directed to that end. There is, again, but one mode in which this can be effected, and that is by taking the sense of each interest or portion of the community which may be unequally and injuriously affected by the action of the government separately, through its own majority or in some other way by which its voice may be fairly expressed, and to require the consent of each interest either to put or to keep the government in action. This, too, can be accomplished only in one way, and that is by such an organism of the government—and, if necessary for the purpose, of the community also—as will, by dividing and distributing the powers of government, give to each division or interest, through its appropriate organ, either a concurrent voice in making and executing the laws or a veto on their execution.[8]

The language is prolix but is easily analyzed and is in no way aberrant or, in its substance, out of the run of ordinary American discourse on politics in its ideological variant.

The fundamental presupposition of the whole paragraph is that society is permanently fragmented into a pluralism of interests. In Calhoun's time, these presumably were in the main sectional interests, but his language indicates he thought them possibly of many sorts: commercial, ethnic, class, or even individual. Certainly that is the pattern in America today. It is also clear that into whatever multiplicity of portions society might be divided, Calhoun believed each of those portions, whatever its individual character or quality, had a natal right to be itself and to pursue, achieve, and protect its "interest." And it is finally clear that in Calhoun's mind, the question of what properly constituted an interest, especially a "vital" interest, as he called it elsewhere, was to be settled by having each recognizable portion of society speak for itself. Only on the basis of conjectural thinking along these lines does the final sentence of Calhoun's paragraph make sense. Why else give to each "division or interest" in the community "an appropriate organ" in the government through which to exercise its concurrent voice or explicit veto?

This is the substantive point of Calhoun's philosophy, that every portion of the community must be given a veto to protect itself against the plans of even the (otherwise) most overwhelming numerical majority. Once the premises are granted, the argument in support of this right to a veto is unassailable. Why would an interest enter government if it were not to protect itself? And if it then finds the government itself to be a threat, then all bets are off, the interest must secede, and the state of nature reigns again. In or out of governmental bonds, the first priority of each interest is unfailingly its own self-preservation.

There is an important caveat to be entered here, a bias in Calhoun's argument that powerfully slants it—and all subsequent derivations from it—in elitist directions. When Calhoun wrote about the interests of the South generally, or of South Carolina particularly, he, of course, meant the interests of the dominant groups established in these areas. He meant what we now call the vested interests. If it crossed his mind to think of the interests of black slaves, he immediately would have assumed that these would be seen to by meeting the interests of their owners. To this day, representative government is representative of the visible interests, the interests big enough, organized enough, skilled and rich enough to demand and get representation. These are the politically relevant interests. By definition and in political fact, the rest do not matter.

This much of Calhoun is Americanized Aristotle. Calhoun's contribution up to this point is his boldness. But he went on to strike a truly original note by advocating the essence of a legislative procedure by which the veto rights of individualized interests could be protected and exercised routinely. This was to be done not only by giving each recognizable interest "an appropriate organ," but also by having each of these organs consulted separately and in series. In this way, instead of having numerical minorities drowned by a chorus of ayes from the majority, each interest, if it chose to exercise its veto right, could count on having its negative distinctly heard and heeded. The voting would proceed interest by interest until a given interest cast its no; then the voting would stop and could not proceed until some accommodation had been reached to persuade that interest to change its vote to an aye. The interest would not change its vote until, at a minimum, it could be persuaded that the proposal had been amended sufficiently to no longer threaten adversely its vital welfare.

In Calhoun's day, he thought the vital interests of the South could be protected only by establishing a dual presidency, one president to be elected by the South, the other by the North, and by requiring the concurrence of both presidents to put into effect any federal law. He had come to distrust the capacities of Congress, so far as southern interests in the moral dimensions of slavery were concerned, to respect the veto rights of minorities.

Events proved him right, and they might again. Congress has difficulty dealing with nonnegotiable demands of the sort American mythic-perceptions can fan into a high heat. But in its pragmatic, ideological perspectives, Congress has developed quite extraordinary capacities for accommodating the practical interests of minorities in great number. In fact, most of the working or successful "majorities" of Congress are best understood as ad hoc coalitions patching together bundlings of minority demands. And the process by which these working or successful coalitions are put together observes the basic principles of serial voting, of Calhoun's doctrine of "concurrent" majority.

How can this be so in a legislative body supposedly dedicated to mythic ideals of majority rule by the sovereign people? The first important clue can be found by noting that, so far as ideology is concerned, myth gets analysis off to a wrong start by looking at Congress from the top down. Myth thinks Congress is dominated from the top, if not by the president, then by its own "leadership," the Speaker of the House, the majority leader of the Senate, and so forth. The supposition is that this "leadership" imposes "discipline" on the members. In fact, ideologically, "discipline," in the sense that an army platoon or established bureaucracy knows that concept, is not an operative idea in the Congress. In ideological perspectives, the two houses of Congress are to all intents headless, undisciplined, in fact undisciplinable, bodies. Viewed from the perspective of their individual members, that is, from the bottom up, the House and the Senate are no more than collections of so many independently situated political actors, each of whom pursues his or her own ends while going about the tasks of servicing the interests he or she most directly represents.

This is their essential, constitutional, structural situation. They each get elected, one by one, by themselves. In pursuit of that election, the individual representative or senator may calculate that it will be helpful to his or her cause to pick up the endorsement of the sitting president or, alternatively, his opponent, of selected fellow members of the House or Senate, and of locally important political figures. Or he or she may calculate that having only a few or even none of these endorsements is the better bet under the particular circumstances of that election. Party identification may be played up or down. Funding to meet campaign expenses can be sought in one or another mix of sources, but almost always with the bulk of it going to the individual candidate personally from client groups personally approached. The point of the matter is that under the American system of independently constituted branches of government and houses of the legislature, elections, fundamentally, must also be independently constituted. Come election time, as a result, it is every man or woman for him- or herself. "Leadership" from the top, whether from the president or from Congress, can only mask this fact. It cannot alter it, no matter how much the media count up victories and pronounce this or that party "the winner."

From this root fact of their constitutional position flow many other characteristics of the lives and labors of representatives and senators. The most obvious is that members of the House and Senate, as independently situated political actors, have voted themselves over the years an array of perquisites like members of no other national legislature anywhere else in the world. To carry out in a professional way their ideological roles, their first requirements are to have adequate office space and staff assistance, both in Washington and in their home districts. The actual number of support personnel they get varies widely, depending on their length of tenure, clout through allies, and other resources.[9] In addition to personal staff, members of Congress have at their disposal:

- the staffs of the various committees and subcommittees (much of which is named by individual representatives and senators personally);

- the staffs of the Congressional Research Service of the Library of Congress and of the Congressional Budget Office (both of which were created specifically to assist members in their legislative work);

- personnel in the offices of the sergeant-at-arms and of the parliamentarian;

- the managerial, professional, and custodial personnel who staff the shops, discount stores, gymnasiums, TV/video facilities, and restaurants and cafeterias that are maintained exclusively for the convenience and comfort of members of the House and the Senate and their assistants.

The total number of all these persons is in the tens of thousands, and housing them fills to overflowing a dozen or so buildings arranged around the Capitol itself.[10] The cost of running the whole of this American national legislative establishment is in excess of one billion dollars annually.[11]

In this light, send any one of the 100 senators or 435 representatives an urgent notice of party discipline, an announcement, for example, of the official party position on a piece of upcoming legislation, together with a request for support, and the proper reply must be, "I'll have my people get on that right away and we'll get back to you when we can. Don't call us; we'll call you."

The American national legislative establishment makes the Congress, easily, the most elaborately and expensively serviced legislative body in the world, absolutely and relatively, in terms of the number of legislators involved and in terms of the total population they represent.[12] The reason for this fact has little or nothing to do with venality, professional vanity, or whatever. The reason quite simply is that individual representatives and senators are heavily, even routinely overworked.[13] And the reason for this in turn is that, because the two houses ideologically are headless bodies, the power assigned them as wholes in law is in practice fragmented into the hands of their individual memberships. Each of those members, on pain of political survival, has to become as nearly as he or she can one-person legislative bodies. Obviously, each of them has to arrive at personal decisions about where to stand on upcoming legislation and to be prepared to defend those decisions on the floor of the appropriate chamber, and, through skilled manipulation of the media, to the public at large. But that is only the start of the game. More subtly and consuming vastly more time, each member of the House and of the Senate must become individually one of Calhoun's "appropriate organs" for the representation of interests drawn from the great pluralism of America's natural fragmentation. This is the individual member's primary ideological assignment and success here is essential to the performance of all other roles.

Becoming an appropriate organ for the representation of a suitably large and diverse collection of client interests has three immediate requirements.

The first is that the member must become a certain kind of person, on the one side, affable, garrulous but a good listener, outgoing; and, on the other side, nondogmatic, even shamelessly nonjudgmental. This must be the member's "real" personality, however much, for mythic purposes, an almost entirely opposite mask may be worn from time to time on the political stage. And the member must train his or her support staff in the same qualities. In a word, they all must be personally accessible. Political scientists like to think of Congress' overall legislative process as a chain of "access points."[14] It is important for every member of Congress to habituate themselves and their staffs into a self-consciousness of themselves as the original and constant access points in this chain.

Second, the individual House or Senate member must make decisions about which interests he or she is going to most represent. Obviously, for mythic reasons, at the top of the list will be the member's own constituents, the "little people" who make up the voting public back in the home district or state. Every representative and senator spends much time playing ombudsman for these people, listening to their views and greeting their children touring the sights on school trips to the nation's capital. But it is questionable how important these people are to the ordinary member of Congress. The views of constituents may be vociferously expressed, but they also largely cancel each other out. Moreover, they cannot be counted on as a source of steady and substantial sums for reelection campaigns. For that kind of money, the member must turn to more organized groups able to make not only larger but longer-term commitments. Sometimes the member will find such groups in his or her own district or state, a major defense contractor, perhaps, or an important ethnic group. Often enough, however, a member's most dependable supporters will be found headquartered far from wherever the member of Congress calls home. Washington is filled with lobbyists of every kind of interest anxious to find and willing to fund generously reliable and understanding voices in the legislative process. Matching clients to legislative representatives is our nation's capital's most fascinating and ongoing mating game. A member's final decisions about which organized interests to represent may depend on chance, philosophical compatibility, mutual need, or, in many cases most important, the member's particular committee assignments and developing legislative and administrative expertise and reputation.

The third immediate requirement for becoming an appropriate, representative organ is that the member and his or her staff will have to become adept at penetrating and manipulating the federal bureaucracy on behalf of constituents and clients. Much of this involves time-consuming casework. But much of it also requires highly knowledgeable, long-term, persistent representation in the bureaucracy to secure changes in the way certain regulations are applied, to ensure favorable consideration for the siting of a major government operation, to obtain a large military contract for a certain firm, or to formulate, plan, and develop a whole new program. It has been estimated that up to eighty percent of the working day of an ordinary member of the House or Senate is spent on this kind of mostly administrative, nonlegislative labor, almost all of it involving some degree of what is called "lateral penetration" of the bureaucracy.[15]

Emblematic of all these efforts to become appropriate organs of representative government is the phrase "iron triangles." The phrase was coined to underline not just the coziness but also the permanence of the relationships that can develop between especially the staffs of long-serving members of the House and Senate, particular client groups, and the middle levels of the federal bureaucracy in which they have a special interest. Once established, these triangular, mutually beneficial relationships, especially if expertly managed by pragmatically minded people with reasonable ambitions, seem impervious to the influence of the president and budget planners and even of other important members of Congress.

The success of "iron triangles" and of many other similar, networklike arrangements in Washington does not, however, depend simply on the skill and accessibility of the individuals directly involved, however important that may be. As important is the fact that relationships of this sort are accepted, even admired, features of the Washington scene, at least by those who live and work there and are conversant with the (ideological) ways of that world. Iron triangles are admired because they work; they make decisions that stick and make sense; they get things done. In a world as chaotic and fragmented as Washington, these are not minor virtues. But the style with which successful iron triangles operate is also the object of much admiration.

This style is the essence of the ideological process of American national government. Although it presumes those personality traits of pragmatic geniality we mentioned before, it goes beyond them. As the various operatives in Washington meet and treat with each other, they quickly learn that, if they are to be successful, they must observe the first law of Washington politics: the law of reciprocity. On its surface, this means, as anywhere else in a liberal democratic economy, that in every deal all parties must win at least something, that for every quo there must be some quid, if not now, then later, or maybe sometime before. Linkages on these matters can be loose and at times mostly promissory. The law of reciprocity implies, to use the old Tammany Hall jargon, that an honest politician is one who, if you buy him, stays bought. But the Washington law of reciprocity means much more than simply honor among thieves. More fundamentally, it means that Washington politics can only proceed on the basis of very large measures of mutual respect. This entails respect for the fact that all Washington operatives are remarkably equal in a basic constitutional sense. Of course, some are senators, others are representatives, one is president, and hordes are bureaucrats. Some have great seniority and others are mere freshmen, and, of course, some are nationally known and others are obscure. All these differences matter. But they do not matter to the point of fundamentally altering the essential fact that in Washington, under a constitutional system that radically fragments and disperses power, virtually everyone has enough power to be an independently situated political actor. Each has his or her own identity, a bailiwick, a bit of expertise, perhaps some staff, and a developing network of connections, concerns, and commitments. Above all, they each have a place, an office, a position from which they can say "yea" or "nay" to what comes across their desks. That demands respect. Put another way, the Washington law of reciprocity says: you honor my turf, I'll honor yours; deal me in and I'll deal you in—otherwise, we may both be left out (an eventuality that happens often enough to keep everybody on their toes).

This is Hobbesian political philosophy raised to a gentlemen's agreement, the war of all to the level of a game, even if one with exceptionally high stakes. It is Calhoun institutionalized in a pervasive and powerful, if mostly informal, tradition. Its most immediate meaning is that, in Washington, any contemplated political action, whether administrative or legislative, cannot be initiated and advanced very far without consulting one by one all interested parties and their representatives, particularly all directly interested members of the House of Representatives and the Senate. Failure to consult will bring not only cries of outrage from those directly offended but rumblings of discontent all across the Washington establishment. This is not to say that the law of reciprocity is unfailingly observed.

It often is not, sometimes deliberately. Sometimes the only way to overcome opposition is to ignore it, run by it, or crush it. But Washington's law of reciprocity is a norm rooted in some of the most fundamental realities of the nation's political system. Its violation will always bring a cost.

Examples of the practical application of the law of reciprocity abound. One example is a rule congressional leaders follow as if by rote: never ask a member to vote against his or her constituents. Another is senatorial courtesy, a tradition that allows a single senator to veto a presidential appointment to a federal position in his state if he and the president are of the same party and there has been no consultation between them. A third is the increasing tendency in both houses of Congress for members to caucus together across party lines if they share some common concern, such as racial, regional, or professional identification. A fourth is the filibuster, including the so-called silent filibuster that allows even a single senator to block a bill from getting on the legislative calendar at all.

But much the most significant example of the law of reciprocity at work in Congress is the committee system. It is here that Calhoun's doctrine of concurrent majority and especially that doctrine's emphasis on serial voting receives its most vivid application.

Despite recent reforms, both houses of Congress have many standing committees, close to two dozen each.[16] With members claiming the right to multiple committee assignments, all these committees tend to be large and unwieldy. Hence, subcommittees. In all, the major committees have together spawned more than 300 subcommittees.[17] The arithmetic of this is significant. There are only 535 members of Congress. The dominant figures on each subcommittee are the chairman and the ranking minority member (the two often work closely in tandem), making a total of more than 600 positions. Even allowing for multiple memberships and chairmanships, the chances that virtually every member of Congress will have a "soap box" of his or her own are good.[18] When the textbooks talk about "fragmentation of power" and the flattening of authority structures in Congress, this is the prime fact to which they point.

In the American Congress, committees, subcommittees, and their leaders have disproportionate significance compared to that of similar groups in other national legislatures. A principle reason for this, intertwined with many others, has to do with procedure. Because the two houses of Congress are headless bodies, because, that is, neither has a leadership structure that can firmly control the legislative calendar, especially with regard to the introduction (first reading) of legislative proposals, members of these two houses are free to introduce whatever they wish—and do. The number of formal legislative proposals arriving on the parliamentarians' desks each year is in the thousands, and regularly tops ten thousand for any two year session.[19] And everything is thrown in together, a bill to fund the whole Pentagon side by side with one to make the bumblebee the national insect. In this situation, arithmetic again becomes controlling. Even in the best of circumstances, the number of (British-type) second readings the houses of Congress could manage in a session could only be counted in the hundreds. That means that something close to eight out of ten introduced bills must die before the second reading.[20] It means, too, that someone must select the one or two in ten that will go forward. Long ago, the two houses decided to assign this responsibility to the committees. The committee stage was made to precede the second reading and was made the first substantive stage in a bill's progress.

This is, on its face, an eminently reasonable solution to a major practical problem. But notice its consequences. First, it makes a shambles of the logic of the British procedure, even of the first reading. Who is going to bother reading and studying and consulting about all bills introduced when only one or two in ten will see the light of day? Second, by depriving the course of a bill through Congress of any interior logic, of clear purposes for each stage, all the formal stages of a bill's progress become vulnerable to many kinds of variation and complexity. Amendments, relevant and irrelevant, can be allowed or, maybe totally disallowed, at virtually any point along a bill's course. Depending totally on the whim of particular circumstance, the whole procedure can be speeded up and compressed, or slowed down, extended, even derailed by filibuster or other similar parliamentary dilatory tactic. The one thing certain is that the more the procedure is adapted for a particular bill, extended and complicated, each step in its way becomes one more "access" point at which the input of some "appropriate organ" speaking for some particular interest can be pressed, recognized, and have its special demands reviewed and, perhaps, acceded to.[21] Bills in Congress tend to look like laundry lists, in fact, like collections of multiple laundry and shopping lists.

Especially illustrative of all these tendencies and principles is the conference committee. These committees are convened at the penultimate stage in a bill's progress through Congress. At this point both houses will have passed, by more or less complicated routes, versions of a bill, but their versions may differ sharply. The conference committee, composed of members drawn from both houses, is convened to resolve the differences. The chairmen and ranking

members of the originally interested committees in both houses—
and there may have been several interested committees in each
house on a big and important bill—will be there as will members
picked to represent the interests of the party leadership and other
factions with special interests in the bill's subject matter. The pressure on the conference committee to come up with an agreed bill
may be intense. The committee may meet for days, even weeks, with
many late-night sessions. It may meet in camera or in the open; it
makes little difference because breaks in the sessions allow members
to drift out and consult with their supporters and leak what is going
on to the press. If it meets in open session, crowded around the
members at the long table will be large assortments of their personal
aides, some armed with portable computers to calculate and recalcu-
late differing versions of various amendments being considered.
Crowded even more tightly, along the walls of the room, will be representatives of the press, and, even more importantly, lobbyists, who
on occasion may signal their reactions to particular proposals with
appropriate facial expressions and hand gestures. Amendments
once accepted can later be considered again and rejected, or vice
versa, because of other changes in the bill made subsequently. All of
this process can be very intense because long tradition and powerful
practical considerations dictate that if a conference committee can
come up with an agreed version of the bill—even if it differs widely
in both substance and detail from what either house once proposed—then that version is the final word, to be voted either up or
down without further amendment by the two houses. So once again,
the ad hoc, coalition-building harmonizing quality of congressional
procedure is emphasized, along with the truth of the old adage that,
as in all games, nothing is over until it is over.

It must be stressed that many of the bills that get this kind of
treatment, in conference committees and before, are not "laws" in
any philosophical sense of the term, that is, they are not enactments
of general principles or rules governing a wide range of human behavior. Instead, they are typically appropriation measures, or tax
code changes, or new formulas for calculating agricultural supports
for peanuts, dairy products, and soybeans. Such bills, in their detailed minutiae, working out exactly who is to get what in long-established programs, are much better understood as acts of public administration than as legislation. In myth, this should be executive
work, best accomplished by the president assisted by his Office of
Management and Budget. In ideology, emphatically, this is congressional labor because, with the president well out of the picture, Congress in its extreme diversity is so much better positioned than he to

have access to all the competing interests and to harmonize and package their diverse claims.

The name of the congressional game is, through all this, compromise, or, more exactly, concurrent compromise, put together serially, piece by piece, interest by interest. This points to another great reason why committees and subcommittees are so important in Congress. To do the work they have to do—most notably, to receive a flood of bills and determine which few will go forward and in what form in the legislative mill—they are specialized by subject matter. The textbooks tell us that this allows members to become specialized experts on their committees' respective kinds of legislation, banking, foreign trade, armed forces, foreign affairs, agriculture—and in the subcommittees, even more specialized and proportionately more expert. This is very probably so (especially as the point is extended to congressional staff people), but there is even more important consideration to be noticed here. By specializing its committees and subcommittees Congress effectively signposts its processes so that interest groups know where to go to get heard and heeded. They and their hired lobbyists can concentrate their efforts effectively and efficiently. This means too that they, as much as the members of Congress, have an overriding interest in seeing to it that the Washington law of reciprocity is closely observed. They translate the law so that their patrons will read it, "You respect what I got for my clients in my committee, and I'll respect what you got for yours in your committee."

Concurrent compromises that build toward majorities as they go along, founded at every point on this client-focused reading of the law of reciprocity, can be either additive or subtractive. A clear example of an additive concurrent compromise bill is the annual appropriation measure funding the Pentagon. The distribution of weapons procurement contracts into virtually every member of the House and Senate's "backyard" has earned these bills the sobriquet of "Christmas-tree legislation."[22] A famous example of a subtractive concurrent compromise was the Unemployment Act of 1946. It started out a strong bill but was progressively weakened into being almost no bill at all. At the end, it was hardly more than a mouthful of platitudes and pious hopes. In fact, most regulatory legislation coming through Congress suffers something like this kind of fate.

This is not to suggest that Congress never passes significant legislation. From time to time it certainly does. What is being suggested is that when a significant bill comes through, analysis of its contents and of the process by which it emerged will show that there is more to the bill—or less—than meets the eye. The usual overall pattern on important legislation is for myth—often through presidential challenge—to suggest some high objective (national security, tax reform, domestic welfare, compassion for the oppressed) and to feed these goals, together with appropriately comprehensive plans for achieving them, into Congress. This will give to the legislative process a powerful tendency. However, as powerful a tendency also exists for the congressional mill to fractionalize those original plans and goals into a scheme of divisible awards to be distributed among the concurring supporters.

In the beginning, in 1787, there was a powerful urge to give the nation a new supreme legislative body. That was high, mythic hope. But before Article I could be drafted, a deal had to be cut. The small states were given equal representation in the Senate; the big states were given representation in proportion to their population in the House; and the slave states were permitted to calculate their population by counting blacks three fifths. And so it was done. Congress has been hearing mythic summonses—and cutting deals—ever since.

The Subjugation of Public Policy

One way to sum up this interpretation of Congress would be to ask a perennial question: why is it that, in a nation dedicated to democracy and majority rule, minorities in Congress nevertheless so often win what they individually want? To form an answer we must begin by observing that majorities in Congress are almost always coalitions of minorities, each one of which must be individually brought aboard, and that this is reflective of the extraordinary pluralism of American society generally. But to complete the answer we must go on to point out that we are now in the world of American ideological perspectives, perspectives that see the houses of Congress as headless bodies, dominated by the law of reciprocity, which in turn is based on principles of representative government, which in turn are premised on Aristotelian understandings of social fragmentation, which in turn, in the American environment, are finally based on the Hobbesian man asking, "What's in it for me?"

The bias in this answer prompts a final set of observations about America's national legislature.

Much of what goes on in Congress is broadly visible and widely reported in the press. Committees vote out proposals, hearings are conducted, floor debates are subject to TV broadcasts. And members of both houses have well-developed and deserved reputations for being accessible, both to the public and to the buttonholing lobbyists. But much of what Congress does is also concealed. Part of this is caused simply by the fact that so much of what Congress does is confusing and extended over such long periods. The procedures are complex, and what is done at one point can be done very differently or even undone altogether at a later point when public attention has wandered off to some other topic. Even when there has been a great victory and a bill has been passed, signed, and put into law, it must be said that often the game is not over because it seems over. The defeated idea can always reappear later, perhaps as an incidental amendment to something completely different. Keeping track of all that kind of thing is asking a lot of even the most skilled reporters. But there is also the fact that much of what Congress does, that has to get done so that work can go forward, is and must be done in private, informally, confidentially. In between votes, before hearings, in the wake of something else, members of the houses caucus among themselves and their staffs about stands to be taken, proposals to be offered, arrangements that can be made. Votes, whether in committee or, even less, on the floor, are a poor guide to the total life flow of Congress. That, if it could be known, could only be learned by tapping into virtually every telephone and "bourbon-and-branch" session on the hill.

Observations along these lines—especially as reinforced by the thought that the Congress, given the ideological realities of the American political system, could not be expected to operate any other way—make many people wonder if American's national legislative body is some kind of private club and, more profoundly, elitist.[23] The quick answer to that is that in real myth Congress is the servant of all the people, but that in ideology it serves the interests, and that, on balance, it does considerably more of the latter than the former. But Congress remains, like so much else in American government, essentially schizophrenic.

This suggestion that Congress may be on balance schizophrenic but in ways that are more elitist than popular in fact raises another and perhaps more serious question. By all accounts, the elites that Congress mostly serves are highly pluralistic. Congress serves them by the processes we have described at length in this chapter, the processes of concurrent majority compromise and the law of reciprocity. The result is a national policy making process that has been aptly described as "incrementalism," a step here, a step there, even a step backward, or two. To every significant pressure, there is some measure of response. The question that this understanding of the national policy making process raises is simply whether national policy made by that kind of process can be in any realistic sense either "national" or "policy." Is not incrementalism, by definition, opposed in principle to any reasonable understanding of the requirements of national public policy making? How can procedures for aggregating interest demands ever be congruent with procedures for defining and implementing the public interest?

8
Grassroots Barons

It would be a serious omission for this book to have no chapter on local government. The American local government system is integral to the national political system as a whole in two important senses.

First, the national system's confederalism/federalism ensures that the eighty thousand or more state, city, county, town, and special-purpose governments of the local government system are, structurally, all members with the federal government in the one overall national network of law and custom.[1] Moreover, they all appear in that one vast network, for all their individual differences in resources and functions, on something like the same footing—in tradition if not literally in law. Local government in America is not some mere appendage to the national goverment.

Second, as a rule, American local governments exhibit in their ongoing operations the same general characteristics and traits that are found in the national government, even if on occasion they carry these characteristics and traits to extremes. Most important, American local governments are as deeply rived as is the national government between mythic and ideological tendencies, and this condition is especially apparent in the schizophrenic quality of its principal actors, persons we will label "grassroots barons."

American local government was born of a familiar kind of compromise. In 1787, the erstwhile colonies all existed as sovereign states, each with its own constitution, history, and honored traditions, as these had by that time developed. All this separatism had to be respected. At the same time, there were powerful aspirations at the Philadelphia Convention to develop a single legal frame that would incorporate all the states and that would promote a single national self-consciousness. The founders in this perspective can be seen trying to have it both ways and, to a remarkable degree, succeeding. The United States from the beginning has aimed to be and is now a fully articulated, single nation-state in which, nevertheless, as former Speaker of the House of Representatives "Tip" O'Neill sagely observed, "All politics is local politics."[2]

This is the theme of the present chapter, that there is, in both myth and ideology, a single flow to American politics that encompasses all elements of the political system, national, state, and local.

148

As we focus our attention on such institutions as the town meeting (the great mythic symbol of American local government) and on the benevolently ruthless big-city boss (the great symbol of the ideological aspects of American local government), we must take care to keep these symbolic figures in the context of the flow of American political life as a whole.

The Local Basis of National Myth

The roots of American national legitimacy lie in a confederal recognition of the American people assembled locally in their natal communities.

Significantly, for the twenty-five years that the Selective Service System fed the nation's male youth into the armed forces, from before World War II through the Vietnam conflict, it was rooted in more than four thousand local boards called by its long-term director General Lewis B. Hershey "little groups of neighbors." The administrative costs of this kind of dispersion of authority were high. The operation of the system was marked throughout its history by confusion, lack of coordination, and uneven application of rules governing who was to go and who was to stay. But these administrative costs were more than offset by the manner and the degree to which this same dispersion allowed the Selective Service System to tap into the well-springs of the nation's patriotic identity.[3]

More comprehensive examples of the ways in which American political thinking presumes a bottom-up understanding of national identity can be found in the Bill of Rights. Both the Ninth and the Tenth Amendments presume a reservoir of authority in the people. More significant in this regard is the opening phrase of the First Amendment: "Congress shall make no law respecting an establishment of religion . . ." The original reason for this language, all subsequent redactions by the Supreme Court to the contrary notwithstanding, was simple: Congress in Washington was not to make laws on religion because the Commonwealth of Massachusetts in Boston (and other states similarly) already had. Washington might be the capital of the mundane and the enlightened. In Boston, God was sovereign.

The balance that puts "real" America in its local heartland, on the hearth at home with God and family, is what makes modern America, even modern urban America, predominantly local, even "small town," in mythic self-perception. That is not a false self-perception or, for that matter, a true one. That national America is predominantly local is a real (if mythic) self-conception that Americans have about themselves as a people. As such, it determines much in the way of their self-understanding and, from thence, their political behavior.

Americans in this mythic world of local life are or strive to be God-fearing, hard-working, and self-responsible—sound Protestant virtues all. These essential virtues are articulated in others: honesty, simplicity, tenacity. As these further virtues are themselves developed in the American imagination and given increasing precision, they take on hues that reveal them as distinctively American and also as decisively political. The God-fearing, hard-working, and self-responsible American is characteristically also something of a natural pragmatist. Not given to theorizing or abstract speculations, the ordinary, local-oriented American prefers to solve immediate problems one way or another without much thought to long-term consequences. Pushed, this pragmatism can emote a powerful anti-intellectualism, which in turn can evolve into an inbred conservatism and a deep suspicion of those who ask too many questions especially about traditional ways of doing things.[4]

Given these tendencies, ordinary Americans of local life, are, socially, instinctive egalitarians but of a restricted sort. They regard themselves as immediately the equal of their neighbors—with whom they maintain, in myth, friendly and protective relations. But the negative side of these attitudes is also important. Ordinary American locals are not only characteristically anti-intellectual; they are also characteristically anti-authoritarian, antistranger, anti-eccentric.[5] Profoundly, they are conformists. On issues involving the rights of minorities and women, they can be bigots.[6] No doubt, on the positive side, American locals are, in myth, generous to a fault, kindly, supportive, in a word, neighborly. But it must not be forgotten that lynch mobs in the South in the 1920s and gangs of white youths in the Howard Beach section of New York City in the 1980s were also "little groups of neighbors" bent on enforcing the traditions and prejudices of their personal communities as they understood them. "Sovereignty of the people," if such groups could have found words to interpret the phrase, meant to them the right and the obligation to assemble and to act to protect the integrity of their neighborhoods.

Politically, such neighborliness means, in the first instance, voting for someone you feel easy about, at home with, someone you can trust, someone much like yourself, as if from around the corner in your neighborhood. The log-cabin myth is often interpreted to mean that in America anyone, no matter how humble in origin, can rise to the presidency. It might be better to interpret it in the other direction: that most American presidents have predominantly projected images of being from "down home." The two great-war presidents, Wilson and Roosevelt, are from the other end of the spectrum and are exceptions. More characteristic are Truman, the man from Independence, Missouri; Eisenhower, from Abilene, Kansas; and Carter, from Plains, Georgia. When Mario Cuomo, governor of New York, made a soaring speech at a presidential convention about his immigrant parents making it in America, he was not only celebrating the American dream; he was putting down his roots and establishing in local footings his national legitimacy. In America, to be nationally authentic, you have to be from somewhere locally.

These observations are testimony to how deep-seated is our social democratic, confederal egalitarianism, an egalitarianism of neighbors and neighborhoods. It is evidenced, obviously, in presidential campaigns, such as Richard Nixon's persistent efforts to market himself as a small-town boy from Whittier, California, and Lyndon Johnson's proclivity for "pressing the flesh" in airport crowds to the consternation of his secret service agents. It is supported as well by the consistency of small-town concerns and regional dialects in TV situation comedies, Hollywood movies, and countless novels and short stories. It explains artists like Norman Rockwell, who, with unsurpassed accuracy, recorded literally the locality of the American myth. Above all, it accounts for the Reagan presidency. Cosmopolitan, sophisticated circles, in their self-centered, professional competence, thought Reagan at best amiable and an ideologue who, simplistically, happened to be right; they thought him at worst an incompetent beyond comparison, a man too ill-educated, lazy, and ignorant to be capable of a principled approach to any complexity. But to the final days of his administration, Reagan retained much of his personal popularity with the public.[7] Cosmopolitan America misjudged him. They thought he was president and so measured him. In fact, with great success, he remained throughout his days in public office always the candidate for reelection, a local folk hero. As ordinary as a California motel, he was supremely America's next-door neighbor. Tip O'Neill, speaking as a politician's professional politician, said Reagan should have been America's king.[8] He would have looked even better in an auto-mechanic's green jumpsuit mowing the White House lawn.

Local Mythic Politics

The mythic notion that each of us is, or, at least, should think of ourselves as, a member of some little band of neighbors is greatly reinforced by the institutions of American local life. Preeminent among these, symbolically, is the New England town meeting. It would be easy to downplay the significance of this proverbial American institution. The operative impact of these meetings on what actually happens in New England towns is small.[9] But the symbolism of these meetings, both in New England and across the country, remains important.

Formal town meetings may operate today only in New England, but their near equivalents appear all across America, in public hearings and open meetings held by school boards, zoning commissions, town councils, and so forth. Many of these meetings are required by law; many others are scheduled intermittently in response to public feeling. Many of them are almost spontaneous and informal. Regardless of whether the issue before such a meeting is bus fares, changes in a high school curriculum, the siting of a new prison, or the institution of a program for the homeless, the central purpose will remain the same: to give the people a chance to assemble and to speak before officeholders and, as much, before each other. It is not enough for these folk to write letters to the editor or to some officeholder. At a public meeting, face to face, in company and concert with others of the community, the will of at least these people is sounded, formulated, and expressed. In many of these meetings no binding decisions are made, or, if they are, they are made only by vote of the officeholders present. But no matter how or when formal decisions are made, if they come after meetings in which "the people assembled" have had their back-and-forth say, the decisions will carry a legitimacy they would otherwise lack.

The name of this game, once again, is confederal social egalitarianism. To understand the dimensions and force of it in American politics, two other aspects need to be mentioned. First is the way the spirit of local egalitarianism spills over and affects the operating style of many of America's nongovernmental institutions. Stockholder meetings in business corporations, even very large ones, often resemble town meetings both in style and substance. At an opposite extreme, so also do the meetings of students in their homerooms to elect class officers and make plans for social events. Studiously, regardless of practical effect, everyone present at such meetings is, at least in planned intent, given a clear chance to hear and be heard. Of particular interest in this regard is the phenomenon known by clergymen in their churches as "creeping congregationalism." In American Jewish synagogues, Roman Catholic parishes, Episcopalian, Methodist, and Presbyterian churches, as much as in denominations where authority is formally placed in the congregation, the whole body of members meets periodically in their particular halls or places of worship. There they constitute, in ways often flatly contradictory to formal expressions of constitutional status, the voice of last resort. This is not to deny that in these religious organizations "real" leadership, whatever that means, is often highly oligarchical. But it is to assert that, under the influence of the American environment, even oligarchies have to seek and at least appear to obtain the mantle of congregational acceptance.

The second important spinoff of the American penchant for local confederal social egalitarianism is the way in which its spirit can be seen infecting the operations of formal governmental bodies well removed from the neighborhood level. State assemblies and senates and councils of major cities, which are in no sense actual neighborhood groups, nevertheless characteristically act as if they were. In most sessions, neighborhood bonhomie is the rule. Obviously, on occasion, passions can rise, tempers can become frayed, even physical brawls can break out on the floors of these meetings. But this sort of bad feeling can happen in the best of neighborhoods without disturbing the norm. And the norm, with surprising consistency around the country at all local government levels, is one of informality and friendliness, of earnest regard for all points of view with an eye to developing a tolerable consensus about what "the people" want.[10] There is even a touch of small-town, local-style bonhomie in the proceedings of the nation's major institutions in Washington, especially the Congress.[11]

This American local government political style, we must keep reminding ourselves, is mythic. It is the measure of how Americans in their localities understand, identify, and legitimate themselves, of what will prompt their fixed moods of pride and hope, or, alternatively, anger and regret. It is a style with which local politicians must become at ease, especially those marked for executive leadership, such as governors, mayors, town supervisors, county executives, and the like. It will not do for these men and women in their official capacities to be aloof, arch, technically explicit, and exact. They must personally cultivate the spirit of confederal social egalitarianism. As leaders they must contrive to be followers, to be always convivial, colloquial, and, above all, able and willing to listen to anyone and everyone.[12] Perhaps most notably, they must appear willing to share their authority and the discharge of their responsibilities with other possible claimants, especially other officers within their administrations, but also figures outside of it.[13]

Local government officers must seek to stand shoulder to shoulder in the community with the other members of the "team," with appropriate groupings of legislative leaders, party organizers, and so forth, but also with leaders of private organizations, school administrators, ministers and prominent church people, and major business leaders and executives. It is even important to cultivate open and mutually supportive relationships with the heads of bureaucratic units, especially the police and fire protection services. In American local government, at the level of the mythic legitimization, a prevailing egalitarianism flattens patterns of deference and hierarchy and blurs jurisdictional distinctions both within and between the public and the private.

It must be particularly noted that local government leaders must be adept at the arts of civil religion as that is understood in American politics.[14] This is, of course, a "low church" business, and zealots of all sorts would be out of place. The name of the divinity must be invoked shyly, even though with some regularity, but always as the companion of us all. Our communities cannot be openly declared Christian, but government leaders often assume them so. Men and women of the cloth are granted a special regard and their help in prayer is regularly requested at public rites of all sorts, high school graduation exercises and even football games. Local government leaders show themselves to be acutely sensitive to the problems of religious freedom and religious education even when federal constitutional bars restrict what they can do in these areas. But most important is the way in which local government leaders from governors to local sheriffs try positively to clothe their governing efforts in the mantle of religious symbols and language. Most of this is accomplished by public speeches and proclamations, and much of it is done, as indicated, shyly and even indirectly. But the repeated use of code words like "family" and "traditional values" makes these inferences unmistakable.[15] We can often be, these speeches seem to say repeatedly, a scattered and weakened people, but when we are moved from within by the spirit of the lord that resides in our natal communities, then we will rise up and achieve great and wonderful things, house the homeless; serve the poor; comfort the lonely, the destitute, the ill, and the aged; and give consolation to prisoners. These are powerful feelings. They are springs that local government leaders are well positioned to tap into and that no survey of American politics can ignore. They are the ultimate root of not just the local myth but of the national myth as well.

The Legal Frame of American Local Government

There is a gap between the spirit invoked by local government leaders in their mythic roles and the practice perpetuated by local government leaders in their ideological roles. To measure this dimension of the schizophrenia of American local politics, we must

analyze how it is that, with one political system confronting in myth
one great problem, how to govern the country, the job in ideology is
given to eighty thousand governments each independently situated
in its own bailiwick.

Start with a paradox. The emphasis in social democratic confederal myth both appears to be and, in fact, is on the multiplicity of
America's discrete neighborhoods. Nevertheless, this loose confederalism is capable, under the arousing leadership of a great charismatic president in times of national crisis, of extraordinary national
unity of both enthusiasm and effort. On the other hand, in both
appearance and fact, in the liberal democratic federal tradition,
America's eighty thousand governmental units are bound tightly
into a single legal frame within which one government, the national
government in Washington, is a colossus that, especially in financial
matters, should be able to curb all the rest into dancing to a single
tune. But despite sometimes heroic efforts to achieve this kind of
centralizing discipline, the national government is rarely able to accomplish it to any measurable degree.

In terms of the second half of this paradox, suppose for a moment
a virtual miracle in Washington: in the face of an economic crisis of
national proportions, all units of the federal government (president,
Congress, Treasury, Federal Reserve Board) agree promptly on a comprehensive program of coordinated actions to increase public spending, lower taxes and interest rates, encourage consumer spending and
business investment, and so forth. Now, what would be required to
bring off a further miracle, getting America's other 79,999 governmental units, those at the state and local levels, to fall cooperatively into
line with the national program? What would be required to induce
them not to go the other way, not to seek to husband their shrinking
resources, not to cut their spending, not to increase their tax rates in
the face of declining revenues, and so forth? All these governments are
liberal democratic entities. They have their interests, and these are defined for them in the context of their particular parochialisms. They
are as intent—and their taxpayers expect them to be as intent—as anybody else on making the powers constitutionally assigned to them work
for them.

On a more restricted level, imagine a major city with an upstate
reservoir. The city's (liberal democratic, operative ideological with
some mythic elements) interest is to draw pure water from that reservoir. But what of the interests of the local governmental units, of
which there may be several dozens or more, that abut the reservoir
and spread out over its catchment area? Independent of any *force
majeure* imposed from somewhere above, these catchment-area governments will have only a "neighborly" interest in seeing the down-

state city get its pure water. Their own immediate interests may well be dominated by perceived needs to encourage tax-base-expanding housing developments—with minimal sewage-treatment facilities.

This is the local government boundary/powers problem. It would not be difficult to daydream solutions to it. As clear is the impossibility of supposing any actual American politician at any level proposing any scheme along such lines. Just to begin, who could suggest the rationalization, let alone the abolition, of the American federal system and the erasure of the dotted lines outlining our current states? New York, New Jersey, and Connecticut exist as if carved out of granite, and each has, therefore, an undisputed share of the government of the New York metropolitan region. Comparable situations exist around Chicago and Washington, D.C. By sheer accident of history comparable situations do not exist around Los Angeles or San Francisco.

On the other hand, all metropolitan regions in the United States endure fragmentation among governments on another scale, that is, each of them has spilled out over not only county lines but also over a host of suburban-community demarcations clustered around the old-city core. It must be further noted that many of these are in turn crisscrossed by school district boundaries following the logic of their own purposes with total disregard for the boundaries of any other authority. It has been estimated that within a suitably generous understanding of the demographic and economic outline of the New York metropolitan region, there are more than fifteen hundred distinct governments with no legal requirement for assuring cooperation and coordination between any of them in the single task of "governing" the region as a whole.[16] The situation around the other major metropolitan areas is considerably worse, if only because of an exceptional accident that occurred in the case of New York City, in 1898.[17] By an act of the legislature in Albany, the then-neighboring cities of Brooklyn and New York were combined together with the boroughs of Queens, the Bronx, and Staten Island. With the possible exception of a somewhat comparable achievement with respect to the city of Miami in Florida, nothing like this has happened anywhere else in the United States. Of perhaps greater significance, even though the city of New York, to say nothing of the towns and cities around it, has multiplied its population many times over since Albany made its extraordinary move, not a whisper has suggested that perhaps it is long since time to rethink the problem. If Queens could with good reason be combined with other boroughs around New York in 1898, why should not Westchester be added today?

The boundary/powers problem is by no means confined to the

major metropolitan areas, however egregious the situation may be
around Boston, New York, Chicago, and Washington. All across
America county lines are as fixed as state lines, and comprehensive
adjustment and reclassification of cities, towns, and villages are rare
to nonexistent.[18] Here and there, one can find a successful case of
"annexation" by which a city is enabled to spread out its boundaries,
and there has been something of a trend toward consolidation of
school districts,[19] but these are exceptions that mostly prove the rule
that the American local government system has neither the will nor
the way to rethink its structure. As measured against even a mildly
rational ideal, the contours and categorization of American local
government from the states on down remain crazy quilt, ramshackle,
and essentially unchanging.

In the context of this book's understanding of liberal democracy
as the operative, day by day, ideology of American politics, it is not
difficult to understand why this should be the case. The extant system is a complex of entrenched interests. These, one by one, are
directly motivated to preserve themselves and enhance their own development. The political system, on its ideological side, is amply
geared from the top to the very bottom both to be sympathetic to
and to facilitate all such efforts. The pitch lies decisively against reformers and against change of any kind, no matter how reasonable.

There is an important spinoff point from this observation. Because the patterns of American local government are so fixed, even
if only in the culture of politics, the legal whip that in formal law
they are all creatures of the states that chartered them is feeble indeed. The horror stories about the various state legislatures, in fits
of political pique, exercising their constitutional right to abolish legally this or that city remain just that, horror stories that, however
often retold in the textbooks, have little general significance.[20] What
does have general significance is that the facts of local government
political entrenchment have effectively extended the character of the
federal relationships that exist among the states and the federal government to the relationships that obtain among all the other local
authorities and between them and their nominal masters in state
capitals and in Washington.

Individual relationships between particular governments are
subject to many kinds of variation. Cities can get into deep trouble,
and states can subject them to various degrees of fiscal tutelage. The
federal government, with its outsized resources of money and other
advantages, can impose, especially through grant-in-aid arrangements, whole programs together with standards for performance on
broad types and classes of local authorities. Or it can intrude its mas-

sive presence by installing a major facility in a particular locality—or close down one already present. The same effect can result from the federal government's letting a large contract to a local supplier or service center. But however various the particular relationships may be, the overriding and persisting constant is the simple presence of all the authorities great and small, their near-absolute individual entrenchment, and their ingrained proclivities to pursue their own interests with only due respect for the rights of others.

This is the real extent of American federalism, an ideologically driven system that includes not only the federal government and fifty states but also, effectively, tens of thousands of other authorities as well, all encompassed in one comprehensive constitutional system of law and tradition. From that one body of law and tradition they receive their powers and their particular bailiwicks, that is to say, their freedom to pursue their own interests in their own jurisdictions as best as they can. If for American local government in myth the name of the game is confederal social egalitarianism, then for local government in ideology the name of the game is federal libertarianism: within the limits of the law, I go my way, you go yours.

A final observation may make this point vivid. In Washington, we all know that placed about the city are the embassies of the major foreign powers to represent, protect, and enhance the interests of their respective governments. These foreign embassies can be thought of as the prototypes for a large number of other groups who place their representatives in headquarters around Washington. For example, it is useful to think of the lobbyists who work for the American Medical Association, the National Rifle Association, and the hosts of other private groups with an active interest in Washington politics as "ambassadors." It is useful also to notice that most of the states in the American federal union have placed these sorts of "ambassadors" in Washington. So too have all the major cities. Moreover, in various ways, the other groups and classes of local government authorities around the country have found ways of making their presence felt in the nation's capital. All are there in deference to the dictates of liberal representative government, and their presence and that of their officers and their staffs says something important about the character of the American federal union.

The American Local Government Process

Fragmentation of power between tens of thousands of governments, fragmentation rendered increasingly haphazard by neglect and the passage of time, best characterizes the structure of American local government. This is a double problem. One aspect of it is simply the question of numbers. It is not only that there are eighty thousand units of government in sum; it is also the fact, to mention one example, that more than thirty-five thousand of these units have their own police forces.[21] These forces range in size from the nearly thirty thousand officers on the New York City force to the one- and two-officer forces characteristically employed by tiny towns and villages all across rural America. The average size is less than a dozen.[22] The consequence is not only fragmentation and confusion that not even the most heroic efforts to achieve coordination and common standards of professionalism can overcome; it is also and more seriously an inevitable understanding of "crime" as a series of isolated, particular acts of wrongdoing, a traffic infraction here, a murder there, each to be "solved" by having the perpetrators apprehended, tried, and individually punished. The meaning of this fragmentation is more than that, it is hard to marshall the forces necessary to confront nationally syndicated crime operations. More fundamentally, it is that the *social* dimensions of America's "crime problem" do not even come into view. This fragmentation means that it is near impossible, in the context of actual police work, even to conceive of a national policy on crime.

Then there is the fact that the fragmentation has become over time so haphazard as to approach the irrational. Why should people who run the city of Boston, the hub of a major metropolitan region, be required to halt their thinking and theorizing about how to develop a tax base to support the increasing cost of public services, about where to route arterial highways, about how to develop abandoned and decaying buildings, and so forth, simply because such thinking and theorizing bumps up against antique, irrationally confining boundaries? One of the most serious of such problems is that of siting public housing for the poor. The inner city needs such housing. But surrounding, prosperous suburbs not only do not need it but are determined not to have it.[23] The result is that either much less of such housing is built, which is one kind of irrationality, or that it is increasingly concentrated in downtown areas, which is another kind of irrationality.

This kind of reflection on fragmentation between local governments is an essential introduction to the internal organization and operation of local governments. However, fragmentation between governments is only half the story. The other half is fragmentation within governments.

The essential patterns of American local government in formal organization are those of the federal government in Washington carried to extremes. Liberal democratic ideology calls for representative government. This is institutionalized as a broad rule into a two-chamber legislature and an independent executive with considerable legislative powers, the whole spelled out and encased in a fixed legal frame maintained by the courts. This is the classic mixed government design, and it is fair to say that it is predominant through American local government. All the states (save Nebraska, whose unicameral "experiment" has never been imitated elsewhere) follow it exactly, as do the mayor/council systems of all the major cities and most of the smaller ones as well.[24] Variations found elsewhere, it can be argued, are all variations from the one basic pattern.

The most common variation is an elected board or commission with a professionally recruited and civil service tenured executive directly responsible to it.[25] This is much the most common pattern for school districts and seems justified by the professionally designed single service these authorities supply. That seems to be the reasoning also behind the adoption of so-called city-manager systems by a scattering of smaller cities, and for comparable systems in many county governments.

What is being appealed to is the sense that local government is the provider of services. In a taxpayers' democracy, what is required is the professional (nonpartisan), expeditious, and efficient provision of services: health care and income support for the indigent; waste disposal, fire, police, water services; zoning and building regulation; roads and parking facilities; library, recreational, and counseling services for youth; financial, planning, and other support services for developers and industrialists; and so forth. If this perspective can be used to argue for placing the management of a school system in the hands of a tenured, professional school superintendent only generally responsible to an elected board (and more fundamentally for the separation of the educational function from the regular local government authority structure into an independently constituted governmental authority), then the approach can be used to argue comprehensively for the squirreling away of all kinds of services into independently situated nooks and crannies of the local government structure where, supposedly, in their isolation they can be freed from political, partisan interference.

This is a fragmentation that breeds fragmentation. In most authorities, as we have seen, the mayor, governor, county executive, or whatever, is already fragmented away from the legislative chambers. These executive figures have further hived off from their nominal authority a succession of responsibilities that are passed on to a wide variety of variously constituted independent boards, commissions, and authorities. Moreover, this formal fragmentation of the executive breeds a mirror effect on the bureaucracy that remains under the nominal direction of the regular executive head. Its various branches develop and entrench a sense of their own distinct professional identity and a claim to manage their own affairs in their own terms. All of this is given a further twist by the long tradition in American local and state government that calls for the election, separately, of not only the leading executive figure (governor, mayor, town supervisor, county executive, etc.) but also of several or more of his or her executive associates (lieutenant governor, attorney general, comptroller, town clerk, sheriff, etc.). Nominally, at election time, the parties put up "tickets" to fill all these offices, with one "team" united under a single banner. But all the participants learn early on that they should stand shoulder to shoulder with their party colleagues only if it is clearly in their personal interest to do so. They know well that in the American liberal democratic environment of representative government, the underlying truth is that it is every politician and his or her clients for themselves.

That is the underlying truth of the whole of this argument. It began by honoring the name of nonpartisan professionalism. But the field of American liberal democracy is pitched more toward the effects of these arrangements than to their rationale. Whatever the professional needs may be, the effect of recognizing them is to split up the public into interests requiring more and more particularized services. The talk may be in terms of educational theory, engineering competence, or fiscal wisdom, but the effect is to cement parents, contractors, insurance agents, and bankers into self-conscious groups able to make their demands felt distinctly and concretely.[26] The name given to the game is "professionalism"; the effect is "representative government" carried to institutionalized extremes.

The general consequence of this whole fragmentation process is to turn American local government into a legal maze through which even experienced lawyers can thread their way only with difficulty and great patience.[27] To maintain distinctions, define responsibilities, and enforce standards, rules are piled upon regulations upon statutes. And with great regularity disputes end up not in election campaigns but in court. In American local government, judges increasingly find themselves immersed in the problems of administrative agencies. The involvement of judges in the administrative problems of prisons and the application of desegregation plans for schools are only the most obvious of such cases. Is this a symptom of a general malaise in American local government? What short of a total recasting of the system could cure it—or at least bring it under control?

Grassroots Barons

What in conclusion can we say about these Americans, the men and women who occupy the elective and appointive offices of the American local government maze and make the system do what it does? They are Protestant Bourgeois people, like all the rest of us, who strive to serve the people as best they can and, at the same time, make the powers of their offices work for them personally and individually. It is this contradiction between goals that earns them the title "grassroots barons."

They answer to the grassroots, in response to the canons of social democracy. They are servants of the people and hail the honor of being so. In this guise, they can—and often do—tap the wells of compassion that drench the heart of the American political psyche. Aided, sometimes even abetted, by private philanthropy but often of their own initiative, and sometimes it must be admitted at the dire bidding of outside authorities such as the federal government, local governments at every level all across America undertake works not just of compassion but of recovery and hope, too. For the nation's unfortunate, all too often local government assistance is not only the last resort but the only support. A very high proportion of the modern American welfare state is operated and administered by local government authorities, even if much of the funding and supervision comes from elsewhere.[28] And much of this work is utterly thankless, as in the care of the vagrant, the unemployable, the psychotic, the congenitally retarded, the permanently handicapped, the terminally ill poor, and the criminally insane.

Yet the picture is not completely bleak. At least some of the great state universities are veritable jewels in the local government diadem. Local government authorities across America have been the source of countless cultural facilities and events, and they have provided parks and other recreational facilities to a standard of which any nation could be justly proud. The record of American local government proves that even at the grassroots there can be a concrete practical response to American mythic ideals of social justice and achievement.

The difficulty is that the record also shows that the response to these mythic needs has been chaotic, dispersed, incomplete, and, on too many occasions and in too many ways, inefficient, corrupt, callous, even cruel and brutal. The unevenness is pandemic. The explanation, once again, is confusion over goals, means, and styles. While striving to be good social democrats, American's local government operatives are at the same time trying to be liberal democrats, and all the while trying to run a system growing more and more out of joint with changes in demographic conditions, technological development, and patterns of private economic organization and production.

A major factor in this situation is often said to be citizen ignorance and apathy. There is some truth to this charge. So far as most citizens care—the proportion is surely well over half—local government is mostly invisible government. While many citizens will know the name of their current local chief executive, especially if he or she is a big-city mayor, and perhaps also the state governor, few could name their state assembly member or senator, their local council member or other elected officials, much less explain why, how, and when these people were elected or what they have been doing since.[29] And the ignorance extends to where local government headquarters are located and what they do. What citizens know seems in most cases to be conditioned by the accident of personal contact over a particular issue: they bought a house, registered a car, paid their taxes. Turnout for local elections is notoriously low, sagging sometimes to less than 10 percent of the available electorate for an isolated primary and rising over 25 percent only if the local contest is coattailing on an exciting national election.[30] One need not look far to find the primary reason for this apathy. No doubt laziness and moral failure are a part of it. But the major factor is the simple fact that local government in America is confusing, complicated, and, frequently enough, irrational and corrupt. It is hard to take an interest in something that fits that description.

On the other hand, the operatives of the system, their friends, relatives, and immediate supporters and clients, know very well what is going on. They are effectively insiders. Shielded by massive citizen inattention, they are left remarkably free to get on with making local government work for them. The situation is not all that different from the liberal democratic elitism we noticed at the national level of American government—except that at the local level it tends to be at once both more extreme and more mundane. Local government barons have their entourages, their personal bailiwicks, their networks of personal relationships, of favors tendered and received, even if all, by national standards, are to an almost petty scale. Likewise grassroots barons practice the political arts of geniality, accessibility, and mutual respect. Perhaps because they are more shielded from public stares, perhaps also because they deal more directly and more frequently with matters that are translatable into mutual rewards, local barons seem more prone to corruption of that characteristically American sort, the kickback and the cut, than their national counterparts. This is the world, after all, that coined the aphorism that "politics ain't beanbag"[31] and that made the distinctions between graft and "honest graft," between "grass eaters" and "meat eaters."[32] Liberal democracy as much as social democracy is an idealism, a vision of how government ought to work. Liberal democracy at the local level as much as at the national level values the honest politician, and in those same terms of "staying bought." It is just that at the local level the price is local, too.

9
The Bureaucracy

We have surveyed thus far in this part of the book the dominant elements of the American political system, its pinnacles of power (the courts, the presidency, the Congress, and their parallels at the state and local levels). We have finally to examine what must seem at times a veritable monster in their midst—namely, ourselves, or at least the vast majority of us, organized rank on rank as the more or less professionalized employees of America's multifarious bureaucratic structures both public and private.

That nearly all of us in modern America are, at least in a technical sense, "bureaucrats" may not be immediately obvious. Yet it is a fact that is easily demonstrated. In any technologically advanced civilization, the great bulk of employed persons earn their livings by performing with definable competence some skill or routine in an institutionalized setting. More difficult to demonstrate is that in America this is a strange fact and, politically, an awkward one.

It is an awkward fact politically because the American federal constitution dates to the eighteenth century. That means that it was composed too early for there to be in it a consistent, focused concern with bureaucratic structures, public or private. Those structures, of course, existed in some profusion in American colonial life, as they had in fact from time immemorial wherever governments and industry went to work in organized ways. But direct, focused concern on these structures, on developing a conceptual vocabulary for grasping their major characteristics and on devising methods for utilizing them efficiently and controlling their operations, did not come among modern nations until well into the nineteenth century. In particular, Americans, whether scholars or politicians, did not learn until that century had come and gone of the work of such theorists of bureaucracy as the German sociologist Max Weber, or more particularly of the development in Great Britain of a legally institutionalized, professionalized civil service. In consequence, neither the American founding document nor the system that was built and entrenched on it made any defined and consistent provision for dealing with the facts of bureaucracy in modern government. The constitution did provide for the nomination of department heads by the president and for their confirmation in office by the Senate. It provided, too, for the president's receiving reports in writing from these officers. And it provided as well for the creation and funding of the departments by the Congress. But all questions about how these departments would be organized and staffed, of how their workloads would be defined, and, most importantly, of how and by whom the administration of them would be overseen, were left not only unanswered but even unasked. The gap left by these questions is the largest hiatus in the Constitution, and its untoward consequences can be seen at every level of American government to this day. Thus, bureaucracy, for all its immensity, in a very real sense arrived in the American political system unannounced, unwelcomed, even undefined. That is an awkward fact.

What makes it also a strange fact is that bureaucracy in America, for all its size and importance, remains also an alien presence, fundamentally at odds with the dominant Protestant and Bourgeois elements of the American political psyche. It is this alien status that makes bureaucracy in America a strange "third term," a threatening, new, and different way of defining government and of organizing and measuring its work.

Bureaucracy in its own perspective means elegance. It means rationality in work. It means efficiency, consistency, comprehensiveness, reliability, accountability, proficiency, and competence; in a word, bureaucracy stands in its own terms for professionalism. But in the perspective of the American political system as a whole, bureaucracy means something more than that—and less. Bureaucracy in America is layered sandwichlike between Protestant/Bourgeois political masters above, in all their schizophrenic confusion, and the great mass of citizens and clients below, in all their individualized hopes and greed, apathy and activism. In this broader context of the American political scene as a whole, bureaucracy is first of all significant for the evidence it provides that the nation really is trying to reach its mythic ideals of social justice and its ideological goals of personal security and the advancement of private enterprise. Through bureaucracies of every size and shape, Americans work hard to fulfill their political commitments. Yet, the system also imposes on the bureaucratic structures within it a weight of contradictory demands. The wondrous goals proclaimed by myth, the bureaucratic mind is bound to find hopelessly imprecise and ill-defined. At the same time, the bureaucratic structures will find their energies and resources milked off for every conceivable ideological range of personal objectives that are as bureaucratically indefensible as they are politically indispensable. Either way, it would seem, bureaucracy—and America—loses.

There is a fundamental tension between the theory, the idea, of bureaucracy and its American environment. Americans with good reason suspect that bureaucracy is a European invention better suited to Napoleonic dreams of a metric system imposed on the order of the nation. Its ideals of flawless impersonality and hyperrationality offend the American sense of a necessary idiosyncrasy in our individualism. Yet "the bureaucratic experience" has come to dominate our lives.

It dominates our lives because of the brute fact that bureaucracy, its principles of human organization, its methods and processes, its instruments and goals, are essential to any community aspiring to modern standards of technological achievement.[1] More than that, even in America, bureaucracy appeals to our shattered sense of community and, at the same time, to our needs for personal accomplishment.

Nevertheless, the fundamental and broad incongruence between bureaucracy and the American political environment remains. The clash between, on the one hand, the ideals of rational, professional competence and, on the other, the Protestant/Bourgeois complex of loving faith and prudent self-interest is a permanent and ineradicable feature of the political system. Its inevitable consequence is that the record of American bureaucratic accomplishment is decidedly mixed. More seriously, it is this ultimate and inner contradiction between the principles of bureaucracy and its American environment that has rendered the American bureaucratized middle class an emasculated proletariat that labors mightily to service and sustain a political system it is powerless to control, reform, or even understand.

The Bureaucratic Mind in America

Stereotypically, the primary feature of the bureaucratic mind is its cool rationality. At the same level of analysis, the primary features of the Bourgeois and the Protestant minds are emotions. The primary positive emotion of the Bourgeois personality is desire, more particularly the desire for things manufactured for human delight. The primary negative emotion of this mentality is fear, insecurity in the possession of things, including one's own life and property, and the free use of these. The primary positive emotion of Protestantism is love, this being defined as an exultant faith in and hope for others. Its primary negative emotions are guilt and grief, shame for self and sorrow for others. To all these emotions, as they stress and pull the American psyche this way and that, the bureaucratic mind is not so much opposed as simply qualitatively different, alien. If it has emotions, they are cool and controlled. Its essential concerns are intellectual, for order, comprehensiveness, regularity, and predictability.

The standardized American, that is, the ordinary, flesh-and-blood, middle-class American acculturated to be in all things a success, plunges into these three stereotypes—Bourgeois, Protestant, and bureaucratic—to give meaning and definition to life and work. As each day dawns, he or she is ambitious for his or her Bourgeois self, and ambitious, too, but wrenchingly, for his or her Protestant soul. Yet the arrival at the bureaucratic workplace (the "office") is like entering still another world. Note these differences of special significance to politics.

In the Protestant/Bourgeois world, politics is power. Political problems all have to do with the creation, legitimization, and use of power. Bourgeois man craves it, power after power, for it is his hope for personal security. Protestants, in their heart of hearts, would surrender it all in service to the lord. Either way, power is the name of the game, power *over* others, power that is arbitrary, absolute, and awful. But in the bureaucratic world, the comparable name is not power but authority. Authority is not arbitrary, absolute, and awful; it is always qualified, always defined, always official, and always, above all else, in ideal, reasonable. That is to say, in the bureaucratic world, authority is always institutional. It is the responsible exercise of right and judgment *within* an institutionalized structure for the achievement of reasonable objectives, appropriate to the welfare of the community as a whole.

Protestant/Bourgeois American citizens resent what they take to be the power of the bureaucratic officials; they take it to be an infringement of their individual moral autonomy. The officials believe, justifiably, that they have been misunderstood; in their understanding, they were just doing their duty, responsibly, rationally, authoritatively.

The contrast between the Protestant/Bourgeois conception of power *over*, as something qualitatively different from bureaucratic authority *within*, points to another issue separating these worlds. The stereotypical Bourgeois person scurries in freedom after a private "interest"; the Protestant elects to dedicate self to loving service to others in the community fellowship. In contrast, abstractly, the bureaucratic mind rationally directs work to satisfy a "public good." What is centrally at issue here is a level of concreteness. The Bourgeois individual seeks a materially experienced self-satisfaction, actual desires for this or that. The Protestant reaches out to love the reality of the destitute and forlorn. But the bureaucratic mind intellectualizes all that. It perceives not real people, wanting and waiting, but "cases" coming in a rationally paced progression up the line. And these cases are in turn perceived not as independent pieces in an aggregate but as elements in an abstractly conceptualized community good. Anything less than that would be skewed sharply toward the concrete sum of actually experienced private interests. The only sure way to the "public good" is by abstraction, by hypothesizing a good that purely reasonable creatures could will in the interest of a generalized humankind.

Then there is the matter of personal success and how it is to be determined and rewarded. The Bourgeois person seeks victory, triumph either up to personal limits or, more likely, over rivals. The Protestant sense of a personal quest is even more powerful, even if the measures of its achievement are more vague and more spiritualized, a personal sense of becoming, of being authentically in relationship with self and others in the essentials of a directly experienced existence. But the bureaucratic personality is somewhere else altogether. Bland, even banal, its goal is simply to do the job that has to be done and to do it with professional competence, efficiency, and dispatch.

The Bureaucratic Idea

The idea of bureaucracy that sits so uneasily in the American environment derives its innate elegance from its aim to rationalize work. The objective is to do this absolutely and comprehensively. To achieve this objective, bureaucracy must succeed at three things: it must thoroughly define the work to be done; it must bring to bear on that work a pure competence to do it; and it must retain total control over that competence as it does its work.[2]

Bureaucracy defines work by conceptualizing it. It puts the job of taking letters back and forth between named individuals into the concept of "home mail delivery." No doubt centrally involved in this process, if only by consequence, is the division of labor. From Adam Smith on, commentators have massed their attention on the improvements in efficiency that the division and specialization of labor engenders.[3] But the dividing up of work into specialized steps is itself the product of a larger idea, the root concept of the routinization of labor.

This is where bureaucracy gets its reputation. On the one hand, routinized labor is infinitely boring. By its reduction to routine, all the excitement goes out of work. Not only its outcome but every step along the way becomes exactly predictable. Anywhere that is not the case is a "failure" and denigratingly attributed to "human error." On the other hand, this is also where bureaucracy achieves the essentials of elegance. To seize in concept the messy world of actual experience is an intellectual feat of great purity. Yet that is exactly what the training manual for the simplest, small-bore pistol does, as does also the whole set of manuals that prescribe correct procedures for the use, maintenance, and repair of huge bombers and all their associated weapon systems. The ever more complex but still essentially equivalent intellectual feat is involved in designing the whole of a highly automated assembly line for automobile engines, or in structuring the offices and personnel, rules and regulations, and forms by which the nation collects its income taxes. The thought—the pure concept—of that last example, of the population of the whole nation in all its variety and individuality being reduced to one comprehensive, integrated process bending pen to paper to pay the government its due is especially a mental wonder, a final, complete picture of intellectual elegance. Just to harbor that thought, let alone to admire its transcendence, requires a certain kind of imagination, a certain kind of character, but one that lies at the heart of the bureaucratic mind.

The standards of bureaucratic success are impersonal. They are set neither by personal selection nor by transcendent commitment. They are set—and judged—objectively, impersonally, by one's professional peers. It is for one's fellow workers in the bureaucracy to decide who should be promoted to the rank of general, district supervisor, resident surgeon, or judge. More generally, it is for duly constituted boards, commissions, and colleges of professional peers to define and impose with total disinterestedness courses of training, standards of admission, and the programs of examination for individual aspirants. The process is an idea, an idea by which a whole army of rational-professionals can be recruited, trained, and employed in the public interest.

In modern governments, including the American goverments, this army—as an idea—is given a political meaning by a political theory that encompasses and contains it.[4] This theory has two sides, one internal to bureaucracy itself, and one relating bureaucracy to its external environment. The theory says that, internally, bureaucracy must be totally coherent. This means that the divisions and stages in the work to be done must be clearly drawn and sharply defined by appropriately written rules, regulations, and descriptions. It means, too, that to ensure that all stages in the work process proceed cooperatively, without overlap or gap, and without conflict or unprogrammed rivalry, workers will be continuously accountable to supervisors operating within clear limits of spans of control. It means finally that the supervisors, in clusters, will themselves be supervised by ascending and narrowing ranks of supervisors to some final pinnacle of control and authority, an ultimate source that by its solitary unity insures singleness of purpose and direction for the whole structure. The pyramidic image approaches a perfection that is, once again, elegant.

Moreover, so bureaucratic political theory continues, the pyramid can be harnessed externally, from both the top and the bottom. In concept, the bureaucratic army is always and essentially a service, whether military or civil. Indifferently, for all and sundry, it works for every one of us, encapsulated as a mass into the idea of the public interest, the common good. The bureaucratic army is working for us even as it collects our taxes, which is precisely why the Internal Revenue Service is called a "service." Even in the extreme case, it is working for us when it arrests one of us for criminal behavior. Obviously, those of us who are law-abiding folk wish criminals in our midst to be apprehended and punished. More to the bureaucratic point, criminals themselves are to be understood as profiting by their apprehension because by this "service," the society of which even they are members is protected—from *their* own criminality.

But it is in the nature of a servant, so the theory runs on, to have a master. The master of the public service is in the first instance the public itself. In a democracy, the theory continues, the public, through the electoral process, is able to make known at least its generalized reactions to the service it has been receiving from the bureaucracy. Through elections, the public can also pick and choose between the policies with which candidates have identified themselves for the future direction of the public service.

Crucial to the articulation of this theory of citizen control over the public service is a distinction between the roles of the elected officials and of the bureaucracy. The line between them is usually called the "political" level, to distinquish between "policy" and "administration." In practice, no absolute distinction between policy and administration can be long maintained, but for the purposes of democratic life, a pro forma distinction between them is essential. Policy is the business of the master, of the elected official. He or she holds office because, with public support expressed through the electoral process, he or she is imposing on the political system the public policies he or she favors. His or her tenure in office is, in concept, contingent on loyalty to those policies and the public support received because of that loyalty. This means most especially that the public official is not elected or sustained in office because of competence, but exclusively for policy leadership.

Meanwhile, the role of the bureaucracy below the ministerial level is or at least should be exclusively concerned with the administration of whatever public policies they are directed by their elected masters to carry out. In utter passivity, they wait to be told what to do and then, having been told, do it, competently, rationally, professionally.

Even in theory, however, there are limits. If a civil or military servant is ordered to do an act that is professionally or personally offensive, he or she even in theory can refuse. If a procurement officer is ordered to award a contract to one party rather than another to facilitate an obvious process of corruption, he or she can refuse on grounds of personal honor. The extreme case demonstrates what can be called the principle of the last scruple. Nevertheless, up to that last scruple, bureaucratic servants are still servants, and without a master they are directionless, lost.

The distinction between policy and administration is made largely by reference to the people responsible for each: elected officials with temporary tenure for the first, the permanently tenured, professionally recruited and trained, merely competent civil service for the latter. There is more to it than that, especially on the policy side of the distinction. Administration is particular, exact, and has to do almost entirely with means and methods. Policy is more complex. On the one hand, it has to do with goals and values, and these can be difficult to specify, both in terms of their own definition and in terms of concrete situations that would constitute their achievement. How does one go about "operationalizing" the notion that all citizens "are created equal"? On the other hand, beyond value orientation, policy setting requires both breadth of scope and consistency of articulation. Policy is something more than just a range of miscellaneous decisions in a particular topic area. Policy is not just an aggregate of accidents. The charge that America "has no foreign policy in the Persian Gulf" means that our activities in that area are simply a scattering of reactions to whatever is happening out there, that we have no coherent, coordinated set of plans and actions for achieving defined and differentiated objectives.

Public policy, in ideal concept, is not improvisation. It is a thought-out program of coordinated initiatives and responses for pursuing in a steady way the allocation of competencies and other resources to achieve a defined good in the public interest. Give that kind of program, a true public policy, to a professionally recruited and trained, rationally organized and disciplined bureaucracy, and the bureaucracy will do the job competently, predictably, and with full accountability.

It is essential to an understanding of the unhappy state of bureaucracy in the American political environment to keep the purity, the elegance, and the step-by-step specification of this bureaucratic ideal in mind. It may be necessary, in fact, to refine it beyond the basic exposition so far presented. For example, to preserve the integrity of the "chain of command" that links the ascending levels of a bureaucratic pyramid, it is essential to theory and almost always useful in practice to distinguish sharply between staff and line positions and confine each to its particular type of operation. Line people are the ones in the field, who actually do the job—producing the goods, fighting the war, whatever—and also the people directly controlling their work, rising in a clear chain up to the chief executive officer in charge of the whole operation. But even in small bureaucracies, the "boss" will need staff help to write letters, answer the phone, make appointments, and so on. In large bureaucracies, beyond the obvious tasks, whole arrays of staff may be required to write speeches, prepare option papers, receive and digest information, maintain records, and transmit commands and recommendations. Troubles begin when the staff people doing all this "eyes-and-ears-of-the-boss" work start going beyond it either by inserting themselves and their personal judgments into the chain-of-command network or by bypassing the people in the field and taking on operational functions themselves. There are enormous temptations for staff people to do this kind of thing, especially on an episodic basis without established patterns of accountability, and people in the field are often virtually paranoid about the possibilities of its happening. What is certain is that its actual occurrence is almost always destructive, one way or another, of established patterns of control and responsibility.[5]

The American Administrative State

The bureaucratic ideal, in all its Platonic elegance, can be carried to the pitch of an absolute extreme: the task of governing the nation, for all its near-infinite complexity, is one task, and, in concept, it should therefore be entrusted to one comprehensive, totally coordinated bureaucracy.

The first blow to this ideal delivered by the American environment is that this country is a democracy, both liberal and social. Either way, the task of governing the nation must be shared between the public authorities and a host of private ones each of which claims both measurable autonomy and a significant bureaucratic structure of its own.

This is no small point, especially in practice. No doubt, it is possible to think of areas of public concern in which private influence is—or should be—minimal, say, the execution of national security policy. In this area, the use of private individuals to carry out public functions, as occurred in certain aspects of the Iran–Contra affair, brings expressions of shock from knowledgeable figures. But these attitudes can be sustained only by ignoring the enormous role that private defense-related industries play in creating usable American military power. These companies steadfastly maintain their private character even when their workbooks bulge for years ahead almost exclusively with government contracts.

Much the more usual pattern occurs when public authorities and their bureaucracies, in very obvious but exceedingly complex and difficult ways, must mesh with a vast number of private bureaucracies. Consider the complex area of health care. Medicine, as practiced by doctors, remains in America a largely private-enterprise system, and the direct involvement of public authorities in the treatment of patients, the Veterans Administration and other public hospitals to one side, is relatively minimal. Nevertheless, the involvement of public authorities at every level of government in the total system of health-care delivery in America is continuous, extensive, intricate, and often chaotic, especially in the areas of service subsidization (as in the Medicaid and Medicare programs), hospital construction, research support, epidemic control, regulation, and inspection.[6] Coordinating the private and public efforts over such a widespread domain of intense human concern would be difficult in any event; it is rendered doubly so by the dominance in the private sector of the traditional American Protestant/Bourgeois morality of love and profit and in the public sector of the more purely rational bureaucratic ideal. The consequence, we can safely assert, is that every program and every decision in the American health-care delivery system bears the marks of a more or less serious and deep-seated confusion.[7] This confusion not only extends across the policy and administration levels but penetrates as well to the level of ethical principles, to the levels of habits of mind.[8]

These examples could be multiplied many times over. Even in police work, a field we are accustomed to regard as almost exclusively the domain of the public authorities (wrongly, it so happens, because private security forces abound all across the country), there is a fundamental disparity. This disparity occurs between the ethical understanding that puts the individual officer through training, into uniform, and out on the beat, and the ethical understanding that guides the lives of the shopkeepers, homeowners, pedestrians, and drivers on the streets that officer patrols. The officer is there to enforce the law and keep the public peace, impersonally, efficiently, in the name of the public interest. But the law says the officer must do all this while observing scrupulously the rights of all citizens to find fellowship with each other and to pursue their own interests with maximum possible freedom. In the eyes of that officer, the people out there are all on the take, one way or another. So why should the police be different? Are we not *all* Americans? Why should the cop be the only one not allowed to say, what's in it for me?

The strain of being public actors in a mostly private world is not the only source of unhappiness for the bureaucratic ideal in America. There is also the problem of fragmentation in the ranks of the public authorities themselves. The public/private strain produces envy, suspicion, and cynicism. But the fragmentation of the governmental authorities, the supposed masters of the civil service, breeds frustration, often monumental and extended.

Fragmentation can be called external when it splits up bureaucracies between governments. Of course, the ultimate bureaucratic ideal of one massive bureaucracy confronting the one task of governing the whole country in every aspect is both absurd and a horror. But does democracy require we go to the other extreme of dividing up the managerial task of government between eighty thousand autonomous units of government?[9] All these governments, whatever their particular sizes, situations, and assignments, are confronting problems that can be regarded as national in scope.

Take the problem of education. A persistent strand in the American political tradition suggests that education is essentially a local concern, perhaps with supervision from the state governments.[10] Certainly, at its beginning, the Reagan administration was of this view, and it came into office determined to abolish the federal government's then recently established Department of Education. But after a few years of grappling with educational problems from the federal government's perspective, it not only desisted from efforts to put the department out of business, it appointed as secretary a noticeably articulate, vigorous, and, moreover, conservative person who made no secret of his intent to show leadership in the field and to encourage what some thought amounted to a revolution in American educational practice. In so doing, the Reagan administration joined a chorus of public figures who had long been accustomed to talking about education in America in national terms, using phrases like "a nation's future is its children."

Furthermore, the Reagan administration's educational philosophy was summed up in the phrase "education for excellence." That is to say, it was prepared to commit federal efforts to realizing a policy that would assign disproportionate resources to educating bright students to very high levels of achievement, with corresponding deductions in effort for those who are less bright. What chance would the federal government have in trying to impose so controversial a policy on the fifty states and the thousands upon thousands of local school boards? It has little institutional machinery beyond what has been called "jawboning"—that is, speech making by the controversial secretary—to effect such a policy imposition. As an added thought, what role in all this should the private school establishment, both secondary and college level, play in this "national" effort?

But fragmentation of bureaucracies between governments may sometimes seem a lesser problem compared to what happens within individual governments. Within every level of American government, definably unified problems are fractured between the work of different agencies and departments. Think of an American ambassador at a major embassy overseas. This individual is charged with representing the interests of our nation in that particular country. He or she will have a hard enough time keeping up with what is going on above his or her head, between the secretary of state in Washington and the host country's foreign secretary, or even above that between the president in Washington and the host country's own chief executive. But what of the situation below the ambassador? In the embassy, there will be the usual assortment of Foreign Service and other State Department personnel over whom the ambassador will have some direct control. But what of the three military attachés? If large American forces are stationed in that country, the responsibilities of these individuals may be considerable. To whom are they answerable, the ambassador or their immediate superiors in the Pentagon? In practice, it is much more to the latter than the former. The Department of Defense's outlook on major national security questions can be noticeably its own. And what of the CIA operatives who may be posted undercover on the embassy's staff? Will they keep the ambassador informed of their activities? And, to keep the argument running, what of the activities of representatives of such departments as Commerce, Agriculture, and the Treasury who may be occasionally or permanently stationed in that country and working out of the embassy building? Just being abroad does not alter their essential character of being, at the operative level, responsible to their own higher commands back in Washington. In sum, the position of the ambassador in an embassy overseas is hardly different except in scale from that, administratively, of the president back at home, chief of everything only in myth.

Take one final example, one that compounds both kinds of bureaucratic fragmentation we have so far been discussing: the problem of the nation's homeless. The sufferings of this element in our society has in recent years attracted much attention, most of it focused on the grossly inadequate and often chaotic, even irrational, care these people receive from the nation's "welfare establishment."[11]

Homelessness is a national problem; no part of the country is without the homeless in its midst. It is also a complex, multifaceted problem, in terms of both its causes and its consequences. The homeless are homeless because, in part, they are poor; but they are poor for many and often very different reasons, because they are unemployed, underemployed, or unemployable. They may end up in one or another of these categories because they have no skills or are not trainable; because they have children or are children or are aged; because they are sick, either mentally or physically, or have character defects so severe no one would hire them; because they are victims of discrimination or are too demoralized to make a favorable impression in a job interview. On the other hand, they may be unemployed or underemployed because there are no jobs, or at least no jobs for persons even approaching their circumstances. But there is a whole other side to this problem. The homeless are homeless not just because they are poor. In major part, they are homeless because there are no homes available for them, homes that even with welfare benefits they could afford. Across the country there is a grave shortage of residential properties for the very poor, in a word, slums.[12] Finally, the problem of the homeless, as already partly indicated, cannot be looked at in isolation. It is deeply entangled with chronic unemployment in the economy generally, with breakdowns in the public school system, with failures of the criminal-justice system, with racism and sexism, and with complex patterns of urban and rural decline and renewal. At times, it must seem that the problem of America's homeless is simply a byproduct of all these other problems.

It would be totally off the mark to suggest that America's homeless population receives no attention. On the contrary, a veritable army of public servants and private charitable organizations are involved. All levels of American government are involved, with a host of their departments, agencies, and bureaus. But the overall result remains a mass of confusion, lapses, contradictions, inefficiency, and countless examples of, on the one hand, gross insensitivity and, on the other hand, acts of patience, kindness, and even love. What is entirely lacking is any defensible, comprehensive, coordinated effort cutting across all bureaucratic jurisdictional lines and attacking the root causes of the problem. That would approach the bureaucratic ideal. Instead, what we have are programs that effectively warehouse the homeless and their psychic and physical problems in more or less temporary shelters under conditions that frequently defy not only description but also rational explanation. And despite it all, many of the homeless simply get left on the streets.

What all these examples of bureaucratic fragmentation and confusion demand is a sense of direction and purpose, a strong sense of institutional leadership that not only is forward looking but that stems from a consistent and comprehensive understanding of the nature of the problems to be overcome. That kind of leadership is especially required over American bureaucracies because of the almost overwhelming tendencies for their structures to be torn apart from the bottom by the multitude of interests they service and in time come to represent. In a liberal democratic society, these interests are plentiful. They are also powerful and can reward and punish as they choose.

It is precisely this kind of leadership that the American political system is ill-equipped to provide. The bureaucratic ideal calls for singleness of purpose and unity of control and direction. What the American political system, in the name of checks and balances, pluralism, accessibility, concurrent majority, incrementalism, and so forth, in fact supplies is fragmentation from the top as well as from the bottom, barely disguised by mythic effusions of greater or lesser relevance.

Most of the mythic effusions come from America's chief executives, the president, state governors, large-city mayors, and so on down the line. One by one, they march to the bridge of their particular piece of the ship of state and call to the helmsman to take it in some general direction. These sweep-of-the-arm statements are not totally without significance. Taken together over time they add up to definitions of the nation's mythic understandings of its needs and challenges. Problems are identified, concerns are voiced and popularized, and perhaps most important, bureaucracies are alerted.

But, as we have seen, America's mythic heroes are far less able than is often supposed to do very much at translating their visions into practical, workable programs. In particular, they are virtually powerless to prevent the major interests from plucking off bits and pieces of the bureaucratic structures they nominally head. Some especially popular and aggressive governors and big-city mayors have marginally more success in this area than others, and particularly more than the president.[13] This is largely because they are somewhat more successful at dominating the legislative bodies that accompany them in the governmental process. But even the most prominently successful of these figures must count their victories in episodic terms that fall far short of the comprehensive standards of the bureaucratic ideal.[14] Moreover, many of them all too often find that the programs and projects they initiated in the space of a few years take on a life of their own and, sustained by the new constituencies they have generated, slip away from central executive control.

Then there is the role of the legislative bodies, especially of Congress, in the administrative process. In a bureaucratic perspective, to whom is a departmental secretary or ordinary bureau chief in Washington responsible? To whom should he or she look for budgetary support, for policy guidance, for security and advancement in his or her own career? Nominally, the words of the Constitution seem to suggest the first loyalty of a career-minded civil servant should be to the president to whom he or she may owe nomination or appointment to office. Moreover, that initial appointment may well have been part of the president's general effort to ensure political control of the whole bureaucracy in terms of his electoral victory.

On the other hand, it takes no long residency in Washington to learn that, other things being equal, the natural allies of any bureau are the clientele groups it services, and such support is most easily translated into ongoing success and good fortune through Congress. It is Congress, or, more exactly, its committee system, that puts the final numbers into the budget and writes the fine print of the statutes authorizing projects and programs.

In the face of these realities, the ordinary bureau chief in Washington will play a double game. Outwardly there will be loyalty to the president. There will be cooperation with the Office of Management and Budget's budget-making processes. There will be supportive appearances before the press and even at hearings in Congress. More covertly, there will be cultivation of close relationships with the relevant interest groups, and, just as assiduously, there will be a careful feeding of information, plans, and hopes, to the necessary members of Congress.[15]

What kind of guidance, what kind of policy leadership, does Congress supply the bureaucracy for its docility in these matters? Piecemeal, patchwork, incremental legislation arrived at through the construction of concurrent majorities. Congress is a legislative body, Congress aspires to give policy direction in conformity with the bureaucratic ideal, only in myth. In ideology, Congress is Washington's primary instrument for harmonizing the diverse claims of the competing bureaus.

This discussion will have left a false impression if it has seemed to suggest anything other than the truth that the great bulk of America's civil servants are honest, dedicated, hard-working, and competent. What it has tried to suggest is that these public servants undertake their work within a political context that from their bureaucratic perspective is far from ideal. As they go about their efforts to do their work, they are confronted by political constraints and contradictions that frustrate them at every turn. They can, mostly, do their immediate tasks: letters do get delivered; weapons get bought; welfare checks get issued; money, to the tune of billions, gets spent. But every larger effort to effect public policies that would be genuinely both "public" and "policy" must face increasing difficulties the higher it aims.

Frustration of dedication, hard work, and competence can take many forms, from apathy to arrogance, from petty corruption to outrageous personal ambition. Often enough it takes the form of the mortality of desire. In the early 1950s, a book by two distinguished American social scientists was published in the wake of the civic idealism unleashed by the end of World War II. Its title, significantly, is *Politics, Planning, and the Public Interest*.[16] It reads like a novel. It is the story of an effort to bring a federal program of low-income public housing to the city of Chicago. The heroine of the story is Elizabeth Wood, a woman of impeccable credentials and elite background, and the federal government's representative for the program in the Chicago community. The book is essentially a record of her selfless devotion to the housing program, her many partial victories, and her final defeat. That is where the book ends. But there is a sequel to the book, word of mouth, perhaps apocryphal. It is said that a friend by chance found Elizabeth Wood some years later operating an art gallery on New York's exclusive East Side and asked her what had become of her career in the federal government. To this Wood is said to have replied, "You can only break your heart so many times."

III
THE POVERTY OF
AMERICAN POLITICS

As we have pushed forward with our analysis of the American political system, the argument has been studded with analytical assertions one by one, for example: that the system is essentially schizophrenic between its religious and secular impulses, that the founding fathers were intellectually and theoretically confused, that the presidency is simultaneously too strong and too weak, that the Congress is a legislative body only in myth, that bureaucracy does not "belong" in America, and many more. Each of these statements was, it is hoped, interesting in itself. But of more importance was the effort to portray them as bound together in one comprehensive, analytical framework. All these assertions were placed on the single canvas of the American political system's being ambiguously a social democracy in legitimizing myth and a liberal democracy in operative ideology.

Constructing and painting that broad canvas was essentially an exercise in explanation. Questions of evaluation necessarily have cropped up again and again. Like the explanations being advanced, the evaluative questions tended to be theoretical: What consequences could a system designed like this have for good or ill? What costs are necessary to its operation? Are they in concept too much? At the risk of having to recapitulate some of our explanatory material, we must now confront these evaluative questions head on and systematically. Explanation by itself is, at best, interesting; when it is made the basis of evaluation it becomes challenging.

As we approach these evaluative questions, we put ourselves under one immediate restraint. From the outset—which is as far as this book can go—we must judge the system in its own terms. The standards that might be set for it by outsiders, by Plato or Marx or pure reason, are for universalists. Before we can get to that level, we must determine what we think of ourselves—whether we have failed ourselves in our own eyes.

10

The Bourgeois Perspective

Life is a quest, personal and urgent. That is the fundamental formulation of American individualism.[1] In this spirit—and not without paradox—the American citizen, as a recognized and defined member of the political system as a whole, looks to it for support and assistance, for all the help he (and, more recently and to a different scale, she) can get. But, exactly as an integral element of the system, the citizen is typically as schizophrenic as the system itself. He—or she—thereby places on its contradictory capacities contradictory demands. These demands in all their complexity become the standards by which we can measure the system against itself.

Does the system deliver as requested? We can anticipate immediately that the answer will be confused. Simplifying, we can say that the process works two ways.

First, straightfacedly, Bourgeois man, as in Section 8 of Article I of the Constitution, makes known his needs. In general response, the American government has given him huge assistance—but far less than what was requested and often in inferior quality. No doubt, much of this process has been obscured by talk about laissez faire and the like, but the overall record is clear, as will be detailed in the first sections of the present chapter.

Comparably, the Protestant spirit in America has reached for every conceivable opportunity to do good, to realize ideals of social justice, to do the work of the lord, and has been actively encouraged and abetted in doing so by all levels of the American political system. But it has also been diminished, demeaned, and frustrated far below reasonable levels of fulfillment, as Chapter 11 will seek to portray.

These two areas of American experience constitute self-measures of the poverty of American politics. To them can be added the direct frustrations experienced by the rational-professional mind, the bureaucracy, in the American environment; this will be detailed in Chapter 12.

Beyond these areas of direct frustration is another range of experience by which American politics can be judged impoverished by self-measured terms. This is where the elements of the American political psyche, crosscuttingly, stand in judgment on each other. When the system permits—or, worse, actively encourages—Bourgeois excess, Protestant conscience is outraged, and the rational-professional mind is appalled. When Protestant demands go to extremes—perhaps driven there—the Bourgeois mind is contemptuous, and the rational-professional mind is mystified. And when rational-professionalism pushes hard through its constraints, both Bourgeois and Protestant condemnations flow unchecked. All of this judgmentalism will also have to be laid out proportionately in the chapters that follow.

In the end, no one is satisfied. All elements of the American political psyche feel cheated. Worse, all feel misunderstood. Justifiably, each of them must believe that the others are congenitally incapable of, that they lack the intellectual vocabulary for, grasping and dealing constructively with identifiable and urgent problems. It is this persistent, unrelievable mood of intellectual impoverishment that most condemns American politics in its own eyes.

Bourgeois Opportunities

The American political system was made for Bourgeois man ("man" once again, because of the inherent male chauvinism of Bourgeois civilization), and Bourgeois man has become what he is because of it. As we have seen, the Constitution itself lists many of his needs. But, as it turns out, meeting Bourgeois man's real needs developed into something vastly more complicated than fending off pirates, coining money, building post offices and roads, and providing for bankruptcies, patent laws, and uniform rules of naturalization.

To do business, to secure the blessings of this life, to enjoy a contented and delectable existence—the great, Hobbesian, middle-class values—Bourgeois man demanded three things from the political system: freedom, security, and a reliable system of transaction and exchange. In practice, these goals often proved to be overlapping and sometimes contradictory. But they are analytically distinguishable and, as such, they constitute not only the first standard to be met by American politics but also the core meaning of such famous remarks as Calvin Coolidge's, that "the nation's business is business."

Freedom, the first element in this business standard, is in the American Bourgeois tradition stemming from Hobbes and Locke (not Rousseau) mostly negative in thrust. It is the right to be left alone, the claim that others should stand clear, should not be an impediment to personal progress. The presumption is that each person is an energy under personal control and that, as of right, each person should be granted the space and time in which to exercise his (or her?) energy freely.

In the American tradition, freedom in this sense is both broadly honored and also given wide practical effect. The two activities must be distinguished. Americans honor freedom without restraint and mostly without definition. The words "freedom" and "liberty," are repeated until they resound across the plains and back from the mountaintops. Empty of content, they get inserted into the nation's most familiar mythic litanies. In myth, to the world, America means freedom. But what freedom means, what having it would let us do, does not get defined in this vague rhetoric.

But if the rhetoric is pressed and freedom is given practical effect in the American context, the mythic context and overtones wash away. What is left is the right to go one's own way. In fact and in aptest metaphor, Martina Navratilova, as a young Czech tennis prodigy, chose freedom while participating in a tournament in Forest Hills, New York. She voted, so the expression goes, with her feet. She lost her first important matches and was pictured weeping alone at courtside. But in a heartwarming story of personal Bourgeois grit, competitive stamina, and extraordinary talent, she went on to become a champion of champions and to claim a life of style, multiple homes, expensive cars, fabulous furs and jewelry, and nutritional hobbies. It was an American success story. How was such wealth gained? By, in this land of real Bourgeois freedom, leaving the competitors in the dust.

In the name of liberal democracy, Americans, relative to the population of any other nation—especially Americans who are white, male, and begin with at least some money—have extraordinary amounts of personal freedom. They can go and come as they please, live as and where they like, marry whom they please, find and exploit their educational opportunities, pursue professions and businesses as best they can, change their minds, start over. And, of course, they have the right to get rich. Over the years, remarkable numbers of otherwise perfectly ordinary Americans have gotten very rich indeed. Even more remarkable, in a historical perspective that includes other civilizations and times, is the huge number of Americans who in their own ways and to their own standards have become at least fairly rich. In this broad perspective, it can be asserted that the American middle class, counted both relatively and absolutely, is certainly the largest and one of the richest of all time.[2]

Many of the rights allowing Americans to get on with their lives are not enshrined in law but are encapsulated in the mores and traditions of our society. Some of these merely social rights, such as the right to travel or to choose one's sexual orientation, are important and subject to limits. But our very fractiousness about such limits—which often leads to stumbling efforts to put them into laws—is proof that the substance of these rights does exist even if not in exact definition.

On the other hand, by the standards of modern nations, an extraordinary number of the personal rights and civil liberties of American citizens are enshrined in law. Think again, in terms of what is said and what is presupposed, of the Fifth Amendment's prohibition against self-incrimination and of the Fourteenth Amendment's stricture that no state, any more than the federal government itself, can deprive its citizens of life, liberty, or property without due process of law or deny equal protection of the laws. Think, too, of the First Amendment freedoms of religion, speech, press, and assembly. What is most obviously presumed by the statement of these freedoms is that we are all very busy people, energetically living our lives; exercising our natural freedoms; using our property; praying, speaking, writing, and assembling with each other. Guaranteeing our legal rights to go on living in this way places a presumptive primary value on our activities as private people. That, in a Bourgeois perspective, is an altogether proper ranking.

It is therefore doubly significant that the famed legal claims we have just listed are all against the public authorities. The original language of the First Amendment is an express limitation on what laws Congress in Washington may make. The intent was to leave especially the regulation of religion to the states and their local authorities. But with the addition of the Fourteenth Amendment, and after a long series of Supreme Court decisions, the meaning of the original language has been extended to limitations on the authority of legislatures and executives from the federal government down to and including, for example, the prerogatives of prison wardens to regulate religious practices of convicts in their custody.[3] The result is to underline and extend the private/public distinction, with priority to the former, even as social conditions grow increasingly dense and intricate.

Obviously, once the basic distinctions and priorities have been set, the efforts to apply them and sustain them in practical situations of great fluidity must become increasingly complex. Courts, especially the Supreme Court, have played a role of growing prominence in attempting to monitor and manage ongoing developments. The Supreme Court's essential strategy has been to attempt to keep a reasonable balance between competing claims. While honoring the priority of the private, it has tried to give an appropriate respect for the preoccupations and programs of government units. The history of these efforts, together with analysis of their various subtleties in the areas of commerce, speech, religion, press, and association, fills volumes.[4]

In sum, what that history proves is that freedom is a precarious business that will not mean much unless it is combined with other actions—which may be restrictive—to give it substantiality. Much the most important of these other actions are those that provide security, the second of the great Bourgeois political values. If I am completely free, the Hobbesian assumption is that I am highly likely to use my freedom to harm you. When the Declaration of Independence talks of the need "to secure" men in the possession of their rights, it was not suggesting that the threat to them came from the Russians, or Latin American drug barons, or spooks under the bed. It was supposing that the biggest threat to your rights came from me, and vice versa. The Declaration, good Hobbesian document that it is, also holds that the primary instrument for securing us in our freedom is the government. What keeps you secure in your home, what guarantees you real domestic freedom, is the cop on the beat.

A point so obvious should not need reiteration. But in an age that talks so much not only about "freedom" but also about "getting the government off our backs," it is hard to make the case that it is the police, both in symbol and in fact, who make us free. But that is the role of the sovereign power in a liberal democracy. And, in our modern, intense, technologically advanced society, vastly more than routine police work is involved in restricting and regulating our freedom to ensure that with it we are also secure. In the name of freedom, we have become one of the most highly government-regulated societies in the world.

In a totalitarian society, we may suppose, there would be little need for regulation in the precise sense of the word. The central reliance would be on command and direction. There would be little need, for example, for slander and libel laws designed to regulate and guard against the dangers of untrammeled free speech. The government would write all the speeches and citizens would simply read what was put in front of them. The same logic would apply in all other areas of life—cultural, religious, commercial, and so on.

But in the kind of free, pluralistic, Bourgeois society that America strives to be on its liberal democratic side, the initiative in all these matters is largely left up to the spontaneous and autonomous individual. Government regulation then becomes a necessary even if secondary effort. In this light, the prosecution even of such crimes as murder and rape can be seen as efforts on the part of the state to curb private initiatives to solving personal problems within minimum limits of civility.

In this framework, the efforts of the public authorities to secure our freedoms fan out in many directions. They not only protect us from invasive crimes; they also protect us from a host of other more indirect assaults, such as by pollutants in our water, air, and food; by toxic chemicals in products we may buy; and by infectious agents that can be transmitted by the contagiously diseased. In the commercial world, masses of legal restraints have been erected, some of which date back centuries, most of which are of much more recent origin, to protect participants from fraud, breach of contract, unfair competition, misleading advertising, malpractice of professional skills, negligence, discrimination, harassment, and so forth. The profusion of this legislation designed to protect the public, the consumer, and also the producer and employees of every sort, all goes to show that, for all our faith in Bourgeois laissez faire, reliance on "caveat emptor" is nowhere near enough.

It should also be noted that in America, at every level of government, but most especially at the federal level, there is a comparable profusion of highly specialized agencies to enforce all this profusion of legislation, especially in its commercial dimensions. The seven major independent regulatory commissions are only the most important and well known of the independent federal agencies doing this kind of work.[5] There are dozens more that are less well known—and thousands more at the state and local levels. After all, local zoning boards protect homeowners from uncontrolled depredations of the environment by developers; in this sense they even protect the developers from themselves. Moreover, at all levels of government there are hundreds of bureaus and offices that issue rules and regulations that are designed to protect us from ourselves and from each other. The Food and Drug Administration and the Environmental Protection Agency are only the most obvious of such agencies at the federal level.

Then there are the monumental efforts the federal government makes to protect America's Bourgeois civilization from threats from overseas. More is involved here than maintaining the nation's armed strength and projecting it into flash points around the globe, although that is a huge effort in which Bourgeois mentalities at home have a direct and continuing interest on any number of counts. The American federal government also acts, through the State Department and its various agencies and through the Commerce, Agriculture, and other departments, to ensure American business access to overseas markets. To recount all this activity in due proportion would take many pages.

To sum up all that has been said so far about Bourgeois needs for freedom and security, let us look at one last example, one that on its face might seem to have nothing to do with what we have been discussing, the issue of abortion. This sensitive issue challenges all of us to take sides. Our concern here is only to notice how the arguments pro and con typically are put. Those who oppose abortion claim that from conception the unborn fetus has a standing of personhood that gives it a "right to life" as substantial as that of the mother—or, for that matter, of the father or any other person protected by the relevant clauses of the Fourteenth Amendment. Such Bourgeois sentiments are hardly surprising in view of the general reputation that Right-to-Life proponents have as "conservatives." But notice the language on the other side of the argument. Here the focus is not on the rights or wrongs of the act of aborting a birth but on the issue of sovereignty, on the question of choice, of who is to decide. Once the focus is thus stated, the answer comes clearly: it is the prospective mother who should choose, who has the right to choose. *My Body, My Decision,*[6] proclaims the book title. Once again, what is of concern here is the language of the argument more than the conclusion it supports. What, formally, is the difference between the language of "my body, my decision" and that of the four-year-old refusing to share his toy and screaming, "My teddy bear . . . ,"? or that of the business magnate saying, "My steel plant . . ."? All talk the language of Lockean property rights, and all, presumably, seek personal freedom to do what they wish behind the security of the state's law.

The language of the Supreme Court's decision on this issue in *Roe v. Wade* (1973) is doubly interesting in this connection. First, the case is far less clear than is its reputation. It not only limited formerly unrestricted federal rights to abortion in the first trimester, it also, through a scattering of comments and implications, connected the abortion decision to a woman's "right of personal privacy." It then went on to declare flatly, "The abortion decision and its effectuation must be left to the medical judgment of the pregnant woman's attending physician." But neither in this statement, beyond calling it a "medical" judgment, nor anywhere else in the decision did the Court give any guidance on how the decision should be made. If the suggestion that it is a "medical" question has any substance, presumably it is that questions of health are involved—but whose? The mother's or the embryo's? How is the health of either to be determined and measured? More likely is the probability that the judges had no clear conception of how the decision would be made, and, moreover, did not think it was their—or the state's—business to make recommendations in this area. Before the private arena, the state must be "neutral." That is the liberal, Bourgeois creed. So far as the Supreme Court was officially concerned, pregnant women and "attending physicians" facing abortion decisions could, if they chose, flip coins. That is what "privacy" and equal protection of the laws basically mean. Your freedom, your security—your choice, however you make it.

The claims of Bourgeois man—and his wife—to freedom with security are essentially negative. The claims to a reliable system in which to buy, sell, use, maintain, manage and develop property are much more positive. As he enters the marketplace, Bourgeois man's wants are much more extensive than for a symbolic policeman on the beat. He expects government to be positively active in creating strong market conditions and to provide a wide range of business services. Central in practical fact but powerfully symbolic as well is the need for government to supply money, both literal coin of exchange and the monetary system within which all forms of monetary exchange take on meaning and measurable value.

In the abstract, there is a paradox involved in money. Its possession is meaningful only if it is in some way private, mine as opposed to yours. Yet the character of money as a medium of exchange is determined by its being public, that is, it is issued and guaranteed by the state, so that it may have the same value for me as it does for you and for anybody else.

The abstract paradox of money may be lost on individual Bourgeois man, however much of this public stuff he privately may have acquired, but its practical dimensions are not. The American Bourgeoisie, right from the beginning, has shown an elaborate concern for both the government mint and for the government's responsibility for the creation and careful management of the monetary system. To make this point, it is enough simply to acknowledge the existence of the Federal Reserve System and to repeat the widely acknowledged claim, even among the most hardened of business conservatives, that the chairman of the Federal Reserve Board is the second or third most powerful public official in America, ranking behind only the president himself and perhaps the speaker of the house.

Mention of the Federal Reserve Bank opens up the vista on the positive services Bourgeois man expects from government. Far beyond roads, post offices, standards of weights and measure, and the like, the Bourgeoisie expect government to provide a host of legal services, for example, specific legal instruments by which property and its use and development can be definitively exchanged, owned, and possessed in a wide variety of ways. Far and away the most important service expected from government in modern times goes well beyond creating and regulating the public infrastructure of the national economy's market place. The modern bourgeoisie wants the government to *manage* that economy for them.

What might be involved in this demand can be gained from a reading of the preamble of the Employment Act of 1946. This act, passed in the wake of World War II and the Great Depression of the 1930s stated:

> It is the continuing policy and responsibility of the Federal Government to use all practical means consistent with its needs and obligations and other essential considerations of national policy, with the assistance and cooperation of industry, agriculture, labor, and state and local governments, to coordinate and utilize all its plans, functions, and resources for the purpose of creating and maintaining, in a manner calculated to foster and promote free competitive enterprise and the general welfare, conditions under which there will be afforded useful employment, for those able, willing, and seeking to work, and to promote maximum employment, production, and purchasing power.[7]

Clearly, the authors of these words were aware of the difficulties that would surround the achievement of their goals. The list of actors and agencies whose cooperation the federal government needs to carry out this assignment is alone enough to underline that difficulty. Nevertheless, what is being called for in this act is clear. There are three demands: (1) free, private, competitive capitalism is to remain the central principle of the American economy; (2) the overall operation of the American economy should be directed to ensure stable, steadily expanding conditions of full employment "for those able, willing, and seeking to work;" and (3) it is the special responsibility of the federal government in Washington to see to it that the first two demands are met.

It is also abundantly clear from the debates at the time the Employment Act was working its way through Congress that the assignment to the federal government of special economic management responsibilities grew out of a relatively sophisticated understanding of modern economic theory and of that theory's determination of what central governments can do in and for free capitalist economies.[8] Central governments are far and away the largest economic actors in their economies. Just by their disparate size, central governments can throw economic resources into particular areas that simply swamp everyone else—or, on the contrary, withdraw them, leaving everyone else to starve. Moreover, central governments are not subject to the restrictions hemming in the activities of private businesses. Private businesses, by and large, are expected to relate sales to costs and show some measure of profit on the proverbial bottom line. But governments, for all the talk about efficiency and "cost-effectiveness," can do things simply because they ought to be done. They can incarcerate for long periods at great cost prisoners found guilty after expensive trials instead of, more cheaply, shooting them on sight; they can send in the marines to defend nothing more valuable than national pride; and they can take a host of actions, many of which can be very expensive in at least the short run, simply because in the long run they will promote the development of a stable, capitalist economy. Finally, governments, by being sovereign authorities, have powers of compulsion and comprehension that cannot be matched by private economic entities. They can force people to pay for services in which they have no direct interest, as when they assess school taxes on the elderly; they can manipulate market conditions both generally and specifically and regulate the money supply and the availability of credit. They can raise taxes for no better reason than restricting consumer spending. They can channel investment outlays into certain kinds of activity by skillfully designed tax breaks paired with alternative penalties.

The list could go on. The point is that through a wide range of variously conceived fiscal and monetary steps central governments, even in the freest of private-enterprise, capitalist economies can prod, push, bump, or, on the contrary, slow and impede economic activity both overall and in particular areas. The opportunities for central government action to "manage the economy" are real, and it was the clear perception of their existence that inspired the fulsome language of the Employment Act of 1946 and, more particularly, of that Act's creation of the Council of Economic Advisors in the Executive Office of the President.

What Does Bourgeois Man Get?

But does Bourgeois man get from American government the freedom, security, and skillful, stabilizing, positive economic management he desires? The answer is mixed but considerably darker than is usually assumed, and certainly darker than one might have supposed for a government so ostensibly dedicated all across its operational side to the satisfaction of quite specifically and exclusively Bourgeois needs.

To put this general answer into an appropriate perspective, it might be well to begin by noting that the American federal government does not now have and never has had difficulty in selling its long-term bonds. That long-term investors seeking principally security regularly make this choice for their savings may be marginally less significant than it at first appears. Where else, after all, could they put that kind of money? Nevertheless, across modern history there have been numerous governments that could not command that kind of confidence, and the fact that the American government does—both at home and abroad—says something that cannot be ignored.

Nevertheless, on the other side of the ledger, in contemporary America, how does Bourgeois man experience all that freedom to pursue his Bourgeois ways? Is the initiative still meaningfully his? Is the race still to the swift? What happens to those who, for one or another reason, are slow off the mark? In all this, what has been the government's role, and has it helped or hindered Bourgeois man's use of his freedom?

In a Bourgeois sense, America is still a free country, and eminently so; but in certain severe ways, the practical meaningfulness of that freedom has been and increasingly is compromised. This is especially the case for the ordinary, moderately well placed individual Bourgeois man, the person Bourgeois liberal democracy always assumed was central to its theory.

Nowadays, to set up a business; to organize, for example, a retail outlet; to start up a newspaper or small magazine; to launch a trucking firm, a construction company, a commercial farm; or even to arrange to practice one of the professions on a private basis, requires far more than ever before in the way of training, accumulation of initial capital, and the making of a wide round of appropriate contacts. The hurdles in the way of this sort of thing are in fact so numerous and so high that the vast majority of us do not try. Instead, we find our niche in some already existing institutional structure and go to work for somebody else. No doubt, in that preexisting firm, we pursue our personal vision of Bourgeois success up some career ladder—but as hired help, not as swashbuckling private entrepreneurs out of the pages of John Locke and Adam Smith. It can be questioned whether our political theory of personal entrepreneurial freedom has kept pace with the development of institutional economics, especially in its contemporary American context.[9]

Then there is the fact that in the modern American context, Bourgeois rights to life, liberty, and property, and to equal protection of the laws, are no longer plain and simple rights subject to common-sense definitions. On the one hand, in a bewildering range of court decisions these rights have been refined and defined and refined again not only to degrees of great intricacy but in ways that are seldom predictable.[10] On the other hand, legislatures from Congress on down to the lowliest village council have issued statutes—and these have been fleshed out by the attendant bureaucracies with volumes of administrative rules and regulations—to the point that the business community believes that it is being smothered by the paperwork required to certify that they have complied in their activities with all relevant restrictions and requirements.[11] This describes the situation only in aggregate terms. To work day by day, any business must confront directly the fragmentation of American government, set out in previous chapters, not only between the federal, state, and local governments, but also within each of these levels with their myriad bureaucratic agencies, many of which have contradictory and conflicting agendas of their own. Freedom, Hobbes said, is the silence of the law.[12] That was three hundred years ago, when it could be assumed the sovereign spoke with a single voice. How much meaningful freedom is left when the law speaks through a hundred tongues?

And it must always be added that this practical situation is no mere accident of accumulated history. It is the necessary consequence of the careful operation of deep-seated principles honored particularly by the Bourgeois mind: federalism, mixed government, and the universal assumption that all political actors are essentially adversaries each pressing a personalized interest. In that kind of world, comprehensive, systematic, regulation of freedom is precluded *eo ipso*. Viewed from a theoretical perspective, it is amazing that the American regulatory state makes as much sense as it does.

What of the security that all this law and regulation is supposed to bring? How secure in America is Bourgeois man, in his possessions, in his home with his family, with his womenfolk on the street, in his ventures in the market, in his nation as it confronts the world? Covenants without the sword, we must repeat from Hobbes, are but words and of no strength to defend a man at all.[13] How strong, how fearsome, how securing is the American sword?

To ask these questions, in the context of our contemporary debates ranging from fears bred by crime in the central cities to anxieties about the gravest issues of national security, is to suggest a line of possible answers. These, when added together, must point to the general conclusion that American government cannot make sane persons feel genuinely secure about either their present being or their hopes for the future—no matter how many long term government bonds they may buy. Combine impressionistic evidence absorbed from news reports of all kinds and relevant personal experiences with batteries of statistics about the incidence of various kinds of crime, of corruption among public officials, of drug addiction and other kinds of substance abuse in all socioeconomic levels of the population, of divorce and other signs of family disintegration, of the kinds and degrees of mental illness occurring especially among the poorest elements of society.[14] Next, add to these statistics a second set painting the underlying factors in American society that in ongoing ways promote the grim picture outlined by the first set: structural unemployment statistics; health-care statistics; statistics measuring racial divisiveness, and other measures pointing to the presence in America of a permanent racial underclass; various measures indicating that the public school system increasingly is unable to socialize in acceptable ways even upper-middle-class children; similar measures indicating declining social confidence in authority figures of every kind (especially tax evasion and nonvoting).[15]

Now turn to the question of whether American government is capable of solving these problems in accordance with reasonable standards of Bourgeois expectations. Clear from the mind all questions of whether other governments of the world do better or worse than we do, of whether the Russians have an unemployment problem, the Swedes a problem of the homeless, the British a problem of crime on the streets such as we do. No doubt, there is much to be learned from how other nations fare and why, but mere comparisons are mostly beside the point. The point is that we have problems, they are our problems, and we have our expectations about what might be done about them.

So recall directly all that has been so far piled up in this book about the general character of American political institutions and their capabilities. Think, first, about the fragmentation of government at every level and within every level, and what that must mean about the sustained capabilities of our governing processes. Think also about the extraordinary capabilities of myth in American politics to obfuscate, delude, and obscure, in short to mask America's ideological, operational politics. Those politics by fundamental design behind the myth do not concentrate on solving social problems; systematically they concentrate instead on harmonizing the conflicting claims of the competing interests. Only in myth was American government designed to "govern." In Bourgeois ideology it was designed to manage conflict—by pitting ambition against ambition.

What is at stake here is the core of the Bourgeois conception of government. Governments in the Bourgeois view are instituted among men to secure them in the possession of their rights and property. The operatives of governments are then induced to work to these goals by, as in all life, making it in their personal interest to do so. That first step in the argument makes government, no matter how much dedicated to security keeping, *fundamentally* vulnerable to corruption and to perpetual insecurity. For what if figures from the world of crime are able to counterinduce government officials from their assigned security tasks? If the price is right, the terms of the equations are the same. What morally is the difference between helping a friend produce and sell soft drinks and helping a criminal produce and sell "coke"—for may not he be a "friend," too? Because of the presence of this fundamental vulnerability in American government to the forces of corruption and insecurity, government is, on its Bourgeois side, open to not just occasional but to systemic corruption and perpetual insecurity. That is not simply the fact of the matter; it is the theory of it.

These paragraphs point us to the root of Bourgeois civilization, Bourgeois man's essential fear of himself and of his neighbor. Hobbes's own character, according to his contemporary, the biographer John Aubrey, was marked by "an extraordinary Timorousness."[16] Liberal democratic culture ultimately rests on that emotion more than any other, on distrust, on my essential fear that without government to hold you in awe you will use your strength to take from me. Government does not abolish that fear, only holds it in check. Bourgeois man's routine anxieties about the menaces of contemporary life all around him are ultimately grounded in his first presuppositions about himself, in an existential angst.

Perhaps this is the answer to a nagging puzzle: by his own standards, Bourgeois man must see America as badly governed even at the most primitive level of providing the citizens with minimum levels of freedom and security; yet he does not seem overly concerned. Is this because, born of fear, he does not believe real security is possible? If this is a factor in Bourgeois man's estimations of issues of domestic security, is it also a factor in his attitude to questions of national and international security?

This is a good context in which to confront the last of the principal demands modern Bourgeois man makes on his government, to manage the nation's economy. We have seen earlier in this chapter that, in the understandings of sophisticated economic theory, the notion that central governments should manage their nations' economies is reasonable, even when the economies in question are highly diffused and depend essentially on private entrepreneurship of all the major capital concentrations. But the particular notion that Bourgeois man can expect American government to "manage" a national economy is, in a word, absurd. No less a figure than Ronald

Reagan, while perhaps not fully appreciating the import of what he was saying, has called major elements in the management process "mickey mouse."[17]

Three major factors are involved in the issue of managing the economy. The first is the question of knowing the brute facts, of knowing what the economy is doing at any particular time, of being able to outline in a timely fashion what management problems it presents, so that on, say, a monthly basis, appropriate corrective steps by the relevant central government agencies could be taken. Some such statistics are immediately available, such as foreign exchange rates. Others can be tracked even under American conditions fairly accurately and rapidly, such as movements of capital in and out of the country. Some business activities can also be canvassed and aggregated quickly enough to make a difference to economic planners, such as the production figures for the major automotive manufacturers and producers of other durable consumption goods. But it becomes more and more difficult to collect accurate figures in a reasonably short time frame as investigators press their inquiries further into the more scattered parts of the American economy. Business investment plans for all kinds of business are a vital fact for the economy as a whole and a critical one for planners, but, since few businesses willingly reveal them, such plans cannot be more than loosely estimated until long after the fact. Even the level of current national factory production and retail sales can only be guessed at. The most notorious of these figures are the regional and national unemployment rates. For all the fanfare and assurance with which these figures are announced each month, the inexactness of the methods by which under American conditions they must be obtained, and the incompleteness and arbitrary quality of the definitions on which they are based, inspire little confidence in either their meaning or their accuracy.[18]

More important than this ignorance about any current state of the economy is the second factor, the question of what the nation's economic planners, given the nation's extant political system, could do about it even if they had full economic knowledge. They have two major paths open to them, monetary policy and fiscal policy, and both, in the American context, are hopelessly confused by the simple questions, Who are these so-called national economic planners and What are their relationships and powers over each other and over the economy?

Of the two, monetary policy presents much the clearer picture. Here the Federal Reserve Board has a solid presumption of primacy. It has positive control over factors that directly determine interest rates and considerable influence over pressures and impediments to the national money supply. Yet it is compelled to share authority over the activities of the great stock and commodity exchanges with other regulatory agencies that are as independently constituted as itself and that have their own interests and policy commitments. Moreover, even on matters as sensitive as interest rates, the Federal Reserve Board can well find itself in head-to-head, not immediately resolvable conflict with the Treasury Department. But much the most serious limitation of the Federal Reserve Board's control over monetary policy is the simple fact that monetary policy, unless coordinated with the government's general fiscal policies, is only of partial significance. That kind of coordination, however, can be obtained only from the president and Congress, and a host of other political actors scattered throughout the American political system.

Fiscal policy, the *intended* qualitative and quantitative relationship between public revenues and outlays, is a feature of American politics that exists in name only, that is, in myth. What happens, in this area of American government, happens; and, given the multiplicity of actors involved and the confusion of their relationships, no one can be said to have intended—much less be held responsible for—the results that occur.

Review the facts as we have presented them before. The federal government is only 1 government in the economy as a whole. There are 79,999 others. Granted, these others lack important powers of a central government as the economic theorists would define it. Nevertheless, all these other governments are public authorities; their spending and taxing policies have, especially in aggregate, major economic implications; and the federal government has only the slimmest kind of direct authority over their behavior. Then there are the incapacities of the president and Congress for enacting coherent national policies. Here the critical question is time, the third factor. Suppose that the president, guided by his Council of Economic Advisors and advised by his Office of Management and Budget, and the Federal Reserve Board, including particularly its chairman, had together, from a shared perspective on the needs of the economy, formed a coherent, internally articulated set of economic policies for the nation. This would be a major achievement in itself, and one that has seldom happened even to the loosest standards of what might constitute a definitive national economic policy. The next step would be to ship these proposals to Congress. The question then becomes, How soon can Congress be brought to act, and at what cost to the integrity of the original proposals? Congress, as we have seen, is fundamentally not geared to act on policy questions as such. Its primary operational tendency is to piece together patchwork solutions that in relatively indiscriminate and dispersed ways satisfy a multiplicity of clients. That takes both time and sustained diffusion of whatever original policy intent was present, as president after president has discovered to his chagrin. If the pressure to act is increased to an extraordinary extent, as it was in the early days of both the Franklin Roosevelt and Ronald Reagan administrations, the result is more than slapdash; the debate about what is to be done takes flights into mythic simplifications and slogans in which all nuances about intelligent, sophisticated economic management vanish.

The general picture of the American central government's attempt to manage the national economy would appear to be this. Most of the time, nothing resembling conscious national economic management takes place, however much the Federal Reserve Board in particular manipulates such controls as it can reach. Certainly, on fiscal policy, taxes in place stay that way, and outlays are voted in seriatim and are only meaningfully added up long after the fact. From time to time Congress may engineer a change here or there to correct a particular problem, often with unexpected consequences. Once in a long while, with a huge buildup of public excitement, major efforts at reform and reconstitution will be made. With unfurled banners of presidential leadership Congress will move. But years later, with reassessments coming in, far less will be found to have happened than was originally thought. Moreover, the unintended consequences may be far more significant than the advertised hopes. Ronald Reagan won the election of 1980 at least in part because he promised to balance the budget by 1984. Instead, the national debt tripled by 1988.[19] Was this Reagan's fault? Certainly he proposed the cuts in taxes and the increases in military expenditures that most observers blamed for the budget deficits. But it was Congress, including a Democratic House, that voted all that legislation. While that was happening, the Federal Reserve Bureau was resolutely pursuing inflation-reducing policies that precipitated a wrenching recession that in turn damped federal government revenues. In this light, the consequences of "Reaganomics" were everybody's responsibility—which is to say nobody's. In the Reagan years, the economy was not so much mismanaged as unmanaged. That is about all Bourgeois man can expect even from the most pro-Bourgeois government in a generation.

The Poverty of the Bourgeois Mind

We have now completed our review of what Bourgeois man as Bourgeois can expect from the design of American government. But Bourgeois man is a figment of our intellectual analysis; he exists only as one aspect of the American political psyche. In consequence, before we can conclude this review of Bourgeois man's response to the whole of the American political environment, we must take notice of his confrontation with his Protestant twin, his Protestant conscience, and with the rational-professional servants that have been conjured into existence to minister to his needs.

For these purposes, it will be enough to notice only one aspect of this confrontation, the issue of the American welfare state, an issue that is broadly indicative of all the most important relationships involved.

The call in America for a welfare state to give public assistance to the socially and economically ill-placed originates in the nation's Protestant conscience, and more particularly, from that conscience's well-focused outrage over Bourgeois man's congenital greed, materialism, and callousness toward the fate of the unfortunate.[20] The welfare state, program by program, has been developed by rational-professional social-service experts striving to place an array of private misfortunes in the context of general principles of social justice and the public interest—matters about which the Bourgeois mind knows nothing.[21] But Bourgeois man, perhaps only after some reflection, can be brought even so to see significant practical reasons why he, too, should support the welfare state both in fact and in principle. In principle, Bourgeois man is prudent enough to see that even he might have reason to value a "safety net" beneath us all, especially since the principle of giving assistance to the "unfortunate" can be extended to major business corporations needing emergency bailout help in the name of national security, or to broad-scale programs to support permanently a whole industry, as does the FDIC for banks, and as agricultural subsidies do for farmers. Then, too, in practice, Bourgeois man has quickly learned that many of his number can make profits from even the poorest of welfare recipients by running welfare hotels for the otherwise homeless or renting them furniture, cashing their checks, taking their food stamps, and so forth.[22]

More broadly, at a level where principle and practice meet, Bourgeois man can come to see that the welfare state is generally advantageous to his requirements, and because of this he has come to sustain it as a permanent and hugely expensive feature of American government. He has in fact given its institution in America a powerfully "conservative" cast. These developments have occurred because, however ungracefully, Bourgeois man in America has learned that his capitalist system is, to put the matter gently, socially untidy. As it has over the decades careened from bust to boom and back again, capitalism in America has consistently left in its wake a considerable mass of shattered lives, broken homes, and smashed hopes, a legion of folk visibly unable any longer to fend for themselves. For Bourgeois man, this situation is patently dangerous, if not also morally bothersome. He thus turns to the Protestant-inspired, professionally run welfare state to correct the problem. In this general Bourgeois perspective, then, the fundamental advantage of the American welfare state lies in its capacity to tidy up after capitalism.[23]

The welfare state thus receives support from all the elements of the American political psyche. But, because of the contradictions between the reasons why and how they give it support, the American welfare state has proved only a mixed blessing. Administratively, it has itself become a very untidy business, chaotic in its operations and callous in its effects, and for these reasons deeply unsatisfying to both the Protestant community and the bureaucracy. But from the Bourgeois perspective, the welfare state in America has served its first purposes tolerably well. It has warehoused enough of the poor to render them politically harmless and has relieved Bourgeois man's business institutions of social burdens they otherwise might well have been forced to shoulder.

Nevertheless, even for Bourgeois man, there are tag-end, moral dimensions of the problem that still generate concern. Bourgeois man would like to see welfare recipients treated as he treats himself. "Workfare" is his instinctive response to their condition: make them work on a straight contractual basis for the benefits they receive.[24] Unfortunately, experience has shown that a large proportion of welfare recipients cannot, because of physical infirmity, psychological illness, character defect, or conflicting responsibilities for the care of children, be fitted into any conceivable workfare program. This, however, is only part of the problem. The real problem, the moral problem, is what is to be done with all these people in the meantime, people for whom workfare programs do not yet exist as an option. Bourgeois man's instinct is to punish those people for not being like himself, hard working, self-reliant, and brave. Somehow, he would transform them, morally transform them. But how can punishments for those already on society's bottom rung be devised and meted out? How and by whom are these people to be transformed? Above all, by what right, in law or nature, are they to be transformed, let alone punished?

Bourgeois man's political vocabulary by which he might grasp this array of problems is confined almost entirely to the relevant phrases of the second paragraph of the Declaration of Independence, the Preamble of the Constitution, and the First, Fifth, and

Fourteenth Amendments. There is nothing in those phrases about how to be your brother's keeper or the keeper of his wretched children. In his confrontation with the poor, as he steps around the homeless beggar in the street, Bourgeois man can only reflect, "This man has his freedom, his opportunities, his immunities and protections within the law. Are these not substantial gifts? Are not these rights what has made America what it is, rich, powerful, and free?" But the homeless beggar is not asking for rights. He is asking for a quarter. This does not mean he is reducing his relationship to the Bourgeois man to a "cash nexus"—a relationship the Bourgeois man could immediately understand. The beggar is not asking for money because he deserves it or earned it, as if there were some hidden, contractual understanding between him and the Bourgeois man. He is appealing to a sense of compassion or to general principles of shared social membership. He is implicitly suggesting that he and the Bourgeois man abandon all suppositions of adversarial and competitive, external relationships. The relationships his appeal would establish are internal, brother to brother, citizen to citizen in a shared social environment. But Bourgeois man has no conceptual vocabulary to comprehend such demands. That is the final measure of *his* poverty. If he parts with a quarter, it can only be with an uncertain feeling that no matter whether he gives or keeps, he is in the wrong. Pounded from above by Protestant conscience to do more and yet more still, and from below to do something professional, sensible, and comprehensive, he can only stare at the beggar's paper cup in befuddlement, with, again, an existential angst.

11
The Protestant Perspective

The contrasts between the demands that the two sides of the dominant American political psyche make on the nation's political system are sharp, and both are qualitatively opposed to the needs of their rational-professional servants in the bureaucracy. Bourgeois men demand freedom with security for their ventures, each of which they approach with the congenital question, "What's in it for me?" Bureaucratic civil servants seek opportunities to do their professional best in a meaningful environment. In contrast, the Protestant spirit seeks very specifically opportunities to do good. With an idealism aglow with faith, the Protestant burns to love neighbor with a glad and generous heart, to infuse the world with charity and hope, and to subdue a raucous self to these sublime ends. But just as the American political system leaves Bourgeois man filled with feelings of guilt and angst, and the rational-professional close to despair, so the political system leaves Protestant souls filled with frustration, in fact suspended in frustration, unable either to resolve underlying tensions or to abandon them. Helpless to desist, the Protestant spirit in America stumbles ever upward in a progress that is always just beginning.

Remember Protestant social idealism. It came to America on an errand into the wilderness. In John Winthrop's words, again, he and his company were to found in America a "city upon a hill."

> For this end, we must be knit together in this work as one man. We must entertain each other in brotherly affection; we must be willing to abridge ourselves of our superfluities, for the supply of others' necessities; we must uphold a familiar commerce together in all meekness, gentleness, patience and liberality. We must delight in each other.[1]

All across pioneering America, Protestant men, women, and children did delight in each other, raising barns together, gathering and celebrating the harvest together, worshiping and reading the Bible Sunday after Sunday together. They fought slavery together, and drink too, and they brought refreshment to the working man, respect and protection for the working woman, and care for their orphaned children. They built hospitals in the cities and visited prisoners in the jails, renaming them penitentiaries. They dotted the

203

American landscape with schools and colleges and infused the public school systems with persisting enthusiasms for learning and right-eousness. And, of course, everywhere and always, the Protestant community raised money and built churches and did good, in profusion, in diversity, in excitement, and in magnanimity.

All this activity gave to American society, including American political society, a recognizable cast and coloration. As much as did the pervasive Bourgeois mentality, American Protestantism gave this country a distinctiveness of national character. In the figures of the great nineteenth-century, early twentieth-century philanthropists such as Andrew Carnegie, the two sets of characteristics, Bourgeois and Protestant, were wonderfully balanced: these men were rich, American, and did much good earnestly.

There can be no question that Protestantism in confrontation with the political system has made its presence and its demands felt throughout American history. The Abolitionists are an obvious example. Even more clear cut is the figure of Abraham Lincoln and the interpretation he gave to the Civil War, especially in the Second Inaugural. But Protestantism, in a quite narrow and specific sense, was also at work in the figure of Woodrow Wilson, in his call for a New Freedom and in his quest for international peace. Only somewhat more broadly it was present in Franklin Roosevelt's summons to the American people to seek through his administration to shelter, to clothe, and to feed the one-third of the nation that was ill-housed, ill-clothed, and ill-fed. In our own day, Protestants, organized and unorganized by the thousands, are demanding that our government abandon its secular, materialistic, bellicose ways, stop the arms race, shed nuclear weapons, and use the public money thereby saved to tend the poor, the homeless, the broken and marginalized in our affluent society.

These are not mere faith-filled demands of a vague religious spirit. In the American political tradition, these are sharply phrased political demands based on fundamental political principles. Pure Protestantism in its political form demands both a radical social egalitarianism and the formation of a radically warm and compassionate social policy. These two principles clash head on with, on the one side, Bourgeois libertarian elitism, and, on the other, the cool professionalism of the established bureaucracies. Much of American political history is a record of Protestant outrage over patterns of Bourgeois discrimination and professional heartlessness.

This chapter does not set out to summarize the record of Protestant protest in America, although instances drawn from that record will come readily to mind as we proceed. Rather, this chapter will attempt to analyze the reasons for Protestant failure, for the consistent inability of the Protestant spirit in America to carry through in a practical way to its objectives.[2] We will focus on two major areas of concern: first, the involvement of the generalized Protestant spirit in America in the ongoing operation of the political system, mostly through its participation in the electoral process, and, second, the more direct areas of church/state relations and the involvement of institutionalized religious groups in political life.

Civic Participation in America

Protestantism, in the sense being used here, is a mass phenomenon in America. It is an empirical, observable fact that there is more than a trace of a distinctively Protestant enthusiasm in virtually every American, a sense of personal commitment to do good, and to live and find a self-identity through that kind of commitment and action.[3] This may be the dominant trait in only a minority of Americans, but even if it only reveals itself intermittently, it is always socially significant, and it finds expression in various ways. Most obviously, it finds expression through formal membership in recognized religious organizations.[4] But often enough the Protestant spirit in America operates powerfully also among the unchurched, in civic volunteerism by housewives, retirees, and even youngsters; in community activism by business corporations, professional organizations, and fraternal groups and clubs of every sort.

More important, this activist, compassionate, congregationalizing Protestant spirit moving through broad reaches of the population is given a warm reception by the political system. The system virtually thirsts for it and, to every intent and appearance, often seems to depend on it to fuel its own energies and enthusiasms. Sometimes the political system only aids and abets what has spontaneously developed in some segment or another of the population, as the federal government tacitly did with the black churches in the civil rights movement of the 1960s.[5] Other times it will attempt to absorb this kind of free-floating Protestant civic energy directly into its own processes. The most obvious and much the most important and persistent example of this is the absorption of Protestant energies and enthusiasms into the political system's social democratic mythic mechanisms of parties, campaigns, and elections.

To focus on this kind of Protestant political participation, we must for the moment exclude from view Bourgeois man's propensities for civic activism, such as his proclivity for lobbying on behalf of clients, and all other such interest-group activities so important to the ideological, liberal democratic side of American politics. That kind of civic activism is widely recognized, accepted, and practiced; it is clearly one way of getting government to do what some citizens want it to do. But its method and goals are sharply different from the means the political system, on its social democratic side, opens to Protestant enthusiasms.

The Protestantized democratic theory involved here is straight-forward enough but, if fully articulated, becomes more complicated than is sometimes supposed. It begins with the Bourgeois notion that the citizen's primary armament for protecting his interest is the bal-lot. It is supposed further that by balancing the size of congressional districts, weighting electoral votes of states by population in presi-dential elections, and dealing similarly with other constituencies, all ballots can be made to have roughly equal significance. (Senate elec-tions, which honor states as territories rather than populations, are the one important exception.) To all appearances, what we have here is a secular egalitarianism insisting on the rule of "one person, one vote."[6]

However, once this secular political egalitarianism entered America's general cultural milieu and came into contact with the na-tion's Protestant enthusiasms—as can be traced through the nation's nineteenth-century development—"one man, one vote" took on in-creasingly a Protestant translation that made it read effectively, "Ev-ery soul deserves to be heard in making up the voice of the people."

Two fundamental doctrines of the Protestant tradition are in-volved here. The first is salvation by faith. To understand this, it is essential to recognize that faith for biblically oriented Protestants is not a philosophical concept. Faith in this tradition is not acceptance "on faith" of certain propositions as true. Faith, rather, is a psycho-logical experience of the soul; it is an outward rush of the soul's inward energy. More than a faith to live by, it is a faith in and for living with enthusiasm and love for others. Thus, the doctrine of salvation by faith points immediately to its twin, the doctrine of the priesthood of all believers. No doubt, negatively, this doctrine is a powerful rejection of sequestered priesthoods and ecclesiastical hier-archies, and that is a reverberating tone that was carried over into this doctrine's political translations. But positively the priesthood of all believers means, even more forcefully, that we must all be priests for each other, that continually we must minister to and with each other's needs and conditions. We must—again continually—be min-istering companions in faith and love (the terms in this tradition are near synonyms) through life's journeys. We are most ourselves when through common prayer, ongoing talk and action, we live with and through each other.

The net result of these two Protestant doctrines is a powerful congregationalism, and it is this congregationalism that in spirit was more and more translated into the general understanding ordinary Americans had of the nation's social democratic processes. Increasingly, in the first direct extension of these principles into the political process, political campaigns came to resemble congregational meditations in which the issues and pains confronting the people and different policies for dealing with them were aired and debated. The pastors of the people and their rivals were made to confront each other and the people themselves in a spirit of common hope and spiritualized concern. This is a context far removed from the language of the Declaration and the Constitution. It is instead the context in which the Gettysburg Address not only was written but has become the paradigm of all subsequent American political orations. It is the context in which the standards are set for "meaningful campaigns" directed to "the issues"—a context in which meanings are understood and issues are defined in terms of Protestant enthusiasms for the significance of the American experience, and for the identity of Americans as a people in history.

To develop these meanings and enthusiasms, so Protestantized social democratic theory soon came to hold, parties, and the competitions between them, were essential. To eighteenth-century, liberal democratic constitutionalists such as America's founding fathers, parties were anathema; but they are indispensable to any Protestant understanding of how democratic ideals can be achieved.[7] Without political parties, campaigns would be impossibly chaotic, and the subsequent elections would serve no purpose.

In this perspective, political parties are seen serving four distinct functions. Parties are to organize and finance campaigns, that is, write and place the advertising, organize the rallies, do the canvassing, arrange for broadcasting time for speeches, commission the polling, and, above all, plot out and manage campaign travels. Second, they are supposed to identify the issues, research and develop alternative policies and, through a variety of means, educate the public about these. Third, they are to recruit and nominate candidates for the relevant offices to be filled by election, selecting these candidates by their ability to champion persuasively the particular policy alternatives with which the parties have identified themselves.

Finally, parties are expected to hold their successful candidates responsible for their conduct in office.[8] If elected candidates do not perform as expected, if they do not carry out their mandates, they will be held to have violated the trust, the faith in the sense defined, that the people put in them. In this light, responsible government— and the role of parties in holding government officials responsible for their conduct in office—become crucial elements in American democratic understandings. Once again, it is a question of faith, of faith won, invested, honored—or lost.

Not a word of this Protestantized democratic theory of the electoral process appears in the Constitution. Nevertheless, all of it assumes that, once in office, under the Constitution elected officials will have meaningful opportunities for executing their election promises, that the constitutional powers of their offices give them adequate leverage on the operations of government to carry out their avowed programs. It also assumes that the parties themselves exist in sufficiently institutionalized and coherent form to shoulder their responsibilities and to carry them out in meaningful terms, not only during the actual campaigns and elections, but in ongoing ways before and after those times. And most important, it assumes that American constitutional mechanisms can identify officeholders with their conduct in office and hold them—and their parties—responsible for it.

What we have before us now is a comprehensive theory of the democratic process, of popular government, rooted in Protestant enthusiasms for the expression of faith in the goodness of shared life. It is possible for even the largest of modern mass democratic societies to believe that by institutionalizing that theory's stages of discussion, judgment, election, and performance, and by fostering the development of competitive political parties to carry them out, they will have measured up to the theory's ideals of government by open discussion and electoral responsibility. More fundamentally, what we have here are the beliefs, institutions, and activities by which the American political system welcomes to its bosom those Protestant surges of enthusiasm and hope for human betterment that float through the free conscience of the American people. It is as if the system were saying to the American people, let your banners unfurl here, let your charismatic heroes preach here, let your crusades begin and go forth in faith, hope, and love from here.[9]

Over the decades, the American people have responded to these calls. Through the portals of politics, the crusading summonses have resounded—to keep hope alive for a New Freedom, a New Deal, a Fair Deal, to Get America Moving Again to a New Frontier, a Great Society, a new beginning. Armies of voters have swept to the polls to give support to the heroes in these prophetic calls, to sustain them as they charted a new course for the nation and congregated us together in history.

It is, in fact, in its vivid actualities exciting. It is difficult not to get caught up in it, as the TV networks give us gavel-to-gavel coverage of conventions, newspapers print every dispatch, and, most importantly, historians and pundits of every description split hairs, sort tea leaves, and analyze every development for its least and most hidden significance. It must also be stated with firmness that, from one perspective, American elections and their fervent campaigns do their job: to a tolerable degree they succeed in relegitimizing the regime. Holders of U.S. Treasury thirty-year bonds must be grateful for that; and, no doubt, they give proportionally to the next electoral campaign for which they may be solicited.

But these are thin grounds for supposing the American elections and campaigns are meaningful in the sense in which they advertise themselves, that is, measured against Protestant, social democratic ideals of meaningful, congregational, responsible government. By those standards, actual American campaigns and elections border on fraud. More exactly, they are myth, masking actualities so contradictory to mythic claims as to make those claims essentially meaningless. It is enough to make modern Protestants go back to their biblical roots and cry out with Amos:

> I hate, I despise your feasts,
>   and I take no delight in your solemn assemblies . . .
> Take away from me the noise of your songs;
>   to the melody of your harps I will not listen.
> But let justice roll down like waters,
>   and righteousness like an everflowing stream.
>
>   (5:21–24)

Many American Protestants know these facts. They learn them and lament them. But the facts are plain; and larger and larger proportions of the electorate respond with frustration, contempt, anger, cynicism, and apathy.[10] But in the American environment, they have nowhere else to go. So, in time and with enough regularity to keep the system going, they return to the polls.

The plain facts Protestantized democrats in America have to face are these. Elected officials in the American political system, as we have seen repeatedly in earlier chapters, can do very little in the way of giving the country meaningful government, of directing or changing its policies. The officials whose elections the public is taught to care most about are chief executives, from the president on down to local town supervisors. But other than giving the appearance of keeping administrations moving, the primary function of these officials is to promulgate the relevant myths, including, most importantly, the myth of their own and their offices' importance. That myth dies hard. Just to mention the presidential level, we are told by textbooks and historians and, of course, by those most persuasive teachers of all, the politicians themselves, that Franklin Roosevelt instituted a new era of big government and changed the map of American government forever, and that Ronald Reagan set off a revolution that rolled back everything Roosevelt began. Once the rhetoric settles, it will soon appear that all such claims are far off the mark. Professor Neustadt's story in which Truman comments on General Eisenhower's advent to office bears repeating for every executive office in the American political system: Whoever it is will walk up to the chief executive desk on the first new day and order, "Do this! do that!" and nothing will happen. Neustadt's story is an anecdote, but it is an anecdote that, no more than the myth that conceals its truth, will not go away.

Legislators also get elected in the hope they will institute new policies, Democratic or Republican, conservative or liberal, humane or stringent. But, again, as we have seen, legislatures in America enact policy choices only in myth. In ideology, at the level of ongoing operations, they are mostly concerned with harmonizing the diverse claims of the competing interests. Elected in name to promote a particular policy, the most a mythically conscientious legislator can do is introduce a relevant bill, and then claim that he or she fought the good fight as best as possible.

The rock of the matter is that Protestantized social democratic electoral theory fundamentally misconstrues what American government ideologically is about. The theory thinks that American government is designed to govern. In ideology, it is up to a different business, that of assuring the established Bourgeois interests that their private needs will be heard and heeded. The clash is between the Protestant enthusiasts who charge the political battlements with cries to bring peace to mankind, succor to the poor, and liberation to the oppressed, and a political system that effectively replies, "That is all fine in theory, but if you want to get along, go along . . . with *us*."

This general analysis of the predicament in which the Protestant spirit finds itself enmeshed as it enters the political system can be given a more detailed explanation. Ask first who gets elected and why? Philosophical stance and policy position have little to do with it. Never was it more important to state the obvious: all candidates for public office in America are Americans. That is to say, all candidates for public office in America who have even a whisper of a chance of winning are, basically, Lockean provincial liberals, one or another variant of the American standard, Protestant/Bourgeois schizophrenic confusion. Insofar as any of them actually enunciate a definable and sustained public policy outlook, within the bounds of general American acceptability, it will be a blurred blend of Bourgeois respectability, a grab bag of policy options that sustain free-enterprise capitalism and fiscal conservatism, and Protestant compassion, a stretch of concerns for the truly needy worldwide. All of which is to say, it is very difficult to find at the philosophical and policy levels consistent and significant differences between candidates.

In consequence of this, there can be little wonder that in American elections issues cast in broad symbolic terms are often given exaggerated significance. With all candidates committed to the sanctity of private property and the welfare of hungry children, differences of opinion on prayer in public schools, the availability of abortion, and the use of capital punishment will take on a considerable saliency. Moreover, stands on these issues can be seen as quick measures of character and personality. Here, differences can be considerable, some candidates amiable and smooth talking, others stiff and formal, some aptly appearing honest and sincere, others seeming false and halting. There can be no wonder either that once this level of electioneering is reached, the debates, the charges and counter-charges will revolve around references to patriotism, leadership qualities, personal achievement, and warmth of personality. In this atmosphere, it is perfectly plausible for voters simply to pick the candidates they like—in the literal sense of that word—best.

But there is one more point to be made about who gets elected in America and why. Far and away the most important single indicator for measuring electability, far outrunning even the issues of character and trust, is simple incumbency. If you are already an elected official in America, regardless of party label, type of office, or any other consideration, your chances of getting reelected if you stand again are better than nine out of ten.[11] The figures are even higher for the House of Representatives in Washington—which fact alone accounts for the prediction that, since the Democrats have built up over the years a considerable majority there, they will continue to "control" that house for as far as the future can be foreseen. The reasons why incumbency has this disproportionate importance include more than that an incumbent has built-in name recognition, and so forth. The essential reason is that, in the Bourgeois, ideological run of things, from the first day in office the incumbent has been nursing the folks, interests, and fellow personalities who need him or her. The incumbent will have built up debts, connections, and hopes that put him or her in a powerfully entrenched position from which to launch a reelection campaign long before any possible opponents have even begun to think about wandering out on the field. By the time the myths begin to fly, the real business of determining how much money is to be raised to buy which kinds of advertising and of reminding which blocs of voters of favors rendered and promised will all have been settled. And of course, the longer the incumbent has held office, the more certain his or her reelection, if it is pursued.

What role in all this do the parties have, these indispensable armies of activist voters banded together to link the voters to their government in disciplined and coherent ways? The verdict is harsh.[12] The parties as coherent organizations of like-minded voters and activists exist only in myth. Of course, the parties exist in some sense. They each have their quadrennial conventions, their national committees, and their state and local organizations. Their candidates "capture" houses and executive mansions. There are even the stereotypes: we all "know" that the Republicans are waspish Protestants and friends of big business, and that the Democrats are still in some faithful measure the party of rum, Rome, and rebellion. But, beginning with the stereotypes, press these propositions against actuality and watch their supposed solidity vanish.

The stereotypes fit the parties, but do the parties fit the stereotypes? Are there not droves of Protestant wasps who call themselves Democrats, and equal numbers of southerners and Catholics who vote, increasingly these days, Republican? Both parties contain ample numbers of Americans of all types, and certainly they cannot— and would not choose to—be distinguished across the country by consistent lines of social class, economic status, ethnic type, or religious preference.

As much to the point is that neither party can be typed either as a grouping of like-minded individuals or as a coherent organization of consistent activists. Both parties are almost random collections of persons with policy outlooks as disparate as the parameters of American politics will allow. Both have their "liberal" and "conservative" wings around "moderates" in the center. The platforms laboriously drafted by the parties at their quadrennial conventions must be classed among the nation's most unread documents and in no way can be seen as binding on the candidates who supposedly run on them. Organizationally, the same kind of analysis holds. Both parties are no more than the loosest kinds of coalitions. In terms of discipline and coherence, the national machinery of the parties might as well not exist, and the same holds true at most state levels. Only at local levels, and even then only here and there and from time to time, can it be said that the parties exist as organizations. Institutionally, the parties are their officeholders and the loose, nameplate alliances that exist between them, alliances that in no way can be construed to limit or inhibit individual officeholders from tending their primary concern—to develop their own constituencies, their own networks of support, their own guarantees of personal survival or longevity. At this level, it often happens that candidates find it in their interests to disavow party labels altogether.[13]

Can parties so defined and constituted in actuality discharge any of the functions assigned them by Protestantized social democratic theories of popular government? Only in the thinnest of myths. Parties at most have minor roles in organizing and financing especially the big, national campaigns. For the most part, individual candidates and their personal staffs do the job themselves. Only weak candidates for lesser offices rely for money on parties. Indeed, it is a truth of American politics that the stronger and more prominent the candidate, the less reliance there is on the party for financing and all other kinds of support. The stronger and more prominent candidates will be particularly careful to research their own stands on issues and to educate the public about them. All party labels and fanfares to the contrary notwithstanding, American elections are not party affairs but personality affairs—and even then, as already argued, are not much more than skin-deep beauty contests. Certainly, the parties and the legendary party "bosses" have little or no hand in recruiting candidates—the candidates as much recruit themselves—and play increasingly smaller roles in nominating them. Primaries do that. Finally, even if they could muster the strength for the role, parties are no more able than anyone else in the political system to hold officeholders responsible for their conduct in office. The American political system is not a system of responsible government. Checks and balances are supposed to take care of that problem. When an election comes up, even the dimmest of officeholders can be counted on to point the finger of blame at uncooperative colleagues, obstreperous agencies down the line, or inauspicious circumstances beyond anyone's control. For all the talk about democracy being a system for holding the governors responsible to the governed, in America there is no effective constitutional machinery for doing so. The closest we come to that is strictly informal, the press conference; and press conferences, it must be noted, can simply not be called for months on end. Even when they are, it is mostly because of perceived opportunities for inflating the public standing of the officials involved. Press conferences that actually press responsibility on a public official are rarities that prove the general rule.

In this context, it is essential to state again that the primary constitutionally established mechanism for holding elected officials to account in America, impeachment proceedings, the threat of which prompted Richard Nixon to resign the presidency, take years to gear up, are cumbersome to focus, and can be brought only on grounds of criminal behavior, not errors of judgment or bad policy choices.[14] Recall elections suffer the same shortcomings and are available only in a few jurisdictions.

The sum of the matter is that the doctrine of responsible government, the Protestant notion that the public trust is a faith entrusted, is, institutionally in America, either nonexistent or inoperable. That may not be the broadest and deepest frustration of the Protestant spirit in American politics; but it surely is the most definable and the most painful.

Nowhere in all this argument is there any assertion that in America elections have no meaning at all. The argument has been that they have virtually no policy meaning, that they fall far short of the criteria for elections laid down by the essential principles of Protestantized social democratic popular government.[15] By these criteria, American elections must be judged charades, farce bordering on fraud. Their meaningfulness is almost exclusively in their capacities to signal the relegitimization of the regime at the mythic level.

In these terms, two points remain to be added, points that reflect sharply on each other. The first is that American elections are expensive. Even by 1984, the cost of elections ran above $1 billion, and subsequent campaigns may have doubled that figure and more.[16] The cost of elections in other nations (Britain, Israel, Japan, and even the Soviet Union) is, absolutely and per capita, radically less.

The second point is that, despite all the money, just as relegitimization exercises, American elections are not entirely successful. Here the important returns are not the totals of who voted for whom, but the numbers of who voted compared to those who never turned out at the polls. In local and primary elections, turnout can range well below 20 percent, with some school board elections summoning fewer than 5 percent. In most state and city elections, the figures rarely get beyond the 30 percent range. Only in the most tumultuous presidential campaigns has participation by the eligible electorate in recent decades topped the 50 percent mark. In all these contests, then, pitting nonvoters against voters, nonvoters win far more often than voters.[17] This fact, surely, says something significant about the health of the American political system. There are many ways to relegitimate regimes, most notably by simple passive acceptance. But in the American context voting is an especially important technique, and it is used disproportionately by those groups wishing to express their support for—their "faith" in—the American way of politics.

These groups have not been able to generate the same degrees of enthusiasm in other elements of American society, however. To one degree or another and in one way or another, many Americans have, in this sense, lost faith in the political system. To that measure, they do not believe the system can or will fulfill their Protestant hopes and their drive to do good. They are no less Americans than anyone else, but, as fed-up members of the politically discouraged, they turn elsewhere.

Church and State in America

Most of them, obviously, turn to apathy, that is, technically, in the political sense, to finding personal and private solutions to or ways around public problems. If in an urban environment streets are filled with crime and schools are bad, the "apathetic" move to the suburbs and commute around the public problems several hours each day to work. If public conditions become unbearable—and a revolution is unthinkable—they may escape into alcoholism or, perhaps on the contrary, pure spiritualism. That kind of absolute withdrawal is the ultimate private solution to political failure. The vast majority of those who elect the privacy option do not go that far. They mostly retreat out of harm's way as best they can, passively refuse to be involved in any kind of social action, and get on with their personal affairs and jobs. At these, they may work hard enough to salve their (Protestant) consciences.[18]

An important variation on this pattern are the people who withdraw their energies and attention from all political life except for one particular issue. On that issue, whether it be civil rights for blacks, aid to Israel, guns for sportsmen, decriminalization of the use of marijuana, or criminalization of abortions, they give their all. Given the veto-sensitive character of the American political system, single-issue politics can be, at least in the short run, very effective.[19] The NAACP is a monument to this truth. Nevertheless, in the longer term, the failure to achieve broad-scale advances can and mostly has rendered the short-term gains insignificant. Without structural redesign, everything else is either socially cosmetic or merely personally advantageous.

In this perspective, we must attach a special significance to those Protestants in America who turn to their churches and seek through them to bring about social advance and human betterment. What we are bringing into focus is not Protestantism as a broad social movement—although our discussion will at every point presume the presence and power of that strand of American political culture. Rather we will be looking at the churches themselves as an institutional grouping and their collective relationship to the state and its works.

When America's religiously committed turn to their churches and temples to find outlet for their social and political frustrations and enthusiasms, they find themselves enmeshed in a situation that is remarkably static, institutionalized, complex, restrictive, and, above all, resistant to even marginal kinds of redefinition and development—and all this regardless of the specific programs and political causes they might individually choose to support.

Nevertheless, on its face, it will appear to be a situation of principled simplicity. On the one hand, there is the state, in the form of our eighty thousand governments, all pristinely secular, going about their particular businesses. On the other hand, there are the churches and temples in their multidenominational diversity, demonstrating in that diversity the reality of religious freedom in America. The two arenas are kept distinct by the doctrine of the separation of church and state, a two-way doctrine that, especially as interpreted by the courts, guarantees both political neutrality and religious toleration. To complete the picture, both arenas, both institutional conglomerates, float on the supporting seas of free, secular citizens on the one hand, and, on the other, devout parishioners (not to mention at this point the American unchurched).

To notice even so that parishioners and citizens are the same people is to introduce complexity into this too-easy picture. This is the ground for a particular and institutional schizophrenia that exactly parallels the larger schizophrenia embedded in America's Protestant/Bourgeois culture. The most obvious evidence of this particular schizophrenia is the consistent use the state makes of institutional religion—all the talk of a principled separation of church and state to the contrary notwithstanding. How else can the secular state command the instinctive loyalty of all those devout parishioner citizens? So, shamelessly, the state has leaned on and borrowed from the churches for its own purposes.

Recent scholarship has accustomed us to the public role that religion plays even in America.[20] In sum, this activity is called civil religion. It ranges from the prayers with which Congress and other legislatures customarily open their sessions, to the work of chaplains in the armed forces, to the invocations of the deity and his divine providence in the speeches of assorted politicians. Civil religion as practiced in America has in fact extended itself into virtually every symbol, ritual, and festival by which the nation proclaims its propriety. Heading any list of examples of this must be the requirement by congressional statute that the phrase "In God We Trust" decorate our money. Perhaps most basic of all is the fact that the nation's myth, its distinctive understanding of itself as a people coming out of history with an identity and purpose different from that of any other nation, is by our national orthodoxy cast in specifically biblical terms.

There is the story itself: we are a great nation of many peoples gathered in exodus from all corners of the earth to be, across the raging seas, a new nation. There is the perpetual sense of crisis, that we have been deeply challenged, that the faith that sustained us of old is fading. There is, however, in our ever-ebbing present, a sense of renewal and recommitment, the charge that we must choose again to go forward onto some divinely set rendezvous with destiny. Especially in foreign affairs and military crisis, this is the stuff of presidential leadership in America, from Lincoln through Wilson and Roosevelt to Nixon and Reagan, in speech after speech, dripping with Protestant allusions and Biblical phrases. Moses and Joshua and Josiah of old (to say nothing of the Book of Revelation) could not have done it better . . . but strange doctrine for a supposedly secular state.

As important as civil religion has been in legitimating and decorating the American state, the churches have also been seen from the beginning as playing an even more direct role in sustaining the political order. They have been charged with the "social welfare" function of inculcating the personal values necessary to the maintenance of the political order.[21] More darkly, but only somewhat less directly, in American political experience the churches have played a sentinel role for the nation's Bourgeois, secular political order. On the one hand, they lauded Bourgeois needs and endlessly praised and otherwise rewarded Bourgeois successes. Middle-class and upper-middle-class churches, both urban and suburban, became bastions of Bourgeois self-congratulation, compliments the Bourgeoisie generously returned with lavish material support for the churches and their various special projects. On the other hand, a soft Christianity of spiritualism and social fellowship served to hide the hard, rapacious character of America's operative political system and its business-oriented civilization. The poor were actively mystified. A flood of good works spilled like syrup over the nation's persistent and fundamental social ills. Americans were told—and largely came to believe—that they were truly and actively a Christian people.

Against this kind of civil religiosity and the debasement they believed it represented of both their churches and of the true social implications of their faith, a minority of Christian radicals could protest only in vain.[22] The primary reasons for their lack of success lay in a skillfully contrived paradox. Even as the hierarchies of government and business shamelessly used religion to legitimize themselves and their activities—and in return generously awarded the churches with tax exemptions and other subsidies—they fastened on the churches not only the doctrine of the separation of church and state but also that doctrine's major religious implication: that religion has nothing to do with politics because religion is a purely personal and spiritual business. So effective was this teaching that even many reformers came to celebrate, as morally indispensable and characteristically American, above all others the right of private conscience.

The centrality of this right to the totality of the American religious experience, of the notion that in America you could believe in your heart anything you liked so long as it did not have consequences in public, that is, in the state's domain, has given to American institutionalized religion a powerful bias toward a highly personalized religiosity. Social awareness, social concerns, even social identity were of only secondary interest; at most, they yielded opportunities for the expression of personal good works and charitable "assistantalism" to the unfortunate. The primary concerns were all directed to the problems of personal commitment. American Christianity radically loosened its grip even on its own institutional constructions. For Roman Catholics, Protestants, and even Jews, religion became a matter of taste, of personal seeking, of hope for private peace of mind and spiritual growth. The end result was an empty ecumenicalism in which on all sides there was devotion simply to belief in believing, faith in faith.[23]

Religion as social conscience armed for social activism and service, let alone political leadership, simply vanished. So too did the great Hebrew God, the God of Abraham, Isaac, and Jacob, the God of Moses who with outstretched arm and mighty sword had liberated the people of Israel from their oppressors in Egypt. That God was a God of history whose prophets—Elijah, Amos, Jeremiah, and Isaiah—had stood in judgment upon the people for their injustice to the poor, their abuse of power, and their idolatrous pursuit of wealth. Even the figure of Jesus was transformed. The story that ends with Jesus saying, "render to Caesar the things that are Caesar's, and to God the things that are God's," was interpreted to split life into public and private realms—with God presumably only in the latter. Forgotten was Jesus' claim to be liberator of the unfortunate and the imprisoned. Gone was Jesus' massive rebuke of the Romans and the Jewish collaborators inherent in his knowing crucifixion. Instead, all became personalized. Jesus was a teacher figure, a friend to each of us in times of sorrow, trial, and death, a source of personal comfort and strength.

The role of law, especially as interpreted and applied by the Supreme Court, in stiffening and sustaining these prejudices has been enormous. A review of the Court's work in this area will also reveal how deeply ingrained in the structures of the American political system these prejudices have become.

The Supreme Court's first great confrontation with church/state issues came in the case of *Reynolds v. United States* (1879). Reynolds was a Mormon who, in pursuit of the teachings of his church, committed bigamy contrary to the federal laws then governing the territory of Utah. Through his lawyers, he contended that Congress was barred by the First Amendment from making any law prohibiting the free exercise of his religion. In reply, the Court laid down the first principle on which Anglo-American, liberal democratic, Bourgeois jurisprudence rests:

> A criminal intent is generally an element of crime, but every man is presumed to intend the necessary and legitimate consequences of what he knowingly does. Here the accused knew he had been once married, and that his first wife was living. He also knew that his second marriage was forbidden by law. When, therefore, he married the second time, he is presumed to have intended to break the law. And the breaking of the law is a crime.

Reynolds, as a legal persona, and his act were thus brought within the vision of the Court. In this light, the Court raised the question of whether religious belief can be accepted as a justification of an overt act made criminal by the law of the land. In support of a negative answer to this question, the Court quoted first from Madison's famed "Memorial and Remonstrance," written in support of Virginia legislation to disestablish the Anglican church in that state: "'Religion or the duty we owe the Creator,' was not within the cognizance of civil government." They then quoted from the legislation itself (drafted by Jefferson): "It is time enough for the rightful purposes of civil government for its officers to interfere when principles break out in overt acts against peace and good order." Finally, they quoted words Jefferson had written in support of the Federal Constitution's First Amendment.

> Believing . . . that religion is a matter which lies solely between man and his God; that he owes account to none other for his faith or his worship;

that the legislative powers of the government reach actions only, and not opinions, I contemplate [the First Amendment] . . . building a wall of separation between the church and State.

Having thus drawn a hard line between belief and action and, correspondingly, between religion and politics and between church and state, the Court need not have gone on to observe at the length it did that bigamy was a noxious practice. Reynolds was a criminal because of the simple fact that as a self-responsible, legally recognized person he allowed his overt behavior to contravene the dictates of a statute duly enacted by the secular state. The Court observed:

> Can a man excuse his practices to the contrary [of a law] because of his religious belief? To permit this would be to make the professed doctrines of religious belief superior to the law of the land, and in effect to permit every citizen to become a law unto himself. Government could exist only in name under such circumstances.

In 1651, Thomas Hobbes had made the argument in reverse.

> But what, may some object, if a king, or a senate, or other sovereign person forbid us to believe in Christ? To this I answer, that such forbidding is of no effect; because belief and unbelief never follow men's commands. Faith is a gift of God, which man can neither give, nor take away by promises of rewards, or menaces of torture. And if it be further asked, what if we be commanded by our lawful prince to say with our tongue, we believe not; must we obey such command? Profession with the tongue is but an external thing.[24]

Thomas Jefferson had made the same point in his inglorious remark that if your neighbor proclaimed there were twenty gods—or one—which in America he was free to do, it would neither pick your pocket nor break your leg.

These arguments take the Hobbesian, liberal democratic position as far as logic would permit. They make absolute a distinction between the public sovereign—and his right to keep the civil peace—and a man's personal realm in which his conscience is sovereign and his religious whims are free. To catch the significance of what is being argued here, it is essential to keep it in historical perspective. Hobbes, and all the rest after him, right down to the Supreme Court justices, are all by common assumption talking about Bourgeois man—who also happens to be Protestant. But he is Bourgeois man first, and as such he is essentially an entrepreneur, going about his business vis-à-vis other men much like himself. As such, in his dealing with these other men, he is rational, prudent, fair, reputable, self-interested, competitive, even, if so minded, just, honest, honorable, but above all, masculine, powerful. But on this stereotypical view, he also has a personal realm, back home, his privacy. That is where he keeps and practices his religion. That is also where he keeps his wife—and hears her feminine voice, loving, nurturing, self-sacrificing, perhaps even romantic. This is where he keeps and rears his children, stables his horse, controls his servants, and in pre–Civil War America in the South, worked his slaves. In this realm, he was—and by traditional family values, still is—patriarch, according to the rules of his house.

The line running through all this argument is that a man's house and all that is in it are not political. Women on this view are not and should not be political.[25] They have no stake or interest in the public realm except through their husbands. Equally, religion is not political; it is instead private, personal. It is also, in a public perspective, trivial.

Particularly in the decades since World War II, the American Supreme Court has addressed dozens of cases involving church/state issues, and not once, either in the majority opinions or in dissents, have the judges seriously confronted the implications for religion of the *Reynolds* decision. On the contrary, for all the wavering about where to draw jurisdictional lines in tightly defined environments, the Court has clung tenaciously to its liberal democratic presuppositions. Above all and without pause, the Court has celebrated the rights of private conscience within strictly controlled contexts. Only in the vexed, so-called exemption cases, has it shown a whisper of concern for religion's practical and public significance. These cases (right of conscientious objection to military service, labor on the sabbath, flag salute, school attendance, etc.) are exceptions that, by their lack of serious social significance, more prove the rule than weaken it.[26]

Thus, in the most quoted of these cases, *Everson v. Board of Education* (1947), Justice Black, for the Court, wrote an opinion enunciating in ringing terms a reaffirmation of Jefferson's thesis requiring an absolute separation of church and state. It included this sentence: "Neither a state nor the Federal Government can, openly or secretly, participate in the affairs of any religious organizations or groups *and vice versa*" (italics added). Nevertheless, Black's opinion somehow found plausible reasoning to support state payments to cover transportation costs of parochial school children. It remained for the dissenters to take the "high wall" version of Jefferson's doctrine with full seriousness. They found state payment of parochial school transportation costs clearly supportive of religious establishments and

closed their opinion with rhetoric as ringing as anything in the majority opinion: "The realm of religious training and belief remains,
as the Amendment made it, the kingdom of the individual man and
his God. It should be kept inviolately private, not 'entangled . . . in
precedents' or confounded with what legislatures legitimately may
take over into the public domain."

The Court showed a fuller understanding of church/state relations in America in *Walz v. Tax Commission* (1970). This decision
aimed to settle long-standing controversies over tax exemption for
church properties. The Court's majority was clearly anxious to sustain the churches' privileges in this regard, but to do so they had to
overcome a powerfully advanced argument from Justice Douglas
that tax exemption effectively taxed nonbelievers to support services
to believers. The majority began by admitting the obvious. In modern America, ancient metaphors to the contrary notwithstanding,
church and state cannot have "walls" built between them. "Separation in this context cannot mean absence of all contact; the complexities of modern life inevitably produce some contact." The Court did
try to minimize its perception of that contact by illustrating it in
terms of "municipal benefits" such as fire and police protection. But
it proved difficult to put a cap on this kind of thinking. The Court
found itself admitting that some churches actively performed, if not
for the state then for the public at large, certain social-welfare services: "family counselling, aid to the elderly and the infirm, and to
children." However, the Court believed the record here was too uneven to justify the across-the-board tax relief the churches have received. The ground for that they found in these phrases:

> The legislative purpose of the property tax exemption is neither the
> advancement nor the inhibition of religion; it is neither sponsorship nor
> hostility. New York, in common with the other States, has determined
> that certain entities that exist in a harmonious relationship to the com-
> munity at large, and that foster its "moral or mental improvement,"
> should not be inhibited in their activities by property taxation. . . . The
> State has an affirmative policy that considers these groups [i.e.,
> churches, hospitals, museums, etc.] as beneficial and stabilizing influ-
> ences in community life.

The *Walz* case is as far as the Court has gone—and perhaps as
far as it can go, given its essentially secular, liberal democratic biases—toward admitting that in the United States church and state
do have a relationship, albeit one that they hold is positive, that is,
"harmonious," "beneficial," and "stabilizing." We can presume that,
locked in its Hobbesian stance, the Court will continue to see this

relationship as essentially contractual, one in which what is good for each is seen as good for both.

Yet there remains something unexplained in a record that has this perception as its conclusion. Even as broadly interpreted by the Supreme Court in recent years, the First Amendment is a restriction only on what Congress or similarly situated public rule-making bodies can do. The relegation of the churches to the realm of private conscience, the denial to them of a forceful public role, the insistence that ministers must not "politicize their pulpits," these things do not arise from the law, however much the judges in their opinions may reiterate their substance. The restrictions have been stated and enforced only by the Internal Revenue Service's regulation no. 501(c)(3), the one that holds that tax exemption can be withdrawn if a tax exempt entity, for example, a church, supports a candidate by name for public office or devotes a substantial portion of its assets or income to legislative lobbying activities. The Court itself has never directly addressed the principle behind that regulation, although it has acted here and there to protect the right of clergy to serve in public office and the right of churches to be protected by free-speech guarantees. If the effect of the admissions running through the Court's majority opinion in the *Walz* case was not (to shift to a new metaphor) to let the cat out of the bag, much of the blame may have to be assigned to the cat.

The pussycat failure of the churches to seize their political opportunities has roots deep in American political culture; the same culture that produced the judges produced the ministry. In the end, it is the ministry itself that has privatized Protestantism in America, trivialized it, muzzled it. That is its ultimate poverty.

Playing Inside the Game

Of course there are exceptions. Of course, Protestantism in America has huge, often untapped energies. But, once again, the system has its own hugeness. It has a huge capacity to absorb Protestant-driven emotions and funnel them into largely meaningless electoral activities that fritter away all that energy in pursuit of self-inflated charismatic heroes repeating slogans emptied of all operational meaning about government by, for, and of the people. It has a huge capacity to allow the Protestant churches to do good works here and there all across the country, provided only that they endlessly allow themselves to be used in celebration of the system and at no point mount any serious challenge to its legitimacy.

None of this is to suggest that Protestantism has not left its mark on the system. Indeed it has, in ways and degrees we have noted throughout this book. Above all, it has left its coloration on the system, on every personality, on every program, on every institution, for praise and for blame. Perhaps, for the sake of balance, we should emphasize that last point more. It may be that Protestantism's most signal achievement has been its record of making everyone feel guilty, no one more so than Bourgeois man himself.

Why cannot Protestantism in America do more? Why are even its best efforts no more than the scattered flutterings of the self-absorbed? How could it do more? It represents America's conscience, not its operational mind, and certainly not the practical work of the system's governing institutions. On these it has no purchase whatsoever. On the other hand, could Protestantism, all heart and soul, do any less than it does, outraged if also forgiving? That seems an impossibility, too. So Protestantism remains an American voice, half of the nation's political energy, stymied in an empty dialogue with its inattentive other half. It is, again, a condition of ultimate impoverishment, an existential angst.

12
The Rational-Professional Perspective

As a breed apart, as a distinct mentality, America's rational-professional community might be thought too isolated, too unconnected to and unrepresentative of America's dominant self-definitions to have an opinion of the nation's political system and its possibilities that would command a general respect. In fact, the situation is quite otherwise. Simply because so many of us in America are active members of this community—earn our livings as trained, tested, and competent members of in one guise and at one level of it or another—the rational-professional critique is easily the most widely accepted and the most widely repeated form of condemnation of American politics. In form, style, and substance, its standards are implicit in virtually every "informed," "thoughtful," "reasoned" critique that can be read in the press, certainly the elite press, and in other equally regarded journalistic commentaries. These implicit values about what constitutes "good government" have even slipped in and out of the preceding chapters of this book. Again and again, we have effectively asked the reader to contemplate questions phrased in terms of, Is this what we should expect of a "modern" government, of a "competent" government?

As we attempt to lay out systematically the essentials of the rational-professional critique of American politics, we must understand why this task must be done.

The rational-professional critique of American politics may be widely accepted among America's "clerisy"—its stock of intellectually alert, socially conscious, professionally trained middle-class persons—but it is rarely presented except in reserved, inconclusive terms. There are many reasons for this phenomenon; it is enough to notice here no more than the fact that for all the prevalence of rational-professionalism in America today, the Protestant/Bourgeois complex remains dominant. Why rational-professionalism has not challenged that dominance is one of the matters this chapter will have to explain, but the continual dominance of the Protestant/Bourgeois mentality even among persons otherwise immersed in rational-professionalism will have to be taken for fact for the moment. In consequence of that fact, the rational-professional critique of American politics confines itself mostly to exposing particular instances of governmental incompetence and failure. When it does stretch beyond these to search for underlying causes, typically it will be careful to avoid all appearance of any full-scale condemnation. It will be content with unexplained assertions that there have been leadership failures, or, alternatively, that the system slipped away from its founding values in the near-term past, in the 1930s and the advent of the New Deal's "big government," or in the period after the Civil War and the nation's sudden switch from a rural to a mainly industrial economy.[1] However put, the clear presumption of such formulations is that all would be well if the political system got back to its basics; there is no transcendent need to reexamine any of the nation's founding values or constitutional principles.

The full truth, however, is that from a rational-professional perspective, the American political system as conceived in 1787 and as we know it today is archaic. It is an eighteenth-century construction that is fundamentally and irreparably at odds with the governmental needs of a modern, technologically, culturally, and morally advanced society.

There can be no backing away from this conclusion. The ground of it is a perception that the root problem in American politics is constitutional, a failure in basic moral commitment. This is essentially a charge against the dominant values of the Protestant/Bourgeois tradition. That tradition, by rational-professional standards, is fundamentally too privatistic to have an operative understanding of either public authority or public need. In its schizophrenic imperatives, it celebrates too much, on the one side, selfish, materialistic greed, and, on the other, a merely personal and spiritual piety. A society founded on those values, by rational-professional standards, pays too much attention to private rights and personal choices even to aspire to the criteria of an advanced, morally developed society. Implicitly, at least, the rational-professional critique of the American political system, taken in full, is a call for a new American social self-definition, for a new 1787. The expressions of outrage, despair, and helplessness by rational-professionals over this or that particular collapse or failure or corruption of American public service all carry with them, again at least implicitly, a demand for a social and political reconstruction of America from the bottom up, a reconstitution dedicated to the creation of a sane and competent politics that could serve without artificial constraint a public interest globally understood.

But as we lay out the arguments advancing these conclusions, we must also take note of the fact that the rational-professional mentality, however bold or not its call for a new day may be, is no more able than its Protestant/Bourgeois masters to articulate what the new order might be. Caught within present arrangements, caught, that is, within limitations that are both congenital and environmental, the American rational-professional mentality can conceive of no viable alternatives either to itself or to the political system that it services. The rational-professional critique of American politics is, therefore, a self-criticism from which there is no escape and no release, a self-imposed impoverishment.

The Critique

The first focus of the rational-professional critique of American government and politics is on a broad array of individual instances of incompetence. This is not to suggest that the critique is bound to say that American government is incompetent across the board, that it is an example of professional failure without limit. On the contrary, rational-professionals in America, especially those who are themselves public servants, will insist that American governments at all levels have done many things—and many kinds of things—remarkably well. Lists of things done right that can be drawn up are long and impressive, and there is no need to even illustrate them here. The problem is that the lists of things done right can always be matched by shamefully long lists of things done badly, or not at all. The lists of things done well mostly serve to set up expectations that far more things could be done well. If there is this much good, why not be the best? But in a rational-professional perspective, American governmental performance is a long way from being the best possible even when all reasonable allowances are made for ordinary margins of error, human frailty, and the brute intractability and complexity of things and events.

Bridges that could have been designed properly aren't. Highway maintenance that could have been provided isn't. A system that should have prevented corruption in high places doesn't. Welfare programs designed to forestall child abuse before tragedies occur don't. Accidents, deaths, and crimes that could have been avoided aren't. Reading daily press accounts of governmentally preventable public and private misery in America is hard going. Two examples will make the general principles involved in these matters plainer.

The military conduct of the American Civil War and of World War I and World War II—which in all kinds of details left much to be desired—nevertheless set standards clearly worth both serious inspection and conscientious emulation. By those standards, that is to say, by rational-professional standards hewn from bitter practical experience, American military conduct in the Vietnam War was a national embarrassment, all the more so for not being openly admitted so. The indictment at this level does not refer to the failures of policy leadership in Washington; it refers only to the conduct of military operations in the field. And here it refers to far more than the all too numerous cases of command breakdown, the misuse and overuse of weapon technologies, the repeated instances of demoralization and indiscipline among the troops. It refers primarily to the progressive breakdown of the American military forces in that conflict as a rationally organized, professionally trained military bureaucracy.

Centrally, this was a collapse of ideas, of patterns of self-conception. The military in Vietnam, from the highest command levels on down, progressively came to think of themselves less and less in rational-professional terms as an organized, ordered force to be used for the deliberate achievement of carefully, narrowly defined objectives.[2] And this progression went forward even while individual commanders and units claimed greater and greater proficiency in the use of particular weapons and tactics.

Thus, more and more often as the war wore on, command centers sent their troops out on what were termed "search-and-destroy" missions. Rational-professional criticism of these operations should focus not on the indiscriminate use of firepower that they generated; the too liberal, almost casual overuse of defoliants, "smart" bombs, and so forth; to say nothing of the overuse of conventional means of killing, burning, and wrecking whatever presented itself as targets for this kind of activity. What is at issue is the concept, the thought, that a military force of a modern, twentieth-century power should be sent out not to subdue, defeat, conquer, or otherwise bring to terms an enemy, but simply to obliterate it. This is to reduce war to its most primitive level, to simple savagery. The commanders who conceived of these operations had explanations for their mindless violence, principally that the enemy was elusive, it would not stand a fight. But none of these explanations touched on the heart of the matter, which was that the very concept of these operations debased, decivilized, above all, deprofessionalized the troops involved in carrying them out.

Even more vivid in this same regard was the invention and use by the American commanders in Vietnam of the concept of "the free-fire zone." In so-designated areas, all fire direction and control was held off. Troops as units and as individuals were free to shoot and kill as they chose anything they saw or heard—or thought they saw or heard. Again, the use of this concept was undertaken with little or no systematic awareness of its implications for understanding military force in rational-professional terms. But it is a concept that would have appalled military scientists as diverse as Karl von Clausewitz and Robert E. Lee. To declare in advance any potential field of battle a "free-fire zone" is to say that in those areas rational-professional criteria for the control and allocation of firepower do not apply. It is as if in those areas the entire command apparatus, the whole of the officer corps, threw up its hands and walked away, leaving the troops, awash in whatever sea of emotions, to fend for themselves. That actual events in the field often conformed to predictable consequences of this kind of calculated command collapse is surprising only to the degree that they did not occur more often.[3]

These instances of rational-professional failure in the field raise a fundamental question. That question is not, in the abstract, why did they occur? Bureaucracies can fail anywhere. The question we must face is why, when exclusively American personnel were involved, did they occur? Obviously, the Vietnam War was a monumentally complex affair; to discuss any aspect of it is to raise hosts of questions not only tragic in every aspect but full of every kind of occasion for shame and blame. Nevertheless, within that wide context, the specific critique of a war misfought, of technical incompetence of a profound sort can be raised. And what is being asked is very specifically, How could a well trained, superbly equipped, generously funded group of American military rational-professionals do so badly so persistently in such fundamental terms?

Our second example of American governmental incompetence raises this same question in even sharper terms. Again it is an example involving issues of great complexity and sensitivity, and is directly concerned with activities everywhere thought central to the nation's international security. This is the issue of the production of the explosive components of the nation's nuclear arsenal, a government monopoly even if major segments of the process were contracted out to private operatives. In the closing months of the Reagan administration, the secretary of the Department of Energy, whose department bore direct responsibility for the production of these materials for use by the Pentagon, allowed the general public access to a series of reports indicating in undisputed terms that the production process was in a sorry state.[4] There was no question here about general policy direction. All established authorities in and out of the government were unanimously agreed that nuclear weapons should be designed, improved and modernized, produced in quantity, operationalized, and stockpiled. Moreover, programs to effect these goals had been funded almost without stint since the days of the Manhattan Project, which produced the first bombs. Yet, over decades of well-documented deterioration, the production process had been allowed to grind to a chaotic halt. Seventeen major installations, some of them very large, were involved, and all of them were in one condition or another of suspended operation. The production of certain critically important elements, not available from any other source, had ceased altogether, and estimates about when production could recommence changed almost daily, always involving further postponements. Other aspects of the situation were even more alarming: (1) all the plants were shown to be more or less antiquated and in sometimes critical need of major overhaul or total replacement; (2) enormous sums were shown to have been already spent beyond current production costs on unneeded facilities, programs that did not work, and installations that were declared obsolete almost on the day they became operational; (3) endemic throughout the program were gross instances of casual operation of facilities with respect to safety regulations and the exposure of workers and also the general public to both nuclear hazards and even, amazingly, completely ordinary industrial toxic substances; (4) because the situation had been allowed to deteriorate unchecked over so many decades, it would take as many more to correct; (5) the costs involved in cleaning up the toxic spills, designing and installing new safety equipment, modernizing still-usable facilities and building needed new ones were astronomical, much of the money being needed immediately; (6) the management of the industry was shown to be sharply fragmented into hostile groups of safety experts, production managers, research scientists, and personality cliques—with the department secretary apparently unable to mediate successfully between them—which may have been the major reason the whole affair became as much public knowledge as it did.

Bureaucratic confusion on this scale is rare if only because bureaucratic operations on this huge scale are themselves rare. It could therefore be plausibly argued that once allowances are made for sheer size, the kinds of mismanagement displayed in the American nuclear explosives industry can be seen as quite ordinary, even as the inevitable concomitants to bureaucratic experience everywhere. They were allowed to get out of hand only to the degree that a penchant for secrecy in the operation from its earliest days shielded it from salutary contact with outside inspection and healthy criticism. But it also could be argued that the special features of the American nuclear explosives industry should have amply protected it from all bureaucratic problems of a merely ordinary sort. For from the beginning this had been a very special industry. It had developed out of an intense wartime effort to move in record time from abstract physical speculations of the most rarefied sort to acute practical possibility. It had succeeded in this because the effort had been encouraged by the highest authorities to attract to it the most dedicated and gifted intellectual resources the nation could command both from home and overseas. Success in this effort, at least many supposed, brought a near instantaneous end to global conflict and the ushering in of a new age in human history. It also brought a sudden and enormous increase in America's international stature, one that, it again was widely supposed, was only preserved in the face of the rise of the Soviet threat, by the sustained rapid development and expansion of the nation's original nuclear arsenal. Thus, the nation's nuclear explosives industry, in the eyes of certainly nearly all Americans, came to carry a weight of historic significance, both practical and symbolic, unmatched by any other bureaucratic structure regardless of size or purpose. For these Americans, it can be surely asserted that the nation's honor, its security, its power in the world at large, stood poised upon this industry and its product. Yet this industry has been allowed to deteriorate over decades into a bureaucratic shambles.

We are thus returned to our original question: how could this happen in America? How could a bureaucratic structure on which so much pure rational-professional concern had been lavished go to pieces over such a long period of managerial incompetence?

Before advancing answers to these questions, it is important to move two other facts again into clear view. First, the bureaucratic failures exhibited in the Vietnam War and also so evident in the nuclear weapons industry are not isolated, exceptional phenomena. Journalistic sources and official reports over the decades give clear evidence that similar situations exist in virtually every aspect and level of American governmental bureaucracy. Stories of corruption, confusion, failure, and foolishness in governmental programs flood the press day after day, ranging from laughable lapses in local government operations to, as we have seen, effective chaos in the processes by which the nation's major institutions put together the federal government budget.

There is no need to detail the facts of these stories in a book of interpretation and theory searching for explanation and evaluation. We do, however, need to keep them in mind, while at the same time also noting that the sheer bulk of these problems points to systemic roots. When enough of these facts are kept uppermost in the mind, it will seem lame indeed to blame the progressive irrationality of the Vietnam War on peculiarities imbedded in the personalities of particular presidents—or the disintegration over the years of the nuclear armaments industry on the gradual departure from its management ranks of internationally famed theoretical physicists. Those are partial and immediate causes only; in the larger picture, larger factors must be seen at work.

Authority Versus Power

The evaluative explanation advanced by the rational-professional mind for the continuing breakdown of bureaucratic structures in American government is that the dominant Protestant/Bourgeois mind controlling those structures fundamentally misunderstands the principles that ought to govern their construction and use. Two matters are centrally at issue here: first, the language appropriate to discussions about the direction and employment of bureaucratic servants, and second, the issue of responsibility.

The Protestant/Bourgeois mind talks in politics the language of power; in its Protestant mode, it says that power is legitimate if it sweeps the American people forward toward goals of social justice; in its Bourgeois mode, it says that power is useful if it advances aggregates of personal interests. In contrast, the rational-professional mind talks a language dedicated to competence in service to a public interest. This contrast is so fundamental that, in Chapter 9, when we were explaining the nature of bureaucracy in the American environment, we made a distinction regarding it, saying that in terms of this analysis the rational-professional mind does not talk the language of power at all but the language of authority. Now we must use this distinction for evaluative purposes.

Power, as defined in this book but also as visibly practiced day by day in the practical experience of American politics, is preemptory. It is Hobbesian. Premised on a practically determined a priori acknowledgement of "who's in charge," it brooks no argument about the expression and implementation of sovereign will. It is simple command backed by sanction: do this or else.

At its most exalted, power in this American Hobbesian understanding decrees that in the name of the nation's might and hope, its providential mission in history, its enemies, in war after war, must simply bow down, surrender unconditionally. At its most pedestrian, power in this tradition is some local councilor demanding and exercising a perquisite of office on nothing more than a personal say-so.

Rational-professional authority is to be understood in an altogether different analytic key. If power in the American tradition is best thought of in terms of being always "power over," then authority in its bureaucratic context should always be thought of as being "authority within."

Bureaucratic authority, as an ideal concept, is both hedged by and permeated with self-limiting contextual understandings. In a bureaucratic context, those with authority may justifiably have it only on a warrant laying out relevant credentials of training and demonstrated competence. It is not enough, it may in fact count against someone, to be shown to be "the people's choice" or to have friends in higher places. And to be sustained in authority that initial evidence of competence must be also sustained. In a sense very different from power's legitimization, authority must always be earned, and earned in ways immediately relevant to the context in which it is exercised. You do not get to be a respected basketball coach by proving you were once a good football player—or vice-president in charge of international operations by demonstrating a strong attachment to family values.

Most important, authority figures in bureaucratic contexts must be able to demonstrate continuous concern for and effectiveness in serving the corporate good. This means, on its negative side, that personal concerns and advantages are eliminated from consideration. It means, on its positive side, that what must be pursued is only the good of the impersonally conceived whole, in its pure institutional and abstract character. Once again, these requirements must be met continually, in every decision and move the authority figure makes. Never must the authority figure be allowed to forget that he or she has authority, has the right to decide this or that, only as an integral part of the whole that created his or her office in the first instance.[5]

These may seem simple points, but it is exactly in terms of them that the rational-professional mind launches its critique of the dominant elements of the American political system. It regrets first the thousands and thousands of jobs that in American government are filled effectively on the basis of cronyism, as favors to reward and promote alliances, and with scant regard to competence, proven or promised. It regrets second and even more that the policy-making process, from initial conception, through general adoption, to particular and extended implementation, is in America shot through, tripped up, deflected, adulterated, fragmented, and constrained by what are euphemistically termed "political" considerations.[6] In plain English, what that means is that to start up and put into place a "policy," the struggling and idealistic bureaucratic authority figure behind it has to ensure that at every turn all the relevant political interests get bought off.

There is nothing original or startling about these comments. Not only do laments along these lines fill the media and the journals, we ourselves have repeated them again and again in earlier chapters. The important point is that, theoretically understood, these must be seen to be systemic criticisms. Whenever an executive in America, whether public or private, complains bitterly that in dealing with the government, "Everybody wants something," the executive may think he or she is merely pointing up the fact that the policy-making process is endless, that there is always one more requirement to be met, one more group whose approval must be won, one more official whose opposition must be overcome. But the implicit point of these complaints is in fact fundamental. Compulsory incrementalism is for all its frustration a celebration of the system as it was designed and as it stands. It is evidence that John Adams instructed James Madison and his cohorts all too well. And it is evidence, too, that no tinkering with the system will change its fundamentals.

That the rational-professional critique goes to the root of the system can perhaps be better noticed in this contrast in how choices are to be made. For the rational-professional mind, the elements in a choice must be stripped of their personal character; effectiveness in achieving an impersonal corporate good should be the only consideration. But think of ways in which the American Protestant/Bourgeois environment turns every issue, from the most trivial to the most socially significant, into "personal choice" issues: as a patient, shall I take aspirin or Advil; as a citizen, shall I vote for this candidate or that one; as a sports fan, shall I cheer for this team or that one; as a religious person, shall I become a Presbyterian or a Methodist; as a prisoner in John Rawls's prisoners' dilemma, shall I make this choice or that one. In every case, it is for me to decide; the choice is mine, rationally, emotionally, whatever. Where in this universe is there room for the person who says, the choice is not mine or for me, the choice is ours for the greater good. Persons on that tack will be labeled in America hopelessly idealistic and perhaps pathetic. In America, rational-professional persons have ample reason for thinking themselves so stigmatized.

Having been so stigmatized, many rational-professionals in America retreat from the commitments and styles of their professionalism into the coziness of the familiar and dominant schizophrenia. They affect the street-smart combination of cynical greed and privatistic spirituality. In short, from the perspectives they have abandoned, they become corrupted. This corruption can take many forms.

It can be the honest corruption of the deliberately shortsighted.

Without thought or conscience, the honest professional just does the job at hand with consummate skill. It is left to others to ask questions. In the moment, the bombs are dropped exactly on the assigned targets, the treatments are given as prescribed, the checks are written as directed, the building is designed as per specifications. This kind of honest but blind professionalism can carry individual rational professionals a long way—and grow. Blindly, it can become, on the one hand, simple careerism. On the other, it can become, again blindly, empire building for whatever office, department, or program is at hand. No doubt, all bureaucratic settings are vulnerable to these kinds of corruption. What they most demonstrate is a loss of contextual sense, the corruption of measured, justified authority into simple power, the one-dimensional pursuit of immediate objectives. That kind of failure of intellectual vision and moral commitment can happen anywhere. But it should be noted how especially vulnerable to these corruptions are bureaucratic structures in the American political environment. And the reasons for this, once again, are congenital.[7]

Bureaucracy requires context, a defined, concretely articulated, programmatic set of policy objectives. It is exactly these objectives that American government, in its Protestant/Bourgeois dominant elements, has great difficulty providing; in fact, it never was designed to provide them. As we have seen, chapter by chapter throughout this book, the policy-making processes of American government are fragmented, inconstant, easily distracted, or hopelessly vague, overly ambitious, utterly idealistic. And these characteristics are not marginal to the mechanisms of American government. They are design flaws, failures of theory.

Beyond their honest corruption, rational-professionals in America can with equal vulnerability succumb to explicitly dishonest corruption.[8] Once again, it must be emphasized that this is a corruption especially perceived as corrupt from the rational-professional perspective itself. Honest dedication to service in the public interest is preeminently a rational-professional criteria of meaningful public employment. It is therefore radically mortifying to the rational-professional mentality when public employees use the advantages of public office for personal advancement. These are not just instances of entrepreneurial indiscretion, mere moral lapses. They are fundamentally irrational repudiations of essential being. In consequence, in a rational-professional perspective, the pandemic vulnerability of the American political system to outbreaks of explicitly dishonest corruption is a grave defect, a perversion of essential character. Madison's formulation, that he would design a constitution that would connect the rights of the office to the interests of the man, is therefore, from a rational-professional perspective, not just an invitation to cancerous invasions of the body politic. It is itself cancerous in concept. It means that the rational-professional mentality, to sustain itself in the American environment, must be perpetually countertheoretical.

The rational-professional indictment of the American political system is, thus, grave and comprehensive. It may proceed in the first instance from outrage over particular instances of incompetence and malfeasance, serious, even monumental, as these individually may be, but from there the critique moves rapidly to matters of substance and principle, and on by necessary implication to systemic dimensions. The whole of this process is paralleled by rational-professional concerns in the American environment over the issue of responsibility.[9]

We have confronted this issue before, in its Protestant version, in Chapter 11. There we saw the citizen, with Protestant enthusiasm, investing trust, faith, even an outrushing of love, in a heroic leader. The leader in turn is expected to reciprocate that affection, to show trustingly sympathy and concern by word as much as by deed. It is essentially a matter of feeling—and of feeling good. Thus, when a presidential rule is cut short by assassination, as in the cases of Lincoln and Kennedy, the outpouring of grief is torrential—and the president is felt to have died nobly. If the leader simply retires after long service, the occasion is still marked by nostalgic farewells in simple ceremonies of separation and sorrow. In no case is there even the pretense of an exact accounting of how performance matched promises and of achievements against declared aspirations.

In contrast, in the bureaucratic context, responsibility is intrinsically an exact business. In the first instance, the individual operatives are exactly responsible to themselves for the position held in terms of the logic of the assignments that put them in those positions. They are responsible next to their fellow workers for getting their jobs done in a cooperative and harmonious way. They are responsible, too, to their subordinates or the publics whom they serve—and who reasonably expect service from them. And they are responsible finally to their superiors not only for getting the job done but also for reporting exactly how and when and with what consequences it was done, whether it was done in accordance with all directives and regulations and whether it achieved the expected goals. In this perspective, responsibility is both an exact and also a rational business, a rationally and fully accountable business. It is the glue, the essential fixative that holds a bureaucratic structure together, vertically up and down the chain of command, and horizontally across the spread of peers within the spans of control. Viewed in this light, responsibility, in the sense of an exact, rational accountability of each and every operative in a bureaucratic structure, may be viewed as the key concept to ensure the achievement of essential objectives, the assured performance of work done in an effective, organized way.

Yet, in the American political environment, the use of this concept is radically compromised, especially at its critically important terminal points. Who, in the end, in America is responsible for bureaucratic operations? Who or what can be the source of that contextual glue that holds bureaucratic structures together?

We have already exploded the notion that the American political system is, in any of the several possible senses, a system of responsible government. The closest the system comes to that is on its Protestantized mythic side in which elected officials are held to be responsible to the electorate. But, as we have seen, in the absence of any formal, effective mechanisms for holding them to account, this notion practically amounts to a charade. Any admission by a chief executive, including especially the president, of personal responsibility for this or that bad policy choice can always be made to evaporate into vacuous rhetoric. As in the Iran–Contra affair, the president can proclaim personal accountability, and then will his own innocence by convincing avowals of ignorance of what was transpiring in his name even by members of his immediate staff. That certain things in fact happened gets lost in swirls of debate about what did the president know and when did he know it.

More interesting are questions of administrative responsibility in the strict, rational-professional sense. Here, in separation of powers myth, the lines of command and responsibility are clear, from the chief executive/administrator president ("The buck stops here!"), through his White House staff and the Office of Management and Budget, to the department secretaries, and thence down through their various management chains, to their respective lowest levels.

It is not enough to dissolve this myth of the executive monolith by pointing to the presence in the so-called executive branch of a myriad number of autonomous or at least semiautonomous boards, commissions, and agencies outside the departmental network. Nor is it, again for present purposes, enough to go on to point to the much more significant facts that in the American political system dominance of the executive machinery by nominal chief executives must always be shared in practice with the relevant legislative bodies.[10] The essential point is that this legislative intervention ("lateral penetration") into administrative structures, whether conducted by individual members, committees and subcommittees, or whole legislative bodies acting as units, is carried out in response to a different and conflicting theory of governmental organization, the language of mixed government and its attendant emphasis on checks and balances. In consequence, what the rational-professional mentality confronts in legislative interference in administration is not just fragmentation of authority and confusion in the lines of command—although those problems are there in almost overwhelming abundance. More ominously, in theoretical terms, the language legislators talk in the check and balance relationships is a language that is antithetical to rational-professional considerations of technical administrative responsibility. To try to hold a committee—or, with perhaps as much or greater justification, its permanent staff—"responsible" for decades of mismanagement and policy neglect is, practically speaking, a near impossibility. How or by whom could its dozen or so independently situated and interested egos be called to account? But that is only at the practical level. The crucial issue is at the theoretical level. There the issue is that the legislators talk not a language of who is responsible for what to whom, but a language of favor and fix, of influence and interest, of negotiation and deal. Moreover, the rational-professionals dealing with these legislators and their staffs quickly learn to talk this Bourgeois language of the American political ideology and themselves become deeply infected (corrupted?) by it, on pain of seeing their ambitions and programs defunded and forgotten.

It is this theoretical fact that, in the end, most appalls rational-professionals as they attempt to go about their work in the American political environment. It must make them believe that in the American environment they are endlessly vulnerable to an existential violation. The individual instances of incompetence and corruption that seem everywhere to occur in American government are always to be regretted. But in the light of the present argument, they must also be seen as symptoms of much more serious and deep-seated problems, problems that must be seen as arising from the fact that the dominant modes of American politics are simply uncomprehending of the requirements of a modern mode of professionalized governmental operations.[11]

The Counter Critique

The rational-professional critique, however muted, even obscured, in practice, is in concept so sweeping and so fundamental that it invites a rejoinder, a countercritique. Like the critiques to which it is in reply, the countercritique is also seldom carried in practice to logically unavoidable conclusions or expressed in fully articulated form. In the American environment, no one wants to say the obvious—completely. Nevertheless, from the scattered and various fuming outbursts against rational-professionalism in America, it is possible to piece together a full argument.

In the first instance, rational-professionalism in America is suspect, specifically from a Protestant/Bourgeois perspective, for its incipient totalitarianism. Protestant/Bourgeois preemptory power suffers from no such taint, however objectionable it may be for being arbitrary, wanton, or even merely whimsically oppressive. Protestant/Bourgeois power is too particularized in its usual objectives. Its broadest claim in principle is simply that of "showing who's boss." But rational-professional authority, with its constant indebtedness to contextualism, can always be feared for harboring ambitions for a generalized control. Its hunger is to impose and implement programs, comprehensive, integrated, and extended. Preemptory power can prove its point by regulating, curbing, constraining here or there. Rational-professionalism, at its very concept, will not be satisfied with anything less than the positive redefinition and reordering of styles of life. It would never be enough for it to give poor families such temporary assistance as would prevent them from starving in the street. For rational-professional mentalities, the objective would in necessary concept be comprehensive: clean, supervised, shelter; health care; the fathers in wage-earning jobs; the children all in school being trained to become orderly, productive, taxpaying citizens. No number of restrictive regulations could achieve goals on that scale. That would take a plan, comprehensive and total, the very thought of which chills the blood of the individualistic, freedom-loving Protestant/Bourgeois American.

All this is an objection to the way in which rational-professionalism thinks about social issues. Protestant/Bourgeois mentalities also object to the way in which rational-professionalism brings its thought patterns to bear on social issues within the actual frameworks of American politics and social life. Here the objection is not only to the grandiose scale of rational-professionalism's daydream solutions to social ills; it is also to rational-professionalism's failure to appreciate the positive virtues, at least as exhibited in the American environment, of the Protestant/Bourgeois way of doing business, incrementalism. There are real advantages, so the Protestant/Bourgeois argument runs, to the step-by-step policy-making process required by the dominant patterns of American legislative/executive institutions at all levels of government. No doubt, there are disadvantages, too; as these things go, the processes are slow and cumbersome, and the results are often complex, overlapping, messy, and always on the margin incomplete. But, again as these things go, the standard American process is remarkably open. Access is effectively offered to an extraordinarily wide and varied range of influences, with few if any groups absolutely and permanently locked out. Moreover, it is generally prudent to require frequent pauses in the development and implementation of public policies. Much too often it has been found that grand initiatives in public policy have had unintended consequences that outweighed their intended effects. Protestant/ Bourgeois policy makers have learned the value of a "wait-and-see" approach, however much frustration that may engender in those impatient to solve problems with broad strokes and comprehensive plans.

Argument along these lines points to deeper issues. The Protestant/Bourgeois mind has a fundamental objection to the way in which the rational-professional mind grasps the citizen in concept. The Protestant/Bourgeois mind has its own difficulties in this area: the Protestant side of it wants to grasp the citizen as neighbor, to be supported, nurtured, and loved; the Bourgeois side of it wants to use the fellow citizen as a client in a deal or defeat him or her in a rivalry. But in either event, the citizen is confronted as a whole human being every detail of whose history, character, and intentions are relevant to the relationship being developed.[12]

In contrast, the instinct of the rational-professional mind is to strip the citizen being met in the course of a service relationship of all inessentials and treat him or her as a simple object placed in the context of the developing project. The railroad conductor must treat his or her passengers all the same without regard for their personal characteristics. If they have paid full fare that is the end of it. And in this process the conductor's own characteristics—gender, age, degree of fatigue, boredom, and so on—must also be kept from view. With massive impersonality, the same goes for the driver seeking a license, the widow seeking a Social Security benefit, the teenager in trouble with the law. Would anyone have it differently? Should the IRS treat the Rockefellers differently from the rest of us? Yet evenhanded, simple, rational-professional impersonalism is essentially a kind of inhumanity, and an inhumanity that can only too easily lead to calculated callousness and on to unforgivable cruelty.

It would be hard to exaggerate the evils that, from a Protestant/ Bourgeois perspective, this line of argument brings into view. Virtually every American has at one time or another—and frequently over and over again—experienced the maddeningly cold impersonality of the rational-professional mind, mostly in grossly mundane ways from teachers and school administrators, police officers, postal clerks, librarians, wherever the testily officious may be found. The very name, "G.I." (derived from "general issue," a World War I term), is a massive, culture-wide, history-deep protest against this kind of experience. But what is at stake here is anything but mundane. It is the deeply felt sense of one's own moral autonomy, the fundamental value of both the American social democratic and the liberal democratic traditions. When the citizen as a whole human being confronts the rational-professional mind and is stripped down to ticketholder, applicant, offender, a mere number, a case among a string of cases, it is precisely that sense of total self that goes, that sense of being in charge of one's life and of having a built-up identity arising from that stewardship. Nevertheless, the fact of the matter, the theory of it, is that for the rational-professional mind, individual moral autonomy is an unthinkable concept. An army of rational-professionals—for whatever purposes—cannot be recruited from the ranks of the morally autonomous.

That what is involved here is more than hurt pride, that what is at stake is nothing less than the citizen's existential status, can be seen from the implications that these points have for the misunderstanding and limitations that the rational-professional mind experiences in the political process. There are two issues here. Both can be briefly stated; but their combined significance is great.

First, because the rational-professional mind is bound, in concept, to strip citizens of their humanity, of their status as individuals in charge of their own lives, that mind can have no genuine understanding of, let alone sympathy for, the political process as it is practiced in America in either its Bourgeois or its Protestant forms. To both of these minds, the political process, for better or for worse, is a sine qua non of self-realization. The Bourgeois citizen joins it in a spirit of negotiation to protect and advance vital self-interests. The Protestant citizen joins it to be swept up in a conversion of faith and love for other. But the impatience that the rational-professional mind experiences in the face of these political goings-on is a measure of its inability to comprehend either their form or their content. The closest this mind can come to an understanding of the political process is to perceive it as a dialogue about appropriate means for securing given ends in the light of available resources, competencies, and time frames. The Protestant/Bourgeois mind, for all its own internal confusion, would call that kind of process a conference of experts—and find in it no place or role for its own talents and objectives. No wonder that in the American political tradition, rational-professionals are pledged to a passion for anonymity. In politics and for politics they have nothing to say.[13]

The second of our final points arises directly from the first. In the perspectives of theoretical interpretation, American democracy is locked in a state of perpetual crisis. Its Protestant, mythic version despises its Bourgeois, ideological practice and vice versa, although both can only offer themselves as an alternative to the other. The contribution to this situation of the rational-professional mind is different. With good reason, over all the decades of its coming to prominent participation in American government, it has complained bitterly and vociferously about the lack of guidance it receives from the dominant elements of the political system. Policy direction of the bureaucracy at every level of American government is ambiguous, fragmented, inconstant, inarticulate, corrupt, devious, or vague and bombastic. But, beyond complaining, the American rational-professional mind has nothing constructive to say about this situation.[14] Having, in concept, no understanding of the political process as practiced in America, it is foresworn from even commenting on it. More to the point even than that, the rational-professional mind, steeped, trained, and competent only to take orders, not give them, only to achieve goals, not define them, has itself no history, equipment, or vision by which to define an alternative democratic process that might give it, in contrast to what it now has, policy direction that is coherent, constant, and specific. Always the servant, never the master, dedicated to servicing a public interest it cannot of itself define, it can signal us no way out.[15]

To this countercritique of itself, the rational-professional mind in America can make no effective reply.

Postscript

It may be wondered in conclusion how a national political system so uncomfortable with itself has so long endured. Why has it put up with itself for so long? How could it endure if, from every available practical moral perspective, it is to a provable degree a failure?

The system endures in part because, for all its limitations and record of failure, it in measure works even if in consistently impoverished ways. Public services of a sort do get provided, most of the wars have been won, leadership of a sort to engender some degree of public confidence is recruited. Perhaps more important, all the major Bourgeois interests get enough of what they want to not fret seriously about opting for a different system, and the American masses are sufficiently "mythed" to resist suddenly being organized for radical change.

More particularly, the American people are sufficiently "mythed" to be only intermittently and incompletely aware of the real operative principles of their political system and of the deplorable record it has left in its wake. In this light, American political myth can be seen as a highly efficient mask, effectively a lie. Accustomed throughout their history to thinking of their collective self only in terms of their noblest aspirations, Americans remain as a people resolutely blind to both the facts and the origins of their sharpest frustrations. They see no reason and can hear no call for a new 1787.

But the overriding reason for the simple endurance of the American political system lies in the central characteristics of that system itself. It is composed of those three conflicting political vocabularies, Protestant, Bourgeois, and rational-professional, none of which is a language of political self-awareness and self-transcendence, a language that could on its own or in tension with the others articulate viable formulas for concrete political change. In consequence, with pain piled upon guilt, and the whole smothered under tattered illusion, Americans adamantly celebrate themselves in politics as the "brightest and best of the sons of the morning."[1] Trapped inside themselves, they can conceive of no alternatives. Even if 1787 were somehow to come again, the American people could only do it

243

again. *In theory*, they could do no other. That is their ultimate political impoverishment.

So, the system endures. But is mere endurance a value to be admired without qualification? Is stability in a sore place a good? The quality of what endures is also to be questioned. Is a perpetually self-impoverishing politics going to be efficient enough, good enough, and competent enough to see the nation into the next century?

Notes

Preface

1. James MacGregor Burns, J. W. Peltason, and Thomas E. Cronin, *Government by the People*, 14th ed. (Englewood Cliffs, N.J.: Prentice Hall, 1990), p. 13.

2. For example, J. Allen Smith, *The Spirit of American Government* (New York: Macmillan, 1907); Charles Beard, *An Economic Interpretation of the Constitution of the United States* (New York: Macmillan, 1913); J. Allen Smith, *The Growth and Decadence of Constitutional Government* (New York: Henry Holt, 1930); William Yandell Elliot, *The Need for Constitutional Reform* (New York: McGraw-Hill, 1935); Walter Dean Burnham, *Critical Elections and the Mainsprings of American Politics* (New York: Norton, 1970); Theodore Lowi, *The End of Liberalism*, 2d ed. (New York: Norton, 1979); Michael Parenti, *Democracy for the Few*, 3d ed. (New York: St. Martin's Press, 1980); Donald L. Robinson, *Government for the Third American Century* (Boulder, Colo.: Westview Press, 1989). The reception given Beard's book is enough to give anyone pause before venturing in his footsteps.

Chapter 1

1. Harold Lasswell and Abraham Kaplan, *Power and Society* (New Haven, Conn.: Yale University Press, 1950), esp. pp. 74–79, 97–102.

2. Methodologically, this book is an exercise in "mundane phenomenology" (the phrase is Fred Dallmayr's). This is a perspective that assumes that: (1) political *reality*, the historically persistent patterns of "mundane" political life (e.g., American individualism, Congress, the Republican party, the state of New York), is a collection of essentially ideal (mental) constructs that persist traditionally in the social (national) collective mind; and (2) political *action* ("behavior," e.g., elections, legislation, a criminal arrest) is the manifestation in the material world, the "acting out," of these conventionalized political ideas.

In this light, this book is an exercise in the apprehension of "theory," the stock of ideas (values, principles, institutions) lodged in the traditional American collective "mind" and by which Americans persistently act out their political lives. The book's method is that of "phenomenological reduction." In the classic example, if you wish to apprehend the "pure" idea of "space," start with an apple, real and actual, and sequentially "reduce" away its color, taste, smell, weight, density, and other phenomenological "accidents" until all that remains is the *idea* of space. Equally, to apprehend the idea of the American presidency, start with Lyndon Johnson, real and actual. Flush away the incidentals and reveal the conceptual outlines of the

presidency as Johnson understood it. What is found there can be checked by
looking at Ronald Reagan. But the aim is not to find statistical patterns; the
aim is to apprehend (and check) as immediately as possible *in the actions of
these figures* the ideas, the "theory," that they, however unselfconsciously,
drew from collective understandings of the presidential office and used to
give structure and meaning to their behavior.

The methodology of practical phenomenology is thus far more a matter
of philosophy, intuition, analysis, and definition than it is an exercise in
history, anthropology, or "political science" in the natural science tradition.

Although a book based on this methodology can hope to be systematic
and conclusive, the actual practice of phenomenological reduction in mundane political life is necessarily unsystematic and never ending. It depends
in essential ways on a continuous reading of the daily press and other
sources of reportage on actual political practice. But this methodology is also
ever open to readers' checking theories claimed to have been apprehended
in past events against their own inspections and apprehensions in future,
actual political developments.

These understandings of political life and the tasks of the political an-
alyst are essentially Kantian. They also owe much to Weber's concept of
verstehen and his theory of "intentional sociology." See Immanuel Kant, *Critique of Pure Reason*, trans. J.M.D. Meiklejohn (London: Dent, 1934), pp. 12,
16, 19, 25; Immanuel Kant, *The Moral Law*, trans. H. J. Paton (London:
Hutchinson's, 1947); George Herbert Mead, *Mind, Self, and Society* (Chicago:
University of Chicago Press, 1934), esp. pt. 3; Alfred Schutz, *The Phenomenology of the Social World* (Evanston, Ill.: Northwestern University Press,
1967), esp. chaps. 1 and 3; Max Weber, *Basic Concepts in Sociology*, trans. H.
P. Secher (New York: Greenwood Press, 1969); and, very important, Peter
Winch, *The Idea of a Social Science* (London: Routledge and Kegan Paul,
1958). For a more extensive discussion, see my *Ideology and Myth in American
Politics: A Critique of the National Political Mind* (Boston: Little, Brown, 1976),
pp. 13–29.

3. Compare this account to Plato's discussion of the "noble lie" in *The
Republic*, trans. Allan Bloom (New York: Basic Books, 1968), pp. 93–94.
Note especially Bloom's comments on this section, pp. xiv–xv and 365–69.

4. These understandings of "myth" and "ideology" owe something to
Karl Marx, preface to "A Contribution to the Critique of Political Economy,"
in *The Marx-Engels Reader*, ed. Robert C. Tucker, 2d ed. (New York: Norton,
1978), pp. 4–5; to the work of certain anthropologists, for example, Mary
Douglas, "The Meaning of Myth," in *The Structural Study of Myth and Totem-
ism*, ed. Edmund Leach (London: Tavistock, 1967); and even to Walter Ba-
gehot's famed distinction between the "dignified" and "efficient" parts of
the constitution in *The English Constitution*, 2d ed. (Garden City, N.Y.: Dol-
phin, [1872]). In these understandings, note again not only the false contrast
that can supposedly be drawn between "myth" and "reality"—against which
we assert that "myth" is as real a part of the political system as any other of
its elements—but also the equally false contrast drawn especially in American politics between "ideologues" and "pragmatists." In fact, as we shall see

in subsequent chapters, the so-called pragmatists of American politics are as ideologically bound as anybody else—it is just that as a breed they are notable for not doing much "myth talk."

Chapter 2

1. Alexis de Tocqueville, *Democracy in America*, trans. George Lawrence, ed. J. P. Mayer (Garden City, N.Y.: Doubleday, 1969); J. Hector St. John de Crèvecoeur, *Letters from an American Farmer* (New York: Penguin, 1981).

2. Frederick Jackson Turner, "The Significance of the Frontier in American History," *American Historical Association* 18 (separately bound, [1893]): 199.

3. Ibid., 226–27.

4. Ibid., 217.

5. Vernon Parrington, *Main Currents in American Thought*, 3 vols. (New York: Harcourt, Brace, 1954–58), 1:vi.

6. Arthur Schlesinger, Jr., *The Age of Jackson* (Boston: Little, Brown, 1945), pp. 118–19.

7. Parrington, *Main Currents*, 1:vi.

8. Samuel Huntington, *American Politics: The Promise of Disharmony* (Cambridge, Mass.: Harvard University Press, 1981), p. 33.

9. Ibid., p. 39.

10. Ibid., p. 33.

11. Ibid., p. 261.

12. Richard Hofstadter, *The American Political Tradition* (New York: Vintage, 1954), pp. vii–viii.

13. Daniel Boorstin, *The Genius of American Politics* (Chicago: University of Chicago Press, 1953).

14. Louis Hartz, *The Liberal Tradition in America* (New York: Harcourt, Brace, World, 1955). Like all prominent scholars, Hartz has come into a good deal of criticism, but none of it has shaken his major propositions. For example, J.G.A. Pocock, *The Machiavellian Moment* (Princeton, N.J.: Princeton University Press, 1975), has a very different understanding of the origins of American political thought. His hypothesis (p. 509), claimed to replace that of Hartz, is that the founders were "civic humanists" in a classical tradition and relied on the "virtue" of the citizens to curb corruption and broaden the horizons of self-interest. Pocock asserts, "A neo-classical politics provided both the ethos of the elites and the rhetoric of the upwardly mobile, and accounts for the singular cultural and intellectual homogeneity of the Founding Fathers and their generation. Not all Americans were schooled in this tradition, but there was (it would appear) no alternative tradition in which to be schooled" (p. 507).

It is worth noting that Pocock's focus, like that of his authorities, chiefly Bernard Bailyn, *The Ideological Origins of the American Revolution* (Cambridge, Mass.: Harvard University Press, 1967), and Gordon S. Wood, *The Creation of the American Republic, 1776–1787* (New York: Norton, 1969), is on the rhetoric of the pamphleteers and not on the detailed provisions of the federal constitution of 1787 or the practical political processes that emanated from its inauguration. Cf. Herbert J. Storing, *The Complete Anti-Federalist*, 7 vols. (Chicago: University of Chicago Press, 1981), 1:5, 83 n. 7; Catherine L. Albanese, *Sons of the Fathers: The Civil Religion of the American Revolution* (Philadelphia: Temple University Press, 1976), chap. 3; John Patrick Diggins, *The Lost Soul of American Politics: Virtue, Self-Interest, and the Foundations of Liberalism* (New York: Basic Books, 1984); Thomas Pangle, *The Spirit of Modern Republicanism* (Chicago: University of Chicago Press, 1988); Richard Sinopoli, "Liberalism, Republicanism and the Constitution," *Polity* 19 (Spring 1987): 331–52. For convincing support for Hartz, see Donald J. Devine, *The Political Culture of the United States* (Boston: Little, Brown, 1972). This book, a remarkable display of methodological ingenuity and thoroughness, is a deliberate effort to provide full-scale "empirical" support for Hartz's theses.

15. Hartz, *Liberal Tradition*, pp. 6, 308.

16. The argument that follows proceeds from that presented in Richard Henry Tawney, *Religion and the Rise of Capitalism* (New York: Mentor, 1947). Tawney derived much of his analysis from Max Weber, *The Protestant Ethic and the Spirit of Capitalism*, trans. Talcott Parsons (New York: Scribner's, 1958). With important reservations, both he and Weber were working in the wake of Marx and Engels. It was the genius of Marx and Engels that focused modern scholarship on the broad revolutionary impact on the modern world of the northwest European middle class. See, for example, Engels's discussion of religion, materialism, and revolution in his "Socialism: Utopian and Scientific," in *The Marx-Engels Reader*, ed. Robert C. Tucker, 2d ed. (New York: Norton, 1978), pp. 683–717.

17. This and all subsequent biblical citations are from the Oxford Annotated Bible, RSV, ed. Herbert G. May and Bruce M. Metzger (New York: Oxford University Press, 1962).

18. The literature on New England Protestantism is disproportionately vast, but for the purposes of this discussion, to illustrate the complexities of John Winthrop's life and times within which the concept of Protestant community arises, consult the standard biographies, e.g., E. S. Morgan, *The Puritan Dilemma* (Boston: Little, Brown, 1958), esp. chap. 7. For quotation in text below, see Perry Miller, ed., *The American Puritans* (New York: Anchor Books, 1956), p. 83.

19. See Seymour Martin Lipset, *The First New Nation* (Garden City, N.Y.: Anchor, 1967), pp. 177–80; Will Herberg, *Protestant-Catholic-Jew* (Garden City, N.Y.: Doubleday, 1960); H. Richard Niebuhr, *The Social Sources of Denominationalism* (New York: World Book, 1957); Robert N. Bellah, "Civil Religion in America," *Daedalus*, Winter 1967, pp. 1–21; Robert N. Bellah, *The Broken Covenant: American Civil Religion in Time of Trial* (New York: Seabury Press, 1975); and George C. Bedell et al., *Religion in America*, 2d ed. (New York: Macmillan, 1982).

20. Luther is preferred over Calvin as spokesman for the Protestant pole of the modern American liberal mind because his type of radical evangelical pietism was much more influential in the development of American religious feeling than was Calvin's more doctrinal theology. Calvin's influence in America was largely confined to New England, and even there was

much diminished by the eighteenth century. In addition, Luther's conservatism in economic and political matters, the natural consequence of the importance of his pietism, underlines the fact that the contradictions in the Protestant/Bourgeois syndrome were present from the beginning. See the discussion of Luther in Tawney, *Rise of Capitalism*, pp. 72–91. For a contrasting discussion of American Protestantism and its relation to American Lockean politics, see, very importantly, Diggins, *Lost Soul of American Politics*.

21. In the famed chapter 13 of *Leviathan*, the one that concludes that life—for "man"—in the state of nature is "solitary, poor, nasty, brutish, and short." For male chauvinism was also integral to this world—even though, exceptionally, both Hobbes and Locke were, *relatively*, liberal on this score. Both specifically noted a respected status for women in the family, and Hobbes even suggested that in the family, the woman should be sovereign if she is bigger. In this world, women were not so much "marginalized" as put in their place, as were also children, servants, savages, and the poor. See Thomas Hobbes, *Leviathan*, ed. Michael Oakeshott (Oxford: Basil Blackwell, 1946), chap. 20; and John Locke, "The Second Treatise," in *Two Treatises of Government*, ed. P. Laslett (Cambridge: Cambridge University Press, 1960), chap. 6. It is important to notice that what Jefferson, writing from the very core of the American version of this world, very probably meant when he said that "all men" are equal was that all heads of households—"men" much like himself—were equal. It is also important to notice that Protestantism with its biblical roots was, however ambivalently, noticeably less strident on feminist issues than its Bourgeois twin. This difference of emphasis would become increasingly significant, especially in the late twentieth century.

22. Locke, "Second Treatise," chap. 6.

23. Since we have argued that, as an instinctual male chauvinist, Locke, when he wrote "man" really meant only male *man*—and was only supposedly using the word in its generic sense of "human being"—it is only consistent that we reproduce his emphasis. For a feminist perspective on this point, consult especially Seyla Benhabib, "The Generalized and the Concrete Other," in *Feminism as Critique: On the Politics of Gender*, ed. Seyla Benhabib and Drucilla Cornell (Minneapolis: University of Minnesota Press, 1987), pp. 77–97, esp. pp. 81, 85, 87.

24. Locke, "Second Treatise," chap.5.

25. Jonathan Edwards, *Puritan Sage: Collected Writings of Jonathan Edwards*, ed. Vergilius Ferm (New York: Library Publishers, 1953), pp. 365–78; Benjamin Franklin, *The Works of Benjamin Franklin*, 10 vols. (New York: G. P. Putnam's Sons, 1887), 1:441–61; Ralph Waldo Emerson, *Essays and Lectures* (New York: Library of America, 1983), pp. 257–82; Elbert Hubbard, *Message to Garcia* (East Aurora, N.Y.: Roycrofters, 1899).

26. The schizophrenic quality of the American political psyche has often been noted. See Gunnar Myrdal, "Introduction," in *An American Dilemma: The Negro Problem and Modern Democracy*, ed. Gunnar Myrdal et al., 2 vols. (New York: Harper and Row, 1944); Michael G. Kammen, *People of Paradox* (New York: Vintage, 1973); Huntington, *Promise of Disharmony*; W. Lloyd Warner, *Democracy in Jonesville* (New York: Harper and Brothers, 1949); but

also for some readers perhaps more persuasively, Lloyd Free and Hadley Cantril, *The Political Beliefs of Americans: A Study of Public Opinion* (New Brunswick, N.J.: Rutgers University Press, 1967): "This discrepancy between operational outlooks and ideological views is so marked as to be almost schizoid" (p. 33).

27. Once again, the vocabulary of this American individualism is essentially masculine. In time, more and more liberally, it becomes an ideal held up to all—male and female (as well as black and white)—but with little change in its essential, white male presuppositions.

28. Garry Wills, *Nixon Agonistes: The Crises of the Self-Made Man* (New York: New American Library, 1969), p. ix.

Chapter 3

1. For a flamboyant example of the degree to which this kind of nationalism was embodied in the rhetoric of the time, see Albert Jeremiah Beveridge's speech on the annexation of the Philippines, in College of Social Science One Staff, *The People Shall Judge* (Chicago: University of Chicago Press, 1949), 2:291–303.

2. See Chapter 2, nn. 21, 23.

3. Thomas Hobbes, *Leviathan*, ed. Michael Oakeshott (Oxford: Basil Blackwell, 1946), chap. 13.

4. Leo Strauss, *Natural Right and History* (Chicago: University of Chicago Press, 1953), pp. 165–66.

5. Alexander Hamilton, James Madison, and John Jay, *The Federalist Papers* (New York: New American Library, 1961), No. 10.

6. Ibid., No. 51, italics added.

7. Frank Coleman, "The Hobbesian Basis of American Constitutionalism," *Polity* 7 (Fall 1974): 57–89.

8. C. B. MacPherson, *The Political Theory of Possessive Individualism* (New York: Oxford University Press, 1962).

9. John Locke, "The Second Treatise," in *Two Treatises of Government*, ed. P. Laslett (Cambridge: Cambridge University Press, 1960), chap. 9.

10. Hobbes, *Leviathan*, chap. 17.

11. Ron Replogle, *Recovering the Social Contract* (Totowa, N.J.: Rowman and Littlefield, 1988), chaps. 6, 7.

12. Chief Justice Charles Evans Hughes: "We are under a constitution but the constitution is what the judges say it is." Dexter Perkins, *Charles Evans Hughes* (Boston: Little, Brown, 1956), p. 16.

13. Hobbes, *Leviathan*, chap. 30.

14. Compare with William Graham Sumner, "Antagonistic cooperation is the most productive form of combination in high civilization," in *Folkways* (Boston: Ginn, 1907), p. 18.

15. The general character of the difference between liberal and social democracy is well established; see George Holland Sabine, "The Two Democratic Traditions," *Philosophical Review*, October 1952; Robert Dahl, *A Preface to Democratic Theory* (Chicago: University of Chicago Press, 1956); Ferdinand Tonnies, *Community and Association*, trans. Charles P. Loomis (London:

Routledge and Kegan Paul, 1955); and Jacob Leib Talmon, *The Origins of Totalitarian Democracy* (New York: Oxford University Press, 1960). Richard Krouse, "Classical Images of Democracy in America: Madison and Tocqueville," in *Democratic Theory and Practice*, ed. Graeme Campbell Duncan (Cambridge: Cambridge University Press, 1983), locates in the American environment two democratic ideals, one from Madison, the other from Tocqueville, that closely parallel those presented here.

16. Carl Lotus Becker, *The Declaration of Independence: A Study of the History of Political Ideas* (New York: Vintage, 1958); Willmoore Kendall, *The Basic Symbols of the American Political Tradition* (Baton Rouge: Louisiana State University Press, 1970); and Garry Wills, *Inventing America* (New York: Vintage, 1979).

17. Once again, we must deal with an implicit emphasis on masculinity. The Bible, from Deborah through Mary, pays far more attention to women than did, for example, the Greek philosophers; and the early Christians, such as Paul, were at least thoroughly confused about the status of women. Nevertheless, the biblical records indicate that all the great prophets, Nathan, Elijah, Jeremiah, Ezekiel, Isaiah, and the rest, as well as all the outstanding leaders, the patriarchs, Moses and Joshua, the major kings from David on down to Jesus himself, were all men. One can hypothesize that the cumulative impact of this record over the centuries has been one factor determining the reluctance of Americans—as descendants of Bible-reading forebears—to entrust major leadership positions to women. In any event, it would seem to justify conducting the present discussion of prophetic leadership in the American context in the masculine mode.

18. Although this phrase is often attributed to Hamilton at the Constitutional Convention of 1787, Rossiter argues that there is little evidence that he said it. Theophilus Parsons, Jr., "said in 1859 that a friend of his had heard Hamilton make this remark at a dinner in 1788 or 1789." Henry Adams contributed to the rumor by putting the phrase in his *History* (1889). See Clinton Rossiter, *Alexander Hamilton and the Constitution* (New York: Harcourt, Brace and World, 1964), p. 162.

19. Under the title "The Higher-Law Background and Popular Sovereignty," Robert G. McCloskey, in *The American Supreme Court* (Chicago: University of Chicago Press, 1960), writes: "This propensity to hold contradictory ideas simultaneously is one of the most significant qualities of the American political mind. . . . With their political hearts thus divided between the will of the people and the rule of law, Americans were naturally receptive to the development of institutions that reflected each of these values separately" (pp. 11, 13).

20. Cyclical patterns in American politics have often been noted. Samuel Huntington, *American Politics: The Promise of Disharmony* (Cambridge, Mass.: Harvard University Press, 1981), pp. 147–48 and 164ff., sees stages of moralism, cynicism, complacency, and hypocrisy. The myth/ideology cycle posited here might be stated formally as stages of quiescence, tension, crisis, and recovery. But the pattern is not fixed, and its sundry variations could only be documented by the historical materials of each instance.

21. Cf. Anne Norton, *Alternative Americas* (Chicago: University of Chicago Press, 1986), esp. "Introduction."

22. See Becker, *Declaration of Independence*, p. 212ff.

Chapter 4

1. Charles Louis Montesquieu, *The Spirit of the Laws*, ed. David Wallace Carrithers (Berkeley: University of California Press, 1977).

2. Clinton Rossiter, *The American Presidency* (New York: Harcourt, Brace, 1956), pp. 26–28; 105–9.

3. Cf. the comment by John Roche, "The Founding Fathers: A Reform Caucus in Action," *American Political Science Review* 55 (December 1961): 816, that the composition of the Constitution was guided "by no over-arching principles." Certainly the founders were practical men, not philosophers. But this does not mean that they had no regard for theories, only that they were heirs to a number of theories that were not always kept straight. Cf. also Max Farrand, *The Framing of the Constitution of the United States* (New Haven, Conn.: Yale University Press, 1913): "No document originating as this one had and developed as this had been developed could be logical or even consistent. That is why every attempted analysis of the Constitution has been doomed to failure. From the nature of its construction, the Constitution defies analysis on a logical basis" (p. 201).

4. For the intellectual milieu of the founders, see Gordon S. Wood, *The Creation of the American Republic, 1776–1787* (New York: Norton, 1969). For their understanding of the problems of government organization, see M.J.C. Vile, *Constitutionalism and the Separation of Powers* (Oxford: Clarendon Press, 1967); W. Gwyn, *The Meaning of Separation of Powers* (New Orleans: Tulane University Press, 1965); George W. Carey, "Separation of Powers and the Madisonian Model: A Reply to the Critics," *American Political Science Review* 72 (March 1978): 151–64; M. Diamond, "Democracy and *The Federalist*: A Reconsideration of the Framers' Intent," *American Political Science Review* 53 (March 1959): 52–68; and D. S. Lutz, "The Relative Influence of European Writers on Late-18th-Century American Political Thought," *American Political Science Review* 78 (March 1984): 189–97.

5. Aristotle, *The Politics of Aristotle*, trans. and ed. E. Barker (Oxford: Oxford University Press, 1946), pts. 4, 5, 6.

6. Alexander Hamilton, James Madison, and John Jay, *The Federalist Papers* (New York: New American Library, 1961), No. 51.

7. Madison thought he had: "The Oracle who is always consulted and cited on this subject is the celebrated Montesquieu," *Federalist*, No. 47.

8. Montesquieu, *Spirit of the Laws*, p. 201.

9. Ibid., p. 202.

10. Ibid., p. 200.

11. Aristotle, *Politics*, bks. 4, 5.

12. Ibid., bk. 6.

13. That the United States political community did not possess clear orders of "rich" and "poor" that could be represented respectively by the Senate and the House was recognized as early as the convention itself

(Carey, "Separation of Powers," p. 153). But that is not what is at issue here. The issue is, Should the legislature be designed to represent interests? This the founders answered affirmatively by (1) establishing the principle of interest representation through the creation of a bicameral legislature and (2) depriving both houses of any mechanism for coalescing behind an executive committed to a single, overriding "public" interest. Both were thereby freed to disaggregate into the particular interests each member might represent. Aristotle's principle was thus carried to an extreme.

14. Arthur Fisher Bentley, *The Process of Government* (Chicago: University of Chicago Press, 1908); Robert Dahl, *A Preface to Democratic Theory* (Chicago: University of Chicago Press, 1956); but also, importantly, N. Jacobson, "Political Science and Political Education," *American Political Science Review* 57 (September 1963): 561–69.

15. Aristotle was familiar with the idea of representation as a formal institutional device (see *Politics*, p. 192, translator's n.2). But it is the more general idea of representation that is being referred to here, the idea that links social class, economic interest, and political participation. This idea underlies the full length of Aristotle's system of constitutional classification (see bk. 3, chap. 8, or, for example, his statement: "The proper application of the term 'democracy' is to a constitution in which the freeborn and poor control the government—being at the same time a majority; and similarly the term 'oligarchy' is properly applied to a constitution in which the rich and better born control the government—being at the same time a minority," bk. 4, chap. 4). It is this conception of "representation" that mixed government theory presupposes.

16. The roots of these contrasting political processes in America are deep. Compare the Pennsylvania Constitution of 1776 with the Massachusetts Constitution of 1780. Compare also the constitutional writings of John Adams ("Defense of the Constitutions of Government of the United States of America" and "Thoughts on Government: Applicable to the Present State of the American Colonies," in *Works of John Adams*, ed. Charles Adams [Boston: Little, Brown, 1851], 4:271ff., 194ff.) to those of John Taylor (*An Inquiry into the Principles and Policy of the Government of the United States* [1814; reprint, New Haven, Conn.: Yale University Press, 1950]). Adams's enthusiasm for mixed government theory collides with Taylor's for separation of powers. But the contrast between their views on specific issues, such as the role of the courts, is especially helpful. Although he did not attend, Adams's influence on the 1787 convention was great. Taylor is centrally representative of that "Jeffersonianism" that flowed through the nineteenth century down to modern times. In this light, Adams was our first and, with the possible exception of Calhoun, our greatest ideologist; Taylor, in contrast, was our first full-scale mythic psalmist.

17. Representative of the assumption of this outlook on American politics is Theodore Lowi, *The Personal President: Power Invested, Promise Unfulfilled* (Ithaca, N.Y.: Cornell University Press, 1985), especially the commentary in the last chapter.

18. The classic and completely unselfconscious exposition of this understanding of American politics remains Bentley, *Process of Government*.

Chapter 5

1. Thomas Hobbes, *Leviathan*, ed. Michael Oakeshott (Oxford: Basil Blackwell, 1946), see esp. chap. 13–17, 26.

2. Ibid., chap. 13.

3. See Robert P. Wolff, ed., *The Rule of Law* (New York: Touchstone, 1971).

4. See Chapter 3, n. 12.

5. Leonard Downie, Jr., *Justice Denied: The Case for Reform of the Courts* (New York: Praeger, 1971), chap. 2.

6. Ibid., p. 23.

7. Lloyd L. Weinreb, *Denial of Justice* (New York: Free Press, 1977), pp. 88–97; Herbert Jacob, *Justice in America: Courts, Lawyers, and the Judicial Process*, 3d ed. (Boston: Little, Brown, 1978), pp. 127–29.

8. Aryeh Neier, *Only Judgment: The Limits of Litigation in Social Change* (Middletown, Conn.: Wesleyan University Press, 1982); David Horowitz, *The Courts and Social Policy* (Washington, D.C.: The Brookings Institution, 1977); Jacob, *Justice in America*, p. 11.

9. C. Wright Mills, *The Sociological Imagination* (New York: Oxford University Press, 1950). Another sociologist defined "apathy" as essentially a determination to find private solutions to public problems. Philip Slater, *The Pursuit of Loneliness* (Boston: Beacon Press, 1970).

10. Deciding the case of a New York City homeless woman held in a psychiatric hospital against her will, Acting Justice Robert D. Lippmann of the State Supreme Court of Manhattan argued, "As to the pathetic condition of her clothes, the logical inference to be drawn from that is that she is poor. The legal question before me is whether Joyce Brown is mentally capable of providing herself with clothes; the question is not whether she is financially able to do so. . . . The predicament of Joyce Brown and the countless homeless raises questions of broad social, economic, political and moral implications not within the purview of this court." *New York Times*, 13 November 1987, sec. B.

11. For example, Ann Stuart Diamond, "The Zenith of Separation of Powers Theory," *PUBLIUS* 8, no. 3 (1978): 45–70.

12. John Taylor, *An Inquiry into the Principles and Policy of the Government of the United States* (1814; reprint, New Haven, Conn.: Yale University Press, 1950).

13. For a classic defense of judicial review, see Alexander M. Bickel, *The Least Dangerous Branch*, 2d ed. (New Haven, Conn.: Yale University Press, 1986).

14. Among other cases on the extent of executive power, see esp. Ex parte Milligan (1866) and Youngstown Sheet and Tube Co. v. Sawyer (1952).

15. Quoted in David V. Edwards, *The American Political Experience* (Englewood Cliffs, N.J.: Prentice-Hall, 1979), p. 280.

16. Baker v. Carr (1962). See also Doe v. McMillan (1973).

17. For example, see Tinker v. Des Moines School District (1969).

18. See Leonard W. Levy, *Original Intent and the Framers' Constitution* (New York: Macmillan, 1988).

19. See Robert G. McCloskey, *The American Supreme Court* (Chicago: University of Chicago Press, 1960), chaps. 5, 6.

20. The Court struck down federal income tax in Pollock v. Farmers' Loan and Trust Co. (1895). In Hammer v. Dagenhart (1918), the Court argued that Congress could not exclude items produced by child labor from interstate commerce because the "harmful results" it wanted to control occurred prior to the interstate commerce.

21. McCloskey, *Supreme Court*, pp. 167–69, 174–79. Justice Roberts's position switching also helped.

22. Sipuel v. University of Oklahoma (1948); Sweatt v. Painter (1950); and McLaurin v. Oklahoma State Regents (1950).

23. Brown v. Board of Education of Topeka (1954); Griffin v. Prince Edward County Board of Education (1964); and Alexander v. Holmes County Board of Education (1969).

24. Swann v. Charlotte-Mecklenburg Board of Education (1971); Keyes v. School District No. 1 (1973). On the other hand, the Court has refused to order integration of metropolitan area schools when school district lines between the central city and suburbs must be crossed. Milliken v. Bradley (1974).

25. On the failure of Brown v. Board of Education to change social reality, see Bickel, *Least Dangerous Branch*, chap. 6.

26. For example, 1986 Federal Bureau of Investigation figures show that blacks make up 62 percent of those arrested for robbery and 48 percent of those arrested for murder and manslaughter but only about 12 percent of the total population. The ratio of blacks to whites in the Nebraska prison population is 15.4 to 1 and in Michigan, 9.5 to 1, according to the Bureau of Justice statistics. The average Scholastic Aptitude Test scores for students from families with incomes between $30,000 and $40,000 are 928 for whites and 742 for blacks. Blacks enter mental institutions at twice the rate of whites. Their incidence of diabetes, nephritis, and hypertension is twice that of whites. Andrew Hacker, "Black Crime, White Racism," *New York Review*, 3 March 1988, pp. 36–42.

The Education Department estimates that in 1987, 9.1 percent of blacks 25 to 29 years old completed four years of college; 2.3 percent completed five or more years. In 1986, 14.0 percent of black families received incomes of less than $5,000, while only 3.5 percent of white families did. Moreover, based on 1986 dollars, the percentage of black families receiving incomes below $5,000 had increased since 1970. Richard Bernstein, "Twenty Years After the Kerner Report: Three Societies, All Separate," *New York Times*, 29 February 1988, sec. B.

27. The average unemployment rate for black men 16–19 years old was 41.0 percent in 1985 and 39.3 percent in 1986. The average unemployment rate for black men 20 years old and older was 13.2 percent in 1985 and 12.9 percent in 1986. Unemployment rates for black women are roughly comparable. For purposes of comparison, the average unemployment rate for white men 16–19 years old was 16.5 percent in 1985 and 16.3 percent in 1986; for white men 20 and older, 5.4 percent in 1985 and 5.3 percent in 1986. U.S. Department of Labor, Bureau of Labor Statistics, *Monthly Labor Review*, January 1988, p. 89.

A 1987 study of recent black graduates of Chicago public schools shows that only 31 percent had jobs; 32 percent were unemployed. Isabel Wilkerson, "'Separate and Unequal': A View from the Bottom," *New York Times*, 1 March 1988, sec. A.

Chapter 6

1. Wilson said and meant "man," and the tradition continues. Even the Geraldine Ferraro experiment is not likely to be repeated soon. The expectation of manliness in the presidency is rooted in the biblical origins of the office's grandeur. For this reason, occupants of the office will be referred to as "he" throughout this discussion. Quoted in Clinton Rossiter, *The American Presidency* (New York: Harcourt, Brace, 1956), p. 64.

2. Theodore Lowi, *The Personal President: Power Invested, Promise Unfulfilled* (Ithaca, N.Y.: Cornell University Press, 1985).

3. Edward S. Corwin, *The President: Office and Powers*, 3d ed. (New York: New York University Press, 1948), p. iii.

4. Arthur Schlesinger, Jr., "Presidential War," *New York Times Magazine*, 7 January 1973, p. 12.

5. *New York Times*, 4 January 1973, p. 36.

6. Philippa Strum, *Presidential Power and American Democracy*, 2d ed. (Santa Monica, Calif.: Goodyear, 1979), p. 80.

7. Richard E. Neustadt, *Presidential Power* (New York: Science Editions, 1962), p. 9.

8. Ibid., p. vii.

9. See n. 1.

10. Harold M. Barger, *The Impossible Presidency* (Glenview, Ill.: Scott, Foresman, 1984); George Edwards III, *The Public Presidency* (New York: St. Martin's, 1983); Barbara Hinckley, *The Symbolic Presidency* (New York: Routledge, Chapman, and Hall, 1989); Erwin Hargrove and Michael Nelson, *Presidents, Politics, and Policy* (New York: Alfred A. Knopf, 1984); Samuel Kernell, *Going Public* (Washington, D.C.: Congressional Quarterly, 1986); Theodore J. Lowi, *The Personal President* (Ithaca, N.Y.: Cornell University Press, 1985); Bert Rockman, *The Leadership Question*, (New York: Praeger, 1984). and Jeffery K. Tullis, *The Rhetorical Presidency* (Princeton, N.J.: Princeton University Press, 1987).

11. James MacGregor Burns, *Roosevelt: The Lion and the Fox* (New York: Harcourt Brace, 1956). President Johnson is an example of the same type of split personality; see Robert A. Caro, *The Years of Lyndon Johnson: The Path to Power* (New York: Random House, 1981).

12. Rossiter, *American Presidency*, p. 24.

13. Ibid., p. 16.

14. Ibid., p. 103.

15. Ibid., p. 250.

16. In 1986, the executive staff of the Executive Office of the Presidency contained over fifteen hundred persons, a decline from levels close to five thousand in the early 1970s. U.S. Bureau of the Census, *Statistical Abstract of the United States, 1987* (Washington, D.C.: U.S. Government Printing Office, 1986.), p. 311.

17. The White House Office employed 351 persons in 1986 and 367 in 1985. Both figures represent a decrease from the 406 persons employed in 1980. The WHO budget was nearly $19 million in 1986. See Matthew Lesks, ed., *Information USA '87* (New York: Penguin, 1986), pp. 1093–94.

18. Howard E. Shuman, *Politics and the Budget: The Struggle Between the President and the Congress* (Englewood Cliffs, N.J.: Prentice-Hall, 1984), chap. 2.

19. The Office of Management and Budget had a staff of 635 in 1986, the largest in the Executive Office. Its budget was set at $37.5 million, also the largest in the Executive Office. Lesks, *Information USA '87*, pp. 1093–94.

20. Rossiter, *American Presidency*, p. 229.

21. Nelson W. Polsby, *Congress and the Presidency*, 4th ed. (Englewood Cliffs, N.J.: Prentice-Hall, 1986), p. 84; Richard A. Watson and Norman C. Thomas, *The Politics of the Presidency* (New York: John Wiley & Sons, 1983), pp. 3–6; and particularly the textbooks, e.g., Milton C. Cummings, Jr., and David Wise, *Democracy Under Pressure*, 4th ed. (New York: Harcourt Brace Jovanovich, 1981), pp. 346–92; and Everett Carll Ladd, *The American Polity*, 2d ed. (New York: Norton, 1987), pp. 174–89.

22. Toward the end of the Reagan administration, analysts remarked on the success of the administration's budget policies in lowering expectations of what the federal government can do in reordering national priorities and in changing the terms of fiscal debate. On the other hand, analysts also noted Reagan's failure to dismantle the welfare state and the huge budget deficits incurred during his tenure. Rudolph G. Penner, former director of the Congressional Budget Office, commented, "It's a record of both incredible accomplishment and colossal failure." Martin Tolchin, "Paradox of Reagan Budgets: Austere Talk vs. Record Debt," *New York Times*, 16 February 1988, sec. A. Interestingly, the *Times* article downplayed the role of Congress in Reagan's budget failures and offered the suggestion that the high deficits were the result of deliberate planning.

23. See, for example, Steven V. Roberts, "Reagan and Wright Caught Up in Feud," *New York Times*, 15 November 1987, sec. A. The article outlines a feud between the president and the speaker of the House, which resulted, according to White House aides, from Reagan's view that the speaker was egotistical and saw himself "incorrectly" as a coequal of the president. The article quotes New York senator Alphonse M. D'Amato, "The confidence level in each other is very fragile. It's kind of like us dealing with the Soviets."

24. See Polsby, *Congress and the Presidency*, pp. 46–47, on Nixon's cabinet appointments.

25. Barger, *Impossible Presidency*; Thomas E. Cronin, *The State of the Presidency*, 2d ed. (Boston: Little, Brown, 1980); H. Heclo and L. Salamon, eds., *The Illusion of Presidential Government* (Boulder, Colo.; Westview Press, 1981).

26. Ben W. Heineman, Jr., and Curtis A. Hessler, *Memorandum for the President: A Strategic Approach to Domestic Affairs in the 1980s* (New York: Random House, 1980), p. 177, quoted in Barger, *The Impossible Presidency*, p. 193.

27. Steven V. Roberts, "Reagan's New Reality: Compromise," *New York Times*, 13 November 1987, sec. A.

28. Fawn Hall, secretary to Oliver North, remarked during the Iran–Contra hearings, "Sometimes you just have to go above the written law." Fox Butterfield, "Key North Memo Altered by Hall," *New York Times*, 10 June 1987, sec. A.

29. See Stephen J. Wayne, "Expectations of the President," in *The President and the Public*, ed. Doris A. Graber (Philadelphia: Institute for the Study of Human Issues, 1982), pp. 17–38.

30. Personal remark made at an American Political Science Convention panel of public opinion and voting behavior experts, 1984. For data on what kinds of activity the public will tolerate in a president, such as wearing jeans in the Oval Office, smoking marijuana occasionally, and using profane language in private, see Wayne, "Expectations" table 2-8, p. 31.

31. For example, the *Gallup Report* of 12 January 1986 shows popular approval of Reagan's "handling of job as president" at 63 percent, while his approval "as a person" was 81 percent (pp. 5, 9). The *Gallup Report* of June 1984 gives the results of a poll taken on 18–21 May 1984. That poll shows Reagan's "approval as President" at 54 percent, while only 37 percent approve of his foreign policy, 49 percent approve of his economic policy, 28 percent approve of his policy on Central American issues, and 46 percent approve of his policy on relations with the Soviet Union, all lower than his rating as president (no. 225, pp. 11–15).

32. Rossiter quotes Henry Jones Ford as calling impeachment a "rusted blunderbuss," *American Presidency*, p. 35.

33. Reagan's spokesman, Marlin Fitzwater, said that the president understood that mistakes had been made, accepted responsibility, and believed that the time had come to move on to other, more pressing issues. David E. Rosenbaum, "Iran–Contra Report Says President Bears 'Ultimate Responsibility' For Wrongdoing," *New York Times*, 19 November 1987, sec. A.

Chapter 7

1. Woodrow Wilson, *Congressional Government* (New York: Mentor Books, 1954), p. 79.

2. Roger Davidson, "Subcommittee Government: New Channels for Policy Making," in *The New Congress*, ed. Thomas E. Mann and Norman J. Ornstein (Washington, D.C.: American Enterprise Institute for Public Policy Research, 1981), p. 99.

3. John Locke, *Two Treatises of Government*, ed. P. Laslett (Cambridge: Cambridge University Press, 1960), pp. 373–74.

4. See, for example, Lyndon Johnson's account, "Congress and the Presidency," in *Congressional Behavior*, ed. Nelson W. Polsby (New York: Random House, 1971), pp. 237–54.

5. Committee on Political Parties of the American Political Science Association, "Toward a More Responsible Two-Party System," *American Political Science Review* 44 (September 1950); Morton Grodzins, "The Federal System," in *Goals for Americans: The Report of the President's Commission on National Goals*, ed. the American Assembly (Englewood Cliffs, N.J.: Prentice-Hall, 1960), pp. 265–82; and Randall B. Ripley, "The Party Whip Organizations

in the United States House of Representatives," in Polsby, *Congressional Behavior*, pp. 225–48.

6. See, for example, Mark J. Green, James M. Fallows, David R. Zwick, *Who Runs Congress?* Ralph Nader Congress Project (New York: Bantam, 1972).

7. "A study of 114 members of Congress has found that nearly 95 percent complained that the legislative process was 'too chaotic.'" Julie Johnson, "Harried Lawmakers Find Congress 'Too Chaotic,'" *New York Times*, 13 January 1988, sec. A. The article went on the say that 87 percent of those interviewed said they would like to remain in Congress. Those responsible for the study could not reconcile the expressed discontent with the willingness to keep working. This book argues that the legislative process is chaotic only in myth. In ideology, it works very well and provides considerable satisfactions to members of Congress.

8. John C. Calhoun, *A Disquisition on Government*, ed. C. G. Post (New York: Liberal Arts Press, 1963), p. 20.

9. In 1987, each member of the House of Representatives was entitled to an annual clerk-hire allowance of $406,560 for a staff not to exceed twenty-two employees. There is no limit on the number of employees a senator can hire, but he or she can only use the clerk-hire or legislative assistance allowance to pay staff salaries. In 1987, the Senate clerk-hire allowance was between $716,102 and $1,438,856, varying with state population. Again in 1987, the legislative assistance allowance was $243,543. In 1986, the personal staffs of representatives and senators totaled 11,694 people. See Norman J. Ornstein, Thomas E. Mann, and Michael J. Malbin, *Vital Statistics on Congress, 1987–1988* (Washington, D.C.: Congressional Quarterly, 1987), pp. 135, 154–57.

10. The congressional staff totaled 31,652 in 1987. For a breakdown by category, see ibid., p. 140.

11. In 1986, the cost of running the legislative branch was $1,783,255,000. Ibid., p. 150; see p. 152 for a breakdown by category.

12. By comparison, the second most heavily staffed legislative branch in the world is the Canadian Parliament. It has a staff of less than 3,500. See Michael J. Malbin, *Unelected Representatives: Congressional Staff and the Future of Representative Government* (New York: Basic Books, 1979), p. 10.

13. Malbin, *Unelected Representatives*, chap. 1; and Davidson, "Subcommittee Government," pp. 109–14. The study of 114 members of Congress discussed above (n. 7) found that almost 80 percent of those surveyed said their jobs left little time for personal or family life. Scheduling and, in the Senate, rules permitting extended debate were frequent sources of complaints. *New York Times*, 13 January 1988. See also Michael J. Malbin, "Delegation, Deliberation, and the New Role of Congressional Staff," in Mann and Ornstein, *New Congress*, pp. 134–77, for the argument that the large numbers of staffers increases the workload of members of Congress.

14. Grodzins, "Federal System"; David B. Truman, *The Governmental Process* (New York: Alfred A. Knopf, 1951).

15. Scholars have been quoting this 80 percent figure since the 1930s, and recent evidence has shown that, if there has been any change, it is in the

direction of a higher percentage. For figures, see John Saloma, *Congress and the New Politics* (Boston: Little, Brown, 1969), tables 6.5, 6.7, pp. 184–85; and Morris P. Fiorina, *Congress: Keystone of the Washington Establishment* (New Haven, Conn.: Yale University Press, 1977), p. 59.

16. In the 100th Congress (1987–88), there were twenty-two standing committees in the House and sixteen in the Senate. In the House, those committees (listed in decreasing order by size of committee staff) are House Administration, Appropriations, Energy and Commerce, Education and Labor, Budget, Ways and Means, Foreign Affairs, Banking, Government Operations, Public Works, Post Office and Civil Service, Judiciary, Merchant Marine and Fisheries, Science and Technology, Interior, Agriculture, Armed Services, Small Business, Rules, District of Columbia, Veterans' Affairs, and Standards of Official Conduct. In the Senate, they are Judiciary; Governmental Affairs; Labor and Human Resources; Commerce, Science and Transportation; Appropriations; Budget; Foreign Relations; Energy and Natural Resources; Environment and Public Works; Finance; Armed Services; Banking, Housing, and Urban Affairs; Agriculture; Rules and Administration; Small Business; and Veterans' Affairs. Ornstein, Mann, and Malbin, *Vital Statistics*, pp. 128–29, 147–48.

17. Counting standing committees, subcommittees of standing committees, select and special committees, joint committees and subcommittees of joint committees, for the 100th Congress there were 118 such bodies in the Senate and 192 in the House. The highest figures for the years between 1955 and 1988 occur for the 94th Congress (1975–76): 205 bodies in the Senate, 204 in the House. Ibid., p. 127.

18. In the 100th Congress, 51.2 percent of all Democratic representatives chaired at least one committee or subcommittee and 87 percent of the Democratic senators chaired at least one committee or subcommittee. Ibid., pp. 131–32.

19. For the 99th Congress (1985–86), 6,499 bills were introduced in the House; 3,386 were introduced in the Senate. Those numbers represent a decrease from recent years. For example, for the 90th Congress (1967–68), 22,060 bills were introduced in the House; 4,400 in the Senate. Ibid., pp. 165–67.

20. For the years 1947–86, for the House of Representatives, about 1.2 bills were passed for every 10 introduced. In 1985–86, in the House, about 1.5 bills were passed for every 10 introduced. The figures are higher for the Senate. On average, for 1947–86, 3.7 bills were passed for every 10 introduced in the Senate. In 1985–86, fewer than 3 in 10 passed. Ibid., pp. 165–67 (averages computed by the author).

21. Evidence of the large number of "access points" provided by the subcommittee system is that, in the 99th Congress (1985–86), there were 4,222 subcommittee meetings in the House and 2,597 in the Senate. Ibid., pp. 165–67.

22. The $604 billion catch-all appropriations bill passed by Congress on 22 December 1987 is a prime example of "Christmas-tree legislation." As soon as the bill was signed, odd proposals added by various members of

Congress began to come to light. One provision, introduced by Robert J. Mrazek, Democrat from Long Island, eliminated $539 million in federal support for the Metropolitan Transportation Authority unless the Long Island Rail Road banned smoking within ninety days (Philip S. Gutis, "L.I.R.R. Told to Ban Smoking or Lose U.S. Funds," *New York Times*, 23 December 1987, sec. B). Senator Ernest Hollings, Democrat from South Carolina, in "a little-noticed action before adjournment," added a barrier to Rupert Murdoch's continued ownership of the *New York Post* and the *Boston Herald* while he owned television stations in the same markets (Alex S. Jones, "Congress Adds Apparent Barrier to Murdoch's Ownership of *Post*," *New York Times*, 31 December 1987, sec. A).

Perhaps the most widely publicized of the personal measures added to secure a majority in favor of the bill was Senator Daniel K. Inouye's (Rep., Hawaii) later rescinded $8 million for parochial schools for North African Jews in France ("Senator Inouye's Christmas Tree Bauble," *New York Times*, 31 December 1987, editorial). Less well-publicized measures include Representative Daniel K. Akaka's (Dem., Hawaii) $250,000 for pig and exotic plant control in Haleakala National Park in his district and Senator James A. McClure's (Rep., Idaho) $6.4 million to spur a Bavarian-style ski resort in Idaho (Julie Johnson, "Picking Over the Pork in 1988 Spending Bill," *New York Times*, 5 January 1988, sec. B). Even President Reagan won the sop of $8.1 million for nonlethal aid to the Nicaraguan Contras (Jonathan Fuerbringer, "Contra Aid Accord Set by Congress and White House," *New York Times*, 21 December 1987, sec. A).

The *Times*'s response to all this is instructive ("Congress Wrong Even When Right," 6 January 1988, sec. A): "It is bad enough that Congress openly stuffs favors into appropriations bills," the editorial page proclaims. "But doing it in the dark subverts honest [*sic*] government."

23. Donald Matthews, *U.S. Senators and Their World* (New York: Vintage, 1964).

Chapter 8

1. George E. Berkley and Douglas M. Fox, *Eighty Thousand Governments: The Politics of Sub-National America* (Boston: Allyn and Bacon, 1978), pp. 81–82.

2. Tip O'Neill, *Man of the House* (New York: Random House, 1987), p. 303.

3. James W. Davis, Jr., and Kenneth Dolbeare, *Little Groups of Neighbors: The Selective Service System* (Chicago: Markham, 1968), pp. v, 3.

4. An early observer of this tendency in Americans was Alexis de Tocqueville, *Democracy in America*, trans. George Lawrence, ed. J. P. Mayer (Garden City, N.Y.: Doubleday, 1969); see also Richard Hofstadter, *The Paranoid Style in American Politics and Other Essays* (New York: Alfred A. Knopf, 1966); Hofstadter, *Anti-Intellectualism in American Life* (New York: Alfred A. Knopf, 1963); Louis Filler, *Dictionary of American Conservatism* (New York: Philosophical Library, 1987); Daniel Bell, ed., *The Radical Right* (New York: Double-

day, 1963); and Nelson Polsby, "Towards an Explanation of McCarthyism," *Political Studies* 8 (1960): 250–71.

5. For example, see Gallup polls of 1987, pp. 34, 47–51, 66; See also Clyde Z. Nunn, Harry J. Crockett, Jr., and J. Allen Williams, Jr., *Tolerance for Non-Conformity* (San Francisco: Jossey Bass, 1978).

6. Bell Hooks, *Feminist Theory from Margin to Center* (Boston: South End Press, 1984); idem, *Ain't I a Woman* (Boston: South End Press, 1981); Audra Lorde, *Sister Outsider* (New York: Crossing Press, 1984); Angela Y. Davis, *Women, Race, and Class* (New York: Vintage, 1983); and Gerda Lerner, *Black Women in White America* (New York: Pantheon, 1972).

7. "Polls Show Bush Sets Agenda for Principal Election Issues," *New York Times*, 14 September 1988, sec. A. According to this article, Reagan's approval rating of 55 percent was his highest for the year. In addition, Reagan's popularity is thought to be reflected in the fact that the Republicans chose to use the president in the Bush election campaign. Steven V. Roberts, "Reagan Invokes Cubs and Kielbasa," *New York Times*, 1 October 1988, sec. A.

8. O'Neill, *Man of the House*, p. 360.

9. See the remarks of almost any of the standard American government textbooks, for example, James MacGregor Burns, J. W. Peltason, and Thomas E. Cronin, *Government by the People*, 14th ed. (Englewood Cliffs, N.J.: Prentice-Hall, 1990), pp. 725–26. For works that celebrate the town meeting, see H. A. Overstreet and B. W. Overstreet, *Town Meeting Comes to Town* (New York: Harper and Brothers, 1938) or the publications of "America's Town Meeting of the Air," 1935–42, first published in New York by American Book Company and later by Columbia University Press. See also Joseph F. Zimmerman, *The Massachusetts Town Meeting: A Tenacious Institution* (Albany, N.Y.: Graduate School of Public Affairs, 1967).

10. Some of the most valuable evidence in support of this is captured by novelists. For example, see Edwin O'Connor, *The Last Hurrah* (Boston: Little, Brown, 1985); and John O'Hara, *Ten North Frederick* (New York: Random House, 1955).

11. Richard F. Fenno, Jr., *Homestyle* (Boston: Little, Brown, 1978); idem, "U.S. House Members in Their Constituencies," *American Political Science Review* 71 (September 1977): 883–917; idem, "If as Ralph Nader Says, 'Congress Is the Broken Branch': How Come We Love our Congressmen So Much?" in *Congress in Change*, ed. Norman Ornstein (New York: Praeger, 1975); David Mayhew, *Congress: The Electoral Connection* (New Haven, Conn.: Yale University Press, 1974).

12. Even the most popular local government heroes must exhibit these qualities. See, for example, Fiorello Laguardia's autobiography, *The Making of an Insurgent: An Autobiography, 1882–1919* (Philadelphia: J. B. Lippincott, 1948); and W. L. Riordan, *The Plunkitt of Tammany Hall* (New York: E. P. Dutton, 1963).

13. C. Rodgers, *Moses: The Man for Democracy* (New York: Henry Holt, 1952); Robert Caro, *The Power Broker: Robert Moses and the Fall of New York* (New York: Random House, 1975); Mike Royko, *Boss: Richard J. Daley of*

Chicago (New York: E. P. Dutton, Inc., 1971); Len O'Connor, *Clout: Mayor Daley and His City* (Chicago: Henry Regnery, 1975); J. C. Thomas, "Restructuring the Periphery: The Quasi-Governmental Neighborhood in Cincinnati," in *Subnational Politics in the 1980s*, ed. L. A. Picard and R. Zariski (New York: Praeger, 1986), pp. 140–51.

14. Robert N. Bellah, "Civil Religion in America," *Daedalus*, Winter 1967, pp. 1–21.

15. For example, see Jack Kemp's basic stump speech for the 1988 presidential primaries, printed in the *New York Times*, 12 January 1988, sec. A. Kemp proclaims: "We support a fundamental belief in the future of freedom and the future of free enterprise and the future of the family and the future of the defense of those values upon which American was based in 1776, 1787, that we fought the Civil War over and had a revolution over. We believe that our rights come to us from our Creator, God, not from the government.

"Those are inalienable rights. They are inextricably linked together. Thomas Jefferson said, 'The same God who gave us freedom gave us our life.' Ladies and gentlemen, the same God that gives life gives freedom. They cannot be separated. They both must be dependent. Life is the first property right. . . .

"The American Dream is not that everybody be level with everybody else by redistributing income. The real dream of this country is to be what God meant us to be.

"That if anyone in this country desired to be mezzo-soprano, or a master carpenter, or a pro-football quarterback, nothing would stand in your way."

16. Robert C. Wood, *The Necessary Majority: Middle America and the Urban Crisis* (New York: Columbia University Press, 1972).

17. Ibid.; See also Ted R. Gurr and Desmond S. King, *The State and the City* (Chicago: University of Chicago Press, 1987) for a comparison with England.

18. For example, the last county created in New York State was in 1914 (George A. Mitchell, ed., *The New York Red Book* [New York: Williams Press, 1978–88]). Only in Alaska, where change might still be expected because it is a newer state and has much room for growth, was there some redefinition as late as 1972, *County and City Data Book* (Washington, D.C.: U.S. Government Printing Office, 1983), p. xix.

19. G. H. Wade and R. C. Nehrt, *Public Elementary and Secondary Education in the United States: A Statistical Compendium*, 1982–83, 1983–84 (Washington, D.C.: U.S. Department of Education, 1987).

20. E. G. Frederic, A. Ogg, and P. Ormon Ray, *Introduction to American Government*, 10th ed. (New York: Appleton-Century-Crofts, 1951), pp. 943–56.

21. Sam S. Souryal, *Police Administration and Management* (St. Paul, Minn.: West, 1977), p. 41.

22. U.S. Department of Justice, Federal Bureau of Investigation, *Uniform Crime Reports: Crime in the U.S.* (Washington, D.C.: U.S. Government Printing Office, 1987), p. 268.

23. See, for example, the case of Milwaukee, where calls by Mayor Henry W. Maier for public housing in the surrounding suburbs were one cause of suburban hostility to the mayor. A Common Council member remarked, "The United States enjoys better relations with the Soviet Union than Milwaukee does with it suburbs." Dirk Johnson, "Milwaukee Mayor Outlives Problems and Politicians in His 28-Year Reign," *New York Times*, 29 March 1988, sec. A.

24. Ira Katznelson, *City Trenches* (Chicago: University of Chicago Press, 1981); Robert Dahl, *Who Governs?* (New Haven, Conn.: Yale University Press, 1961); G. William Domhoff, *Who Rules America?* (Englewood Cliffs, N.J.: Prentice-Hall, 1967); G. William Domhoff, *Who Really Rules?* (New Brunswick, N.J.: Transaction Books, 1978); and Howard Woolston, *Metropolis: A Study of Urban Communities* (New York: D. Appleton-Century, 1938), pp. 161–63.

25. Charles Adrian, *Governing Urban America*, 2d ed. (New York: McGraw-Hill, 1961), chap. 8; see also readings by Don Price, Leonard White, and Charles Adrian in *Urban Government*, ed. Edward C. Banfield, (New York: Free Press, 1961), p. 238ff.

26. See, for example, Robert Dahl, *Who Governs?* (New Haven, Conn.: Yale University Press, 1961).

27. N. A. Huelsberg and W. F. Lincoln, eds., *Successful Negotiating in Local Government* (Washington, D.C.: International City Management Association, 1985).

28. Lawrence M. Mead, *Beyond Entitlement* (New York: Free Press, 1986); Francis Fox Piven and Richard A. Cloward, *Regulating the Poor: The Functions of Public Welfare* (New York: Vintage, 1971); Francis Fox Piven and Richard A. Cloward, *The New Class War* (New York: Pantheon, 1982); and Diana DiNitto and Thomas R. Dye, *Social Welfare Politics and Public Policy* (Englewood Cliffs, N.J.: Prentice-Hall, 1987), p. 218. For statistics on federal and local social-services spending, see *Congressional Quarterly, Health Policy* (Washington, D.C.: U.S. Government Printing Office, 1980), p. 3; and U.S. Bureau of the Census, *Statistical Abstract of the United States, 1984* (Washington, D.C.: U.S. Government Printing Office, 1983), p. 367.

29. Sidney Verba and Norman Nie, *The Changing American Voter* (Cambridge, Mass.: Harvard University Press, 1976); and Martin Harrop and William L. Miller, *Elections and Voters: A Comparative Introduction* (New York: Macmillan, 1987).

30. Bruce I. Newman and Jagdish N. Sheth, *A Theory of Political Choice Behavior* (New York: Praeger, 1987), chap. 6.

31. Finley Peter Dunne's observer of Chicago politics, Mr. Dooley, quoted in E. J. Dionne, Jr., "Sticks and Stones Are Flying as Bush–Dole Rivalry Heats," *New York Times*, 11 January 1988, sec. A.

32. Riordan, *Plunkitt*, pp. 3–6; Michael Armstrong, et al., *The Knapp Commission Report on Police Corruption* (New York: George Braziller, 1972). The Knapp Commission, which investigated corruption among the New York City police in 1969–72, reported that the men on the force distinguished between "meat-eaters" and "grass-eaters." "Meat-eaters" are officers

who take corruption seriously and who spend many on-duty hours aggressively seeking out situations they can exploit for personal financial gain. Among "grass-eaters" graft is small scale, almost casual, but regular.

Chapter 9

1. Max Weber, "Bureaucracy," in Hans Gerth and C. Wright Mills, eds., *From Max Weber: Essays in Sociology* (New York: Oxford University Press, 1958); Dwight Waldo, *The Administrative State* (New York: Holmes and Meier, 1984); and Ralph P. Hummel, *The Bureaucratic Experience* (New York: St. Martin's Press, 1987).

2. See Weber, "Bureaucracy," in Gerth and Mills, *From Max Weber*, pp. 196–244.

3. Of course, the division of labor has many severe critics as well, notably Marx and Petr Kropotkin. See, for example, Andrzej Walicki, *A History of Russian Thought* (Stanford, Calif.: Stanford University Press, 1979), pp. 287–89.

4. See Norton E. Long, "Power and Administration," *Public Administration Review* 9 (Autumn 1949): 256–64; Joseph A. Schumpeter, *Capitalism, Socialism, and Democracy* (New York: Harper and Row, 1976), chaps. 18, 22; and William J. Keefe, *Parties, Politics, and Public Policy in America*, 4th ed. (New York: Holt, Rinehart and Winston, 1984).

5. Prime examples of this occurred in the Iran–Contra scandal, especially in connection with the activities of Col. Oliver North. See his own testimony as reported in the *New York Times*, throughout the summer of 1987.

6. See Diana M. DiNitto and Thomas R. Dye, *Social Welfare, Politics and Public Policy* (Englewood Cliffs, N.J.: Prentice-Hall, 1987), pp. 206–32, 265–85. DiNitto and Dye note the following obstacles to the implementation of social welfare policies: poor communications, resource failings, conflicting attitudes of public authorities involved in policy implementation at each level of government, and bureaucratic inertia. See also Harold Seidman and Robert Gilmour, *Politics, Position, and Power*, 4th ed. (New York: Oxford University Press, 1986); and Randall B. Ripley and Grace A. Franklin, *Congress, the Bureaucracy, and Public Policy*, 4th ed. (Chicago: Dorsey Press, 1987).

7. When Dr. William B. Walsh, a prominent physician on the Presidential Commission on the HIV Epidemic, complained about foot-dragging and the "vast amount of duplication" in governmental efforts against AIDS, a more experienced bureaucrat, Ralph Bledsoe, executive secretary of the Domestic Policy Council, responded, "Welcome to the federal government." Philip M. Boffey, "AIDS Panel Marvels at Government's Efforts," *New York Times*, 11 September 1987, sec. A.

8. An example of this can be seen in action taken in the U.S. Senate in January 1988. The Senate passed two amendments to the Civil Rights Restoration Act. Each concerned whether federally funded hospitals and clinics would be required to provide abortions. Although the purpose of one amendment was to negate the other, a number of senators voted for both. *Congressional Record*, V134 N4, 28 January 1988.

9. See Chapter 8.

10. See J. Anthony Lukas, *Common Ground* (New York: Alfred A. Knopf, 1985).

11. Jonathan Kozol, *Rachel and Her Children* (New York: Crown, 1988).

12. See Robert E. Forman, *Black Ghettos, White Ghettos, and Slums* (Englewood Cliffs, N.J.: Prentice-Hall, 1971); Joseph P. Fried, *Housing Crisis U.S.A.* (New York: Praeger, 1971).

13. Take the housing issue. New York City passes five- and ten-year plans, attempts at comprehensive policy on the issue. Each year small victories are won, the city secures grants from the Federal Community Development Block Grants, and year by year a record number of dwelling units are rehabilitated. Nevertheless, full-scale policy objectives do not come through, and there has been a rise in the numbers of homeless anyway. Compare goals and actual victories in Charles Brecher and Raymond D. Horton, eds., *Setting Municipal Priorities* (New York: New York University Press, 1980–86) and "Department of Housing Preservation and Development" chapters in *The Mayor's Management Report* (New York: City Books, 1980–88). More generally and on a recurrent theme in this book, see Howard E. Shuman, *Politics and the Budget, The Struggle Between the President and the Congress*, 2d ed. (Englewood Cliffs, N.J.: Prentice-Hall, 1988).

14. See Roger H. Davidson, "Breaking Up Those Cozy Triangles," in S. Welch and J. Peters, eds., *Legal Reform and Public Policy* (New York: Praeger, 1977), pp. 30–53; J. Freeman, *The Political Process: Executive–Bureaucratic–Legislative Committee Relations* (New York: Random House, 1965); and Morris Fiorina, *Congress: Keystone of the Washington Establishment* (New Haven, Conn.: Yale University Press, 1977).

15. Martin Meyerson and Edward C. Banfield, *Politics, Planning, and the Public Interest: The Case of Public Housing in Chicago* (Glencoe, Ill.: Free Press, 1955). See also Theodore Lowi et al., *Poliscide* (New York: Macmillan, 1976); and Jeffrey Pressman and Aaron Wildavsky, *Implementation* (Berkeley: University of California Press, 1973). For a contrasting view, see Edward C. Banfield, *The Unheavenly City Revisited* (Boston: Little, Brown, 1974), esp. pp. 271–286.

Chapter 10

1. The paradigm metaphor for this individualism is Samuel L. Clemens (Mark Twain), *The Adventures of Huckleberry Finn*, ed. Sculley Bradley et al. (New York: Norton, 1962). The central theme of this novel, politically, can be interpreted as a meditation on American slavery, the subjugation of the black race by the white. Characteristically, Clemens declines this historical and sociological issue in all its enormity to a personal narrative, to a personal choice issue: what is Huck to do about Jim? The metaphor is vividly underlined by having the prepubescent lad confront this question while he and his black friend are isolated on a raft drifting down a wide river through the nation's midsection. As characteristic is the tension that Clemens perceives in his hero's mind between two imperatives, to treat Jim as a runaway "nigger" to be returned under law to slavery, or to treat Jim as his friend and help

him escape to "freedom." The tensions between these Bourgeois and Protestant poles of Huck's conscience are treated repeatedly throughout the book, especially in the second half of chapter 16, and in chapter 31, where, in a burst of schizophrenic confessionalism, Huck resolves the issue with the supremely ambiguous assertion, "All right, then, I'll *go* to hell," and decides to protect (love) Jim as his friend. The book's lame conclusion, in which it is discovered that Jim had been legally freed long since, is also characteristic. It is as if Clemens knew full well that Jim's being "free" would no more change his status in Huck's world than Lincoln's Emancipation Proclamation would fundamentally redefine in the nation the relationship between the races.

2. U.S. Bureau of the Census, *Statistical Abstract of the United States, 1988* (Washington, D.C.: U.S. Government Printing Office, 1987), esp. sec. 14, table 685ff. Compare *International Marketing Data and Statistics, 1987/88* (London: Euromonitor Publications Ltd., 1987), esp. pp. 1ff. and 295ff.

3. Cooper v. Pate (1964).

4. For example, see Lucius Barker and Twiley Barker, *Civil Liberties and the Constitutional Cases and Commentaries* (Englewood Cliffs, N.J.: Prentice-Hall, 1986); Bernard Schwartz, ed., *Statutory History of the United States Civil Rights* (New York: Chelsea House Publishers in association with McGraw-Hill, 1970); and Paul R. Benson, Jr., *The Supreme Court and the Commerce Clause, 1937–1970* (New York: Dunellen, 1970).

5. The seven major independent regulatory commissions are the Federal Reserve Board, Securities and Exchange Commission, Federal Communications Commission, Federal Trade Commission, Interstate Communications Corporation, Civil Aeronautics Board, and National Labor Relations Board.

6. Lindsay R. Curtis et al., *My Body, My Decision* (New York: New American Library, 1987).

7. *United States Statutes at Large* (Washington, D.C.: U.S. Government Printing Office, 1947), p. 23. See also S. K. Bailey, *Congress Makes a Law: The Story Behind the Employment Act of 1946* (New York: Columbia University Press, 1950), esp. the concluding chapter.

8. For the origins of these understandings of government's role in the management of the economy, see J. Maynard Keynes, *The General Theory of Employment, Interest, and Money* (London: Macmillan, 1936).

9. Thurmand Arnold, *The Folklore of Capitalism* (New Haven, Conn.: Yale University Press, 1937); Louis M. Hacker, *The Course of American Economic Growth and Development* (New York: Wiley, 1970); Robert L. Heilbroner, *The Limits of American Capitalism* (New York: Harper and Row, 1966); and Robert Benne, *The Ethic of Democratic Capitalism* (Philadelphia: Fortress Press, 1981).

10. Consult the whole history of the Court's interpretation of Congress's power to regulate interstate commerce from Gibbons v. Ogden (1824) forward.

11. Take the Avetax case. This producer of rayon fiber was sinking in the attempt to keep up with the legal requirements. The plant in Virginia

was bailed out at the last minute by government contractors. *Daily News Record*, 1 November 1988, p. 1; 3 November 1988, pp. 1, 11; 4 November 1988, p. 2; 10 November 1988, p. 1; 15 November 1988, pp. 2, 8; 17 November 1988, p. 3; 7 December 1988, p. 8.

12. Thomas Hobbes, *Leviathan*, ed. Michael Oakeshott (Oxford: Basil Blackwell, 1946), chap. 21.

13. Ibid., chap. 17.

14. A start on collecting statistics of this sort may be made by consulting *Statistical Abstract, 1988*, secs. 1–5.

15. Ibid., but also secs. 8, 13, 14; consult also *Uniform Crime Reports for the United States* (Washington, D.C.: Federal Bureau of Investigation, 1986). In particular note that social scientists estimate that about one-third of all taxpayers cheat on their federal income tax. Daniel Goleman, "The Tax Cheats: Selfish to the Bottom Line," *New York Times*, 11 April 1988, sec. A. Also, table 420 in *Statistical Abstract, 1988* shows voter turnout in some state gubernatorial and senatorial primaries often dipping below 5 percent and in one instance down to 1.5 percent.

16. John Aubrey, *Brief Lives*, ed. Oliva L. Dick (Ann Arbor: University of Michigan Press, 1957), p. 156.

17. Quoted by John Herbers, *New York Times*, 29 May 1982, sec. A.

18. *Handbook of Labor Statistics* (Washington, D.C.: U.S. Department of Labor, 1985), bulletin 2217, "Technical Notes: Current Population Survey (Household Survey)," passim.

19. *Statistical Abstract, 1988*, p. 291.

20. John Dewey, *Individualism, Old and New* (New York: Minton, Balch, 1930); Reinhold Niebuhr, *Moral Man and Immoral Society* (New York: Scribner's, 1936); Robert E. Goodin, *Reasons for Welfare: The Political Theory of the Welfare State* (Princeton, N.J.: Princeton University Press, 1988).

21. Willard C. Richan, *Social Service Politics in the United States and Britain* (Philadelphia: Temple University Press, 1981); Paul E. Weinberger, ed., *Perspectives on Social Welfare* (New York: Macmillan, 1974); and Harold L. Wilensky and Charles N. Lebeaux, *Industrial Society and Social Welfare* (New York: Russell Sage Foundation, 1958).

22. Daniel Patrick Moynihan, *Family and Nation* (San Diego: Harcourt Brace Jovanovich, 1986).

23. Francis Fox Piven and Richard A. Cloward, *Regulating the Poor: The Functions of Public Welfare* (New York: Pantheon, 1971).

24. Lawrence Mead, *Beyond Entitlement* (New York: Free Press, 1986).

Chapter 11

1. "A Model of Christian Charity," in *The American Puritans*, ed. Perry Miller (New York: Anchor Books, 1956), p. 83.

2. Cf. Robert Booth Fowler, *Religion and Politics in America* (Metuchen, N.J.: Scarecrow Press, 1985); and A. James Reichley, *Religion in American Public Life* (Washington, D.C.: The Brookings Institution, 1985).

3. See Chapter 2, above.

4. U.S. Bureau of the Census, *Statistical Abstract of the United States, 1988*

(Washington, D.C.: U.S. Government Printing Office, 1987), p. 52, shows total membership of American churches declined only slightly from 64 percent of the total population in 1960 to 60 percent in 1985 in nearly 350,000 church units.

5. Martin Luther King, Jr., *Stride Toward Freedom* (New York: Harper, 1958); Kenneth B. Clark, *The Negro Protest* (Boston: Beacon Press, 1963); and James C. Harvey, *Black Civil Rights During the Johnson Administration* (Jackson: University of Mississippi Press, 1973).

6. Baker v. Carr (1962); and Reynolds v. Sims (1964).

7. The religious (Protestant, biblical) origins of political democratic enthusiasm in the Anglo-American tradition are best exemplified by the Putney Debates in Cromwellian England. See especially A. D. Lindsay, *The Modern Democratic State* (New York: Oxford University Press, 1947), chap. 3, and idem, *The Essentials of Democracy* (London: Oxford University Press, 1929). Consult also Michael Walzer, *The Revolution of the Saints* (Cambridge, Mass.: Harvard University Press, 1965); Christopher Hill, *The World Turned Upside Down* (New York: Viking, 1972); and Melvin Richter, *The Politics of Conscience: T. H. Green and His Age* (Cambridge, Mass.: Harvard University Press, 1964).

8. Ernest Barker, *Reflections on Government* (London: Oxford University Press, 1958); E. E. Schattschneider, *The Semisovereign People: A Realist View of Democracy in America* (New York: Holt, Rinehart and Winston, 1960); Austin Ranney and Willmoore Kendall, *Democracy and the American Party System* (New York: Harcourt, Brace, 1956), esp. pt. 1 and chap. 22; and Committee on Political Parties, American Political Science Association, "Toward a More Responsible Two-Party System," *American Political Science Review* supplement (September 1950).

9. Note that this argument does not deny that the social democratic electoral experience could be theorized in secular terms (e.g., Joseph Schumpeter, *Capitalism, Socialism, and Democracy* [New York: Harper, 1950]). What is maintained is that *in America* this framework was filled up and shot through with Protestant enthusiasms.

10. Francis Fox Piven and Richard A. Cloward, *Why Americans Don't Vote* (New York: Pantheon, 1989); and Kim Ezra Shienbaum, *Beyond the Electoral Connection* (Philadelphia: University of Pennsylvania Press, 1984).

11. Norman J. Ornstein et al., *Vital Statistics on Congress* (Washington, D.C.: American Enterprise Institute, 1984–85), p. 53.

12. Arthur N. Holcombe, *The New Party Politics* (New York: Norton, 1933); Charles E. Merriam and Harold F. Goswell, *The American Party System*, 4th ed. (New York: Macmillan, 1949); V. O. Key, *Politics, Parties, and Pressure Groups*, 5th ed. (New York: Crowell, 1964); and Leon D. Epstein, *Political Parties in the American Mold* (Madison: University of Wisconsin Press, 1986).

13. See Chapter 7, above.

14. Raoul Berger, *Impeachment: The Constitutional Problems* (Cambridge, Mass.: Harvard University Press, 1973).

15. See Samuel J. Eldersveld, *Political Parties in American Society* (New York: Basic Books, 1982), esp. pts. 4 and 5, pp. 269–433.

16. Herbert E. Alexander, *Money in Politics* (Washington, D.C.: Public Affairs Press, 1972), see esp. chart p. 319; and Brooks Jackson, *Honest Graft: Big Money and the American Political Process* (New York: Alfred A. Knopf, 1988).

17. See above, n. 10. Compare especially Sidney Verba and Norman H. Nie, *Participation in America* (New York: Harper and Row, 1972), pt. 1, chap. 1, pp. 1–121.

18. Philip E. Slater, *The Pursuit of Loneliness: American Culture at the Breaking Point* (Boston: Beacon Press, 1970).

19. James N. Rosenau, *Citizenship Between Elections* (New York: Free Press, 1974); and Bruce Cain et al., *The Personal Vote: Constituency Service and Electoral Independence* (Cambridge, Mass.: Harvard University Press, 1987).

20. Robert Bellah and Philip E. Hammond, *Varieties of Civil Religion* (San Francisco: Harper and Row, 1980).

21. See below, Walz v. Tax Commission (1970).

22. Walter Rauschenbush, *Christianizing the Social Order* (New York: Macmillan, 1912); also, idem, *Christianity and the Social Crisis* (New York: George Doran, 1907).

23. Will Herberg, *Protestant–Catholic–Jew* (Chicago: University of Chicago Press, 1955).

24. Thomas Hobbes, *Leviathan*, ed. Michael Oakeshott (Oxford: Basil Blackwell, 1946), chap. 42.

25. Seyla Benhabib, "The Generalized and the Concrete Other," in *Feminism as Critique: On the Politics of Gender*, ed. Seyla Benhabib and Drucilla Cornell (Minneapolis: University of Minnesota Press, 1987), pp. 77–97.

26. West Virginia State Board of Education v. Barnette (1943); Everson v. Board of Education (1947); United States v. Seeger (1965); Donnelly v. Lynch (1984); and Thorton v. Caldor (1985); and so on.

Chapter 12

1. Willmoore Kendall, *The Basic Symbols of the American Political Tradition* (Baton Rouge: Louisiana State University Press, 1970).

2. George Herring, *America's Longest War* (New York: Wiley, 1979); Richard J. Barnet, *Roots of War* (New York: Atheneum, 1972); and Daniel Ellsberg, *Papers on the War* (New York: Simon and Schuster, 1972).

3. For example, the My Lai incident in which more than two hundred Vietnamese civilians were "wasted" by an American company under the command of Lt. William Calley. See Ellsberg, *Papers*, p. 234ff.

4. The story on the nuclear arms industry may be said to have broken with charges by two congressional committees that serious accidents at weapons plants had been concealed for over thirty years. See *New York Times*, 1 October 1988, sec. 1. Subsequent stories appeared weekly, sometimes daily, for months thereafter.

5. Cf. Peter Blau and Marshall Meyer, *Bureaucracy and Modern Society*, 2d ed. (New York: Random House, 1971).

6. Dwight Waldo, *The Administrative State*, 2d ed. (New York: Holmes and Meier, 1984).

7. Anthony Downs, *Inside Bureaucracy* (Boston: Little, Brown, 1967), esp. chaps. 8, 9.

8. Jack D. Douglas and John M. Johnson, *Official Deviance: Readings in Malfeasance, Misfeasance, and Other Forms of Corruption* (Philadelphia: J. B. Lippincott, 1977).

9. Cf. Aaron Wildavsky, "A Cultural Theory of Responsibility," in *Bureaucracy and Public Choice*, ed. Jan-Erik Lane (London: Sage, 1987).

10. Robert C. Fried, *Performance in American Bureaucracy* (Boston: Little, Brown, 1976), pt. 3.

11. Ronald M. Glassman et al., ed., *Bureaucracy Against Democracy and Socialism* (New York: Greenwood Press, 1987), esp. essays by Glassman and Swatos.

12. Much of the argument of these paragraphs is drawn from the insights of Ralph P. Hummel, *The Bureaucratic Experience* (New York: St. Martin's Press, 1977), p. 4ff.

13. Cf. Alvin W. Gouldner, "Metaphysical Pathos and the Theory of Bureaucracy," in *The Politics of the Federal Bureaucracy*, ed. Alan A. Altshuler (New York: Dodd, Mead, 1968), p. 4ff.

14. Cf. Joseph LaPalombara, "Bureaucracy and Political Development," in the volume he edited, *Bureaucracy and Political Development* (Princeton, N.J.: Princeton University Press, 1967), p. 34ff. See also the section titled "The Passing of the Pyramid," in George E. Berkley, *The Craft of Public Administration* (Boston: Allyn and Bacon, 1975), p. 465ff.

15. Cf. Blau and Meyer, *Bureaucracy*, chap. 8.

Postscript

1. Reginald Heber, "Brightest and Best of the Sons of the Morning," *Pilgrim Hymnal* (Boston: Pilgrim Press, 1958), No. 126; also David Halberstam, *The Best and the Brightest* (New York: Random House, 1972).

Index

Abortion, 189, 211
Adams, Abigail, 56
Adams, John, 44, 56, 234, 253n. 16
Adventures of Huckleberry Finn, The
  (Twain), 266n. 1
Alternatives, xiii–xiv, 42
Amos (Old Testament), 209
Appomattox, 61
Apter, David, 106
Aristotle, 44, 72, 76–78, 133
Articles of Confederation, 66
Authority, 168, 272

"Barons," local, 162–64
Bentham, Jeremy, 38
Bible, 34, 35, 38, 55, 251n. 17; and
  biblical nationalism, 54
Bill of Rights, xiv, 149
Blacks, 103–4
Bourgeois ethos, 32, 37–39; defined,
  37–38; frustration of, 202; needs of,
  184–92; political role of, 43
Brown v. Board of Education of Topeka
  (1954), 69, 102–4
Bureaucracy, 7, 81, 85; defined, 166;
  fragmentation of, 175–77; leadership
  needs of, 178–80. *See also* Rational-
  professionals
Bush, George, 60

Cabinet, U.S. president's, 119
Calhoun, John C., 133–36, 140
Calvin, John, 248–49n. 20
Capitalism, 191–92
Carnegie, Andrew, 204
Carter, Jimmy, 60, 107
Charismatic hero, 52–54
Checks and balances, 4, 68–72. *See also*
  Mixed government
Civil War, American, 25, 26, 31, 44, 59,
  61–62
Civis Americanus (the American citizen),
  8, 82–83, 183

Committees, Congressional, 118, 126,
  141–43
Communitarianism, 54–55
"Concurrent majority" (Calhoun), 133
Confederalism, 64–68, 148, 155;
  defined, 65–66
Congregation, 53–55
Congress, 7, 126–27; elitism of, 145–47;
  first duty of, 85; legislative process of,
  129–30, 140–43; members of, 137–
  38; organization of, 128–29; staff of,
  136–37; symbolism of, 127
Constitution, U.S., 2–3, 33, 44, 66, 68,
  71, 87, 101, 165, 226
Constitutionalism, 50, 57, 79, 99
Constitutional review, 69–70, 79, 97
Coolidge, Calvin, 184
Cooper v. Aaron (1958), 103
Corruption, 196, 234–36
Corwin, Edward S., 106
Cotton, John, 27
Council of Economic Advisors, 114
Courts, 6–7, 70; first duty of, 83, 85,
  88; judges in, 88; mythic role of, 88,
  99–104
Crèvecoeur, J. Hector St. John de, 25

Dahl, Robert, 106
Dallmayr, Fred, 245n. 2
Declaration of Independence, xii, 2, 13,
  25, 33, 37, 52
Democracy. *See* Liberal democracy;
  Social democracy
Discipline, party, in Congress, 135, 137

Edwards, Jonathan, 27
Eisenhower, Dwight D., 107–8
Elections, 81, 171, 206–15
Equality, 3–4, 34–35, 104
Evaluation, criteria for, 181
Everson v. Board of Education (1947), 221
Executive budget, 118

273